Forgotten Books

Toward Soviet America

By

William Z. Foster

Published by Forgotten Books 2012

PIBN 1000032241

TOWARD SOVIET AMERICA

TO ESTHER

TOWARD
SOVIET
AMERICA

wwwwwwww

William Z. Foster

SPECIAL EDITION
PRINTED FOR
INTERNATIONAL PUBLISHERS
BY
COWARD-McCANN, Inc.
NEW YORK

WORKERS LIBRARY DISTRIBUTORS
1413 West 18th Street - Room 13
CHICAGO, ILLINOIS

PREFACE

THERE is a great and growing mass demand in this country to know just what is the Communist party and its program. The masses of toilers, suffering under the burdens of the crisis, are keenly discontented and want to find a way out of their intolerable situation. They are alarmed at the depth, length and general severity of the crisis. They begin to realize that "there is something rotten in Denmark," that there are fundamental flaws in the capitalist system. Their growing realization of this is further strengthened as they see the spectacular rise of Socialism in the Soviet Union. The masses are beginning rightly to sense that Communism has an important message for the human race, and they want to know what it is.

Capitalism is deeply anxious that the masses do not get this message. Hence, from the outset it has carried on a campaign of falsification of the Russian revolution entirely without parallel in history. There has been a veritable ocean of lies in the capitalist press against the U.S.S.R. The American Federation of Labor leadership and the Socialist party, defenders of the capitalist system, have outdone even the capitalists themselves in this wholesale vilification. The effort of the capitalists and their labor lieutenants has been to set off the Communists as willful enemies and destroyers of the human race. But the masses begin to see through this misrepresentation and they want to know the truth.

The present book is an attempt to meet this mass demand by a plain statement of Communist policy, avoiding technical complexities and theoretical elaboration. It outlines simply the program, strength, strategy and perspectives of the Communist party of the United States. It undertakes to point out what is the matter with capitalism and what must be done about it. It indicates where America is heading and it makes a practical application of the lessons of the Russian revolution to the situation in this country. Its central purpose is to explain to the oppressed and exploited masses of workers and poor farmers how, under the leadership of the Communist party, they can best protect themselves now, and in due season cut their way out of the capitalist jungle to Socialism.

WM. Z. FOSTER

New York City
May 1, 1932

CONTENTS

TOWARD SOVIET AMERICA

CHAPTER I

THE DECLINE OF CAPITALISM

THE MOST striking and significant political and social fact in the world today is the glaring contrast between the industrial, political and social conditions prevailing in the capitalist countries and those obtaining in the Soviet Union. Throughout the capitalist world, without exception, the picture is one of increasing chaos and crisis. The capitalist industrial system is paralysed as never before. Tremendous masses of workers are thrown into unemployment and destitution. The standards of living of the producing masses have declined catastrophically, mass starvation existing in every capitalist country, including the United States. War is already here in Manchuria and preparations go ahead upon an unprecedented scale for future wars against the Soviet Union and among the capitalist powers themselves. To enforce their regime of hunger and intensified exploitation, the capitalists everywhere are increasingly developing their dictatorship from its masked form of bourgeois democracy into open systems of Fascist terrorism. And against all this the revolutionary upsurge of the workers and poor farmers becomes worldwide; revolutionary struggle growing acute in many countries. Capitalism is manifestly in serious crisis.

On the other hand, the Soviet Union, born in the midst of the capitalist world slaughter of 1914-18, presents a picture of growth and general social advance. The Russian industries and agriculture are expanding at an unheard-of rate, the Soviet Union being the only country in the world not prostrated by the economic crisis. The masses of producers of factory and farm are all employed; their standards of living and culture are rapidly rising. They are building a new and free proletarian democracy. In short, as capitalism goes deeper and deeper into crisis, the Soviet Union forges ahead faster and faster upon every front.

The meaning of all this, as will be developed in the course of this book, is that the capitalist system is in decline and is historically being replaced by a new social order, Socialism. Capitalism, based upon the private ownership of industry and land and the exploitation of the toiling masses, has exhausted its social role; the revolutionary forces, under the leadership of the Communist International, are gathering to sweep it away and to build in its place a social system based upon the common ownership of the means of production and the carrying on of production for social use. Out of the welter of crisis and mass misery and war, a new

social system is born. We are living in the historical period of the revolutionary transition from
capitalism to Socialism.

The Present Economic Crisis

LIKE a tornado the present economic crisis struck
the capitalist world. It is a crisis of over-production. The first signs of this threatening over-production manifested themselves in Germany and
central Europe generally in the latter part of 1928.
The industrial decline began in the U. S. towards
the middle of 1929, followed by the great October
Wall Street crash, after which every capitalist
country was swiftly drawn into the vortex. The
inevitable result is the worst economic crisis, by far,
in the whole history of capitalism. It is the deepest, the most far-reaching and the longest. Every
branch of industry, every capitalist country is
affected. Only the Soviet Union is immune. And
as Stalin says, "The crisis has struck deepest of
all at the principal country of capitalism, its cita-
del, the U.S.A." The crisis is setting in motion
forces that threaten the very existence of the capitalist system.

Statistics constantly pile up to indicate the entirely unparalleled severity of the economic crisis.
In industry the drop in production has been catastrophic and, after 30 months of crisis, it still declines. Production in the basic industries has

fallen more than 50% below 1929 levels and more than 30% below 1930. Steel has dipped to 20% of capacity and "even order inquiries for tacks are seized hopefully." Building is off about 70% since 1928, notwithstanding "emergency" building programs, etc. In 1931 American exports declined about one-third, or $1,418,000,000. The total national income fell from 89.5 billions in 1929 to 52.4 billions in 1931, or 41%. The drop in wholesale prices, 24% between 1929 and 1931, is wholly unprecedented, the previous record being 7% in the crisis of 1873-75. New financing decreased from $6\frac{1}{2}$ billions in 1929 to $2\frac{1}{2}$ billions in 1931. The general business index, at this writing registering 60, a drop from 113 in Aug., 1929, is the lowest in American economic history, the nearest low to this being 72 in 1894.

Internationally there is a similar picture, world production levels at this time being about those of 1913. According to League of Nations' figures, world trade has fallen off 40% from the Spring of 1929 until the end of 1931, a decline entirely without precedent.[1] In England production is at 65, or far below pre-war levels. In Germany, says the German Institute for Business Research, "Industrial production is about as large as it was in the years 1900-03." Production in France has dropped 20% since the middle of 1930. Poland and Austria have declined 28% and 31% respec-

[1] *The Phases and Course of the World Depression.*

tively since 1929.   The Balkans are deep in crisis, Japan's industries have been similarly paralysed.

Unemployment has developed internationally upon an unheard-of scale.   In Great Britain there are 3,000,000 unemployed, in Germany 6,500,000, in France unemployment registers an all-time record, and in the United States over 12,000,000 are unemployed.   There are almost as many more part-time workers.   Throughout the capitalist countries there are not less than 40,000,000 unemployed and the number constantly increases.

In agriculture the crisis is no less ravaging and general.   According to the Department of Agriculture bulletin of Dec. 16, 1931, the value of farm products declined from $8,765,820,000 in 1929 (which was already about 50% below 1919) to $4,122,850,000 in 1931, as against a decline of only 10% in prices of commodities that farmers must buy.   The terrific fall in the prices of agricultural products is graphically illustrated by the fact that on Oct. 4, 1931 wheat reached 44½ cents a bushel on the market, the lowest point since the Civil War, with farmers getting as low as 25 cents.   And world agriculture in the capitalist countries is in a similar crisis, prices received by the peasants having fallen from 40% to 70% for the great staples, wheat, cotton, rice, rubber, silk, coffee, etc.

In finance the world economic crisis also manifests itself with devastating effects.   Whichever way one looks there is a spreading ruin and wreckage. The whole financial system of capitalism is tottering. Internationally, there is a great wave of bankruptcy, many of Europe's oldest and greatest banks and industrial concerns collapsing. Great Britain, Japan and various other countries have been driven off the gold standard. Stock exchange prices in many countries have dropped 50% to 75%, the general average in France declining from 437 in 1930 to 230 at the end of 1931. Huge deficits exist in all the national government budgets. Repudiation of international debts is the order of the day, with the United States standing to lose, counting war debts and other loans now in default, from 10 to 15 billion dollars.

The United States, home of the world's strongest capitalism, presents a similar picture of financial crisis. During 1931, 2,290 banks with deposits of $1,759,000,000 closed their doors, and 17,000 retail stores failed. In 1931, bank deposits declined by seven billion dollars. From the middle of 1929 to the end of March, 1932, the average prices of 30 leading industrial stocks on the New York Stock Exchange dropped from $381.17 to $61.98.[2] The total loss in security "values," according to B. C. Forbes, was 75 billions. New York, Chicago, Philadelphia, Detroit and hundreds of smaller cities are bankrupt. The Federal government faces a deficit of about two and one-half billion dollars. And, most significant of all, the Federal

2 *New York American,* April 12, 1932.

Reserve Bank system, a financial fortress of supposed Gibraltar strength, has manifestly proved unable to stand the strain, the Hoover two billion dollar Reconstruction Finance Corporation being an attempt to buttress up the reserve bank system by a further concentration of the State power behind the great bankers and by a policy of inflation. Mazur says: "1931 has witnessed a substantial debacle of both the orthodox currency basis and the established banking system of the world." [3] And the end is not yet, with the crisis deepening internationally.

The Mass Impoverishment of the Toilers

"We in America today are nearer to the final triumph over poverty than ever before in the history of any land."
President Hoover, Aug. 11, 1928.

THROUGHOUT capitalism the policy of the ruling class is to try to find a way out of the crisis by throwing its burden upon the shoulders of the working class, the poor farmers and the lower sections of the city petty bourgeoisie. This is being done by a vast system of starving the unemployed, wage-cuts, speed-up, inflation schemes, taxes directed against the masses, etc. In consequence, with the development of the crisis, there has been an enormous increase in the impoverishment of the toiling masses.

[3] *Current History*, November, 1931.

Wholesale starvation, spreading like a plague, is the order of the day in all capitalist countries. The bourgeoisie, intent only upon its own pleasures, cynically shrugs its shoulders at the whole terrible misery, when it does not hypocritically direct the masses towards religion for consolation. Nor are there "scientists" lacking to justify this mass starvation. Thus Prof. E. G. Conklin of Princeton University says: "Some of the weaker, according to the law of nature, will naturally die under the stress of the times. Others will not propagate their kind. The strong and hardy will survive and reproduce, and thus the human race will be strengthened." [4]

Since the onset of the present economic crisis American workers and poor farmers, through unemployment, part-time work, wage-cuts, reduced prices for agricultural products, tax increases, etc., have suffered a general decline in their living standards of at least 50%. Prof. Leiserson estimates that the total income of industrial and office workers was about 22 billion dollars less in 1931 than in 1929, and this is supported by the figures of *Business Week* (Feb. 10). This is by no means offset by the decline in living costs which, according to the U. S. Dept. of Labor, amounted to 11.7% from June, 1929, until June, 1931. On the farms, the Alexander Hamilton Institute says, the average income per household has dropped from

4 *New York Times,* Jan. 28, 1932.

$887 in 1929 (already a crisis year in agriculture) to but $367 in 1931.

By these gigantic reductions in their real income masses of toilers of field and factory have been forced down to actual starvation conditions. Even before the crisis the working masses stood at the very threshold of destitution. The average wage of industrial workers during the height of "prosperity" did not exceed $23.00 per week. Consequently, the vast body of American toilers existed from hand to mouth. They had very little reserves. Paul Nystrom says that 9,000,000 people in the United States lived below the subsistence level.[5] Then came the economic hurricane.

The result is real destitution, verging into actual starvation, on a broad scale in the United States. "Only in countries like India and China are there today larger numbers of workers suffering from mass unemployment, hunger, semi-starvation, disease and other manifold evils of wholesale poverty than in the United States — the richest country in the world," says the *Statement of the National Hunger Marchers* to Congress, Dec. 7, 1931. "One-third to one-half of our population is at various stages ranging from hunger to the pressing danger of losing homes and farms," says Governor LaFollette. The *New York American,* (Feb. 21, 1932), says: "Food is lacking in 81 per cent of the New York City homes that have been stricken by

[5] *Economic Principles of Consumption.*

unemployment, the Emergency Unemployment Relief Committee reported last night." William Hodson, executive director of the Welfare Council of New York City, informs us: "Relief in New York City is now on what might be called a disaster basis . . . the spectre of starvation faces millions who never were out of work before." The *Baltimore Post,* (Mar. 11, 1932), declares; "40,000 face starvation in Baltimore." An Associated Press dispatch of Mar. 23, 1932, from Tulsa, Okla., says: "Ten thousand persons have been living here since Nov. 1 on a charity ration costing six cents a day per person."

So it is all over the country. The cities are full of "Hoovervilles" and breadlines, where tens of thousands of homeless, hungry workers are compelled to exist in tin can shacks and to stand for hours to get a miserable bowl of soup. Workers fall famished in the streets in front of stores and warehouses that are crammed with the necessaries of life. Daily we read in the capitalist press of families actually starving to death. No longer is it "news" for a confused and desperate unemployed worker to blow out his brains or to do away with his family.

The workers are losing wholesale the houses, radios, furniture, etc., that they so laboriously got together during the upward swing of American capitalism; thousands of farmers are losing their farms to the usurers. *The Nation,* (Mar. 23,

1932), says that in Detroit alone 50,000 workers lost their life savings in the collapsed banks, and similar huge losses have been suffered all over the country. In 1931, according to the *New York Journal,* (Jan. 28), 198,738 workers' families were evicted from their homes in New York City for non-payment of rent. The worker's life has become an endless round of worry and misery. The jails are filled to overflowing, thousands preferring prison rigors to life under the Hoover regime of "rugged individualism." Prostitution spreads like a poison weed in every American city. Tuberculosis runs riot among the half-starved masses, and the hospitals are packed with sufferers of diseases bred of under-nourishment, etc., etc. To such a debacle has come the Hooverian pre-election promises of the "abolition of poverty," "a chicken in every pot" and "an automobile in every garage" for the workers. And daily the whole maze of poverty, starvation, misery and death gets worse.

Manifestly, a fundamentally necessary measure against actual starvation among the workers is the establishment of a system of federal unemployment insurance, financed by the government and the employers. This must be of a permanent character, because what we have to deal with is not a temporary condition of unemployment, but a huge mass unemployment on a permanent basis. This, however, has not been done. The capitalists and their government have forced the workers into wholesale starvation which is now infesting the country like a plague.

The entire question of unemployment relief has been reduced to a charity basis. Although the worker has spent his life producing the wealth of the country, now when the capitalist system has broken down he is treated as a mendicant and a criminal. He is thrown a beggarly handout like a starving dog. Mr. Gifford, head of Hoover's Emergency Employment Committee, boasted that in the 1931 Fall relief drive about $150,000,000 had been raised in the various localities. So far as the Federal government is concerned, this money (what the workers get of it after the grafters are through) has to last the unemployed for the whole year. Thus it figures out at about $1.00 per month for each of the 12,000,000 unemployed. In New York, richest city in the world, after a disgusting campaign of begging, $18,000,000 of Gifford's fund was raised. This would give about $1.50 per month to each of New York's 1,000,000 unemployed.

The unemployed relief program of the Hoover Government is a real hunger plan. It is the policy of the capitalist class and it has the support of both big parties and the A. F. of L. That the Progressives also agree fundamentally with it is shown by the new unemployment insurance law in Wisconsin. This law adds insult to injury. According to its beggarly provisions unemployed workers can receive only a maximum of $100 yearly. And this applies only to those now employed, for whom insurance funds will be gradually built up. As for the masses of those totally unemployed now and part-time workers, they are left out of consideration altogether.

If the capitalists have callously forced the toiling masses into starvation conditions they have, however, very carefully looked after their own interests. "During the first nine months of 1930, our national industrial and business system was able to and did pay $432,000,000 more in dividends and $191,000,000 more in interest than it did in 1929; in the first nine months of 1931, the second year of the depression, it paid $347,000,000 more in dividends and $338,000,000 more in interest than it did in the first nine months of 1929." [6] The Publishers Financial Bureau, (*New York American,* Mar. 19, 1932), states that the industrial dividends paid in 1931 are "the largest for any year previous to 1929." Anna Rochester says: "In September, 1931, the *New York Times* reported that of 5,000 companies, 50% had continued dividend payments without reduction; 20% were paying smaller dividends; and only 30% had omitted payments entirely. . . . For October, 1931, the total dividends plus bond interest by a large group of corporations were only 4% below the high record

[6] *America Faces the Future,* p. 370.

of October, 1930." [7]   Besides, every appeal of the bankers and other capitalists to the government for assistance has met with immediate response. The two billion dollar Reconstruction Finance Corporation has been organized and the Glass-Steagall inflation bill is being prepared to absorb the worthless paper of the banks and to underwrite the dividends of industrial corporations. And in the new Federal taxes the capitalists are further shielded from the economic effects of their own bankruptcy.

In the other capitalist countries starvation conditions also grip the masses. In Germany, with wages down 30% since the hunger period of 1929 and millions getting no unemployment benefits, actual famine exists in many cities. The great masses in England are almost as badly-off. In Poland miners got 69 cents a day and have recently had another wage-cut. And the offensive to cut wages and reduce unemployment benefits and social insurance in general goes on ever faster throughout Europe. In the colonial and semi-colonial countries crisis conditions also prevail. Famine stalks in China and India. In Brazil, says E. Penno, Brazilian Public Health Director, "30,000,000 people are slowly dying of starvation, malaria and syphilis." The world over, the bankrupt capitalist system is physically destroying the producing masses. The general crisis bids fair to

[7] *Profits and Wages*, p. 8.

outdo in numbers of human victims even the murderous World War itself.

All this is a picture of a society in decay. Great
mills and factories standing idle and warehouses
piled full of goods, while millions of toilers starve
and lack the necessities of life — that is plain bankruptcy. Never until capitalism appeared upon the
world scene was such an anomoly possible — starvation in the midst of plenty. The present great
crisis is not only a glaring exhibition of the decline
of capitalism, it is a crime against the human race.

Capitalist Fear and Confusion

THE WORLD economic crisis has dealt a shattering
blow to capitalist complacency. Greatly alarmed,
the capitalists dimly perceive its seriousness, without understanding its causes. Chadbourne, the
sugar expert says: "Those who speak about these
world depressions coming in cycles and this being
one of these cycles are talking sheer nonsense.
This is a depression for which there is no precedent." [8] Judge Brandeis says: "The people of the
United States are now confronted with an emergency more serious than war." Pope Pius XI declares: "The international crisis is too general to
have been the work of men. It is evident that
the hand of God is being felt."

Over the world system of capitalism there grows

[8] *Speech in Brussels,* May 9, 1931.

a brooding fear of revolution. The capitalists cannot cure their deepening crisis and have been unable to check its progress. The old tricks and slogans for making capitalism "go" are no longer potent. Pessimism and confusion begin to appear in the ranks of the bourgeoisie. They start to see, not prosperity, but the revolution, "just around the corner." Spengler asserts: "It is no mere crisis, but the beginning of a catastrophe.[9] The chief economist of the Stock Exchange, Dr. Irving Fisher of Yale, in a speech cited by the United Press on Jan. 3, of this year, issued "a warning to capitalism 'to clean the dirt of depression' from its foundation or be devoured by some form of Socialism." In the recent debates in the House on the sales tax Rep. Rainey declared that the American people "are right up against Communism." Mr. Raymond Fosdick, (*New York Times,* Dec. 27, 1931), shrinks at the prospect of a revolution, stating that: "Western civilization (read capitalism, WZF) has begun to look furtively around, listening behind it for the silent tread of some dread specter of destruction." W. F. Simms, Scripps-Howard Foreign Editor, in a dispatch of Oct. 5, 1931, says:

"The object of these epochal comings and goings (the various international conferences), it is admitted behind the scenes, is nothing more or less than to prevent, not merely the collapse of this or that particular country,

9 *The American Mercury,* January, 1932.

but of the white man's universe as a whole.   For recent events have driven Washington, London, Paris, Berlin and Rome to the startling realization that only some sane accord on international finances, economics and armaments — and that promptly — can prevent a general smash."

Such elements among the bourgeoisie become especially lugubrious when they think of the Soviet Union. They begin to sense Communism as a higher and inevitable order of society. They more and more realize, as their own society goes deeper into crisis, that the U.S.S.R., forging ahead, is having a profoundly revolutionary effect upon the masses of starving workers and poor peasants still under capitalism. Prof. Pollock, a bourgeois scientist, at the 1931 World Congress for Social Planning, said:

"The Soviet Union has filled millions of workers and peasants with hope and belief in a better future and of the possibility of further progress.   With us, on the contrary, things get worse every year.   If capitalism is not capable of arousing equal enthusiasm and readiness for sacrifice in the masses, then there can be no doubt that they will finally choose the path of the Soviets."

It is well known, of course, that the European bourgeoisie, animated by such fears, are taking many precautions for their personal safety. But it is "news" that American capitalists feel the need for similar measures. In *Liberty,* Jan. 2, 1932, Cornelius Vanderbilt, Jr., says, speaking of the ultra-rich: "They see the possibility of long vistas of hungry faces in breadlines again this winter, and they fear the red specter of revolution. . . It is interesting to note that since the beginning of the depression the yachts of society millionaires (in New York Harbor) have invariably been anchored in places where their owners could board them on short notice."

These dark forebodings are true expressions of the fear eating at the consciousness of the capitalist class. They serve to stimulate the offensive against the workers. But, of course, the general policy of the capitalists does not limit itself to spreading such pessimism. On the contrary, especially in the United States, they systematically cultivate optimism. As the capitalists intensify their drive against the workers' standards of living, they at the same time increase their propaganda about the impending return of prosperity. The burden of their song is that this is "just another crisis," that the crises of the past have been overcome and have been followed by "prosperity," and that the same thing must happen again. The cultivation of such prosperity illusions is one of the principal methods of the capitalists to break the resistance of the workers against wage-cuts, starvation, relief systems, etc.

This pollyanna propaganda is best illustrated in the policy of the federal government. President Hoover started out, at the time of the Wall Street crash, by assuring everyone that this was only a financial bubble, that the great "prosperity" was safe. Then, when the industrial crisis was upon us on all sides, he assured us, March 8, 1930, that "the depression will be over in 60 days." And from that time on every department in the government has harped upon a similar string. Undoubtedly, the effect of sowing such illusions has been to facilitate the wholesale cutting down of the workers' living standards that has taken place. The theory that the crisis will cure itself and that all will be well again, is further classically illustrated by Prof. Taussig, who advises us: "Don't spend too much; don't hoard; don't worry; just live normally and everything will right itself in due time as it has always done." [10]

The capitalist optimists are wrong; the fears of the pessimists are justified. What we have to deal with is not "just another crisis," which will soon liquidate itself and be followed by a higher and worldwide wave of "prosperity." It is a profound economic crisis developing on the basis of a rapidly deepening general crisis of capitalism. Arising out of fundamental weaknesses of the present social system, it is setting on foot forces that are drastically undermining the very economic, political and social foundations of capitalism, and hastening that system ever faster towards the proletarian revolution.

[10] *Radio Broadcast,* Jan. 23, 1932.

Cyclical Crises

IN ORDER to understand what is the matter with the capitalist system, why it is torn with economic crises, war and revolution and why it is sentenced to death as a social order, it is necessary to take at least a brief glance at the basic processes of capitalism. If this is done it is readily seen that the capitalist system is a shaky house built upon sand. It is full of incurable internal contradictions which cause its conflicts and crises, which deepen with the development of capitalism, which produce its decline and decay, and which must culminate in its revolutionary overthrow. Over 80 years ago Marx pointed out these innate weaknesses of capitalism.

The basic contradiction of capitalism, the source of all its weakness and of its final dissolution, is found in the fact that this system does not carry on production for the benefit of society as a whole but for the profit of a relatively small owning class. The great industries by which society must live are owned by private individuals who ruthlessly exploit the masses who work in these industries. Under capitalism production is regulated not by the needs of the masses but by whether or not the capitalist class can make a profit by such production; commodities are not produced primarily for use, but for profit.

The system of private ownership and production for profit generates the whole series of contradictions and conflicts — economic, political and social — which torment present day society, causing disruption in the economic life and violent struggles between individual capitalists, between social classes and between capitalist States. This maze of conflict turns around the two major contradictions into which the basic contradiction of capitalism resolves itself. The first of these is economic, the tendency of capitalist production to exceed the buying capacity of the masses and thus to cause crises of over-production. The second contradiction is social in character, the division of capitalist society into classes of exploiters and producers, with resultant class struggle between them. The first contradiction, making for the disruption of capitalist economy and the impoverishment of the masses, provides the objective conditions for eventual revolution; the second, organizing the political struggle of the toiling masses, prepares the subjective factor, the revolutionary working class.

Now let us examine briefly the first of these major contradictions, the tendency of capitalist production to outstrip the markets, to cause over-production. Over-production is inherent in the capitalist system because the toiling masses, robbed in the industries by the employers, are paid back in the shape of wages only a fraction of the value they create. The wage of the worker remains essentially at the subsistence level, regardless of his productive capacity.

This exploitation results in a piling up of commodities in the hands of the capitalists, for naturally a worker getting a wage of three to five dollars a day cannot buy back the ten to twenty or more dollars' worth of commodities he has produced. This gap between his producing and buying powers widens by the constant increase in the workers' productive capacity through machinery and the speed-up and also by the lowering of their standards of living. The gigantic booty in the possession of the capitalists is further increased by their wholesale robbery of the poor farmers by paying them low prices for their products, charging them monopoly prices for the commodities they must buy, loading them down with exorbitant taxes, usurious loans, etc.

The capitalists waste huge masses of these stolen commodities through luxurious living, by the creation of hordes of parasitic occupations, by immense military establishments and wars. They seek to dispose of them by export trade. But the surpluses are not exhausted by these means. There is an inevitable tendency to glut the market with unsaleable commodities. Even though, as now, the millions of producers, who make up the bulk of the population, may actually starve and die for want of the barest necessities of life, the market suffers from over-production.

This basic tendency of capitalism to over-production (while the masses starve) results in actual economic crisis because of the competitive character of the capitalist system. Under capitalism there is and can be no general plan of production to fit social needs. Capitalist production is anarchic. The innumerable individual capitalists and companies, ruthlessly exploiting the toiling masses, produce whatever they think they can sell by dint of sharp competition with each other. The results are, the impoverished masses not being able to buy back what they have produced, over-expansion of the industries, a general flooding of the markets and a hastening of the capitalist crisis of over-production.

But the basic tendency of capitalism towards over-production does not result in immediate and chronic industrial stagnation, because it is partially offset by a counter tendency towards the expansion of the capitalist market. Among the principal factors historically in this market expansion have been the extension of capitalism upon a world scale, with a consequent wide development of transportation and communication industries, the gradual conquest of the peasant and handicraft occupations and their re-organization upon a capitalist basis, the large increase in population in all countries, the building of elementary public services such as water and lighting plants in many countries, the huge growth of munitions making and the military establishment, etc.

These developments of the capitalist market have

provided outlets for the investment of the capital robbed from the workers in the shape of surplus value. But the tendency for the market to expand has always lagged behind the tendency to clog the market with over-production. In consequence there is periodic need for the readjustment of these mutually antagonistic tendencies. These readjustments are the cyclical crises of capitalism.

Marx made the first analysis of the causes and consequences of these crises. Cyclical crises are common to all capitalists countries, including the United States, which has experienced 15 of such major economic disturbances since 1814. In the various countries the cycles have averaged from seven to nine years. The development of the capitalist system has not been even and steady, but by a series of jerks. The zigzag graph made by the cyclical crises is the normal graph of capitalist growth the world over.

The general course of the capitalist cycle is quite familiar. First, the upward trend, a period of industrial expansion, with rising prices and wages, an era of good employment, "prosperity" and optimism, gradually developing into a boom, with its characteristic orgies of feverish production, stock speculation, etc.; secondly, the downward trend, with the gradual surfeit of the market from excess production, slowing down of industry, wage-cuts, fall of prices, mass unemployment, financial "panics" and general economic crisis; and thirdly, the trough of the crisis, in which the productive forces are diminished and the choking surplus of commodities, in the low state of production, are consumed or wasted in various ways and the markets thus cleared for a fresh race between the swiftly expanding productive forces and the more slowly developing capitalist market.

But the cyclical crisis is more than an economic disturbance. It also greatly sharpens the major social contradiction of capitalism, the ever-active antagonism between the working class and the capitalist class. In economic crises the capitalists always seek to shift the economic burden onto the workers through wage-cuts, etc., and this still further stokes the class struggle. Hence, the capitalist cyclical crises have been especially periods of great strikes fiercely fought, growing class consciousness of the workers, etc.

The present economic crisis bears this cyclical character, but it develops under the special conditions of the deepening general crisis of capitalism, which profoundly change its character and deepen its effects in every direction.

The General Crisis of Capitalism

THE TREND of capitalist development is not, however, a simple repetition of cycles, with capitalism necessarily having a broadened base and stronger sinews after each cyclical crisis. It is a bourgeois fallacy that production and exchange, in the long run, automatically balance each other under capitalism, that the capitalist market mechanically expands to accommodate the increased production. On the contrary, as we have seen, the capitalist system, in its very essence, leads to over-production. This tendency to over-production is vastly strengthened as capitalism develops. The productive powers of the workers more and more outrun their consumptive capacity. Thus the major economic contradiction of capitalism, that between production and exchange, becomes ever deeper and more devastating, and with it, like its shadow, grows an intensification of the revolutionary class struggle.

Capitalism can live only by a rapid extension of its market, so that the ever-increasing masses of surplus value robbed from the workers may be disposed of through new capital investment. Therefore, the widening of the gap between the productive forces and the consuming power of the impoverished masses progressively brings the whole capitalist system into broader and deeper crises, into sharper class struggle, and eventually into decay and decline. Karl Marx clearly foresaw the development of this general crisis of capitalism when, speaking of the manner of liquidating the cyclical crises, he said it was "paving the way for more extensive and more destructive crises and diminishing the means whereby crises are prevented." As Varga says: "Each cycle is at the same time a step in the history of capitalism, bringing it nearer to its termination." [11] So far, in fact, has this general trend gone that the world capitalist system can be said definitely to have entered its period of decay. That is, capitalism no longer has to deal simply with cyclical crises, each of which left it upon a higher plane, but a growing general crisis, political as well as economic, which marks its decline as a world system.

The history of capitalist development may be divided into two general eras, industrial capitalism and imperialism. The former was the period of "healthy" capitalism, of its rapid rise and extension; the latter is the period of its decay and decline. As Lenin says, "Imperialism is the final stage of capitalism." Regarding the early phase of capitalism, the *Program of the Communist International* states:

"The period of *industrial capitalism* was, in the main, a period of 'free competition,' a period of a steady development and expansion of capitalism throughout the entire world, when the as yet unoccupied colonies were being divided up and conquered by armed force; a period of continued growth of the inherent contradictions of capitalism, the burden of which fell mainly upon the systematically plundered, crushed and oppressed colonial periphery."

Imperialism is the era of monopolistic capitalism. It has been analysed by Lenin in his *Imperialism,*

[11] *International Press Correspondence*, No. 27, 1931.

which may be summarized as follows: (a), the concentration of industry and the development of trusts and other monopoly forms; (b), the concentration of banking capital and its amalgamation with industrial capital under the hegemony of finance capital; (c), the export of capital from the imperialist countries; (d), the division of the world among monopolistic unions of capitalists, cartels, syndicates and trusts; (e), the territorial division of the world among the great imperial powers.

The correctness of this elementary analysis is clear. It would serve no purpose to summon statistics to show the gigantic growth of trusts and powerful banks in all capitalist countries, and the supremacy of finance capital. The significance of the export of capital is that when it takes place it means that the faster developing productive forces have quite outrun the slower developing home market in the given country and that it becomes necessary to find foreign markets for the excess of capital and other commodities. All the great capitalist countries have reached this stage, England being the earliest and most classical example. The growth of the international trusts and cartels and "spheres of influence" are a matter of common knowledge. And as for Lenin's final proposition, the division of the world among the capitalist powers with the growth of imperialism, he says: "In 1876 three powers had no colonies; and a third one, France, had hardly any. In 1914 those four powers had acquired a colonial empire of 14,100,000 square kilometers, or approximately one and a half times greater than the area of Europe, with a population of some 100,000,000 souls . . . the division of the world was 'completed' by the dawn of the 20th century." [12]

The United States began clearly to show its imperialistic character about 1900. This was evidenced by the intensification of the growth of trusts, the rapid rise to dominance of the great banking interests, and by the beginnings of a system of colonies through the seizure of the Philippines, Cuba, Porto Rico, etc., and the development of "spheres of influence" in China, Latin America, etc. All these tendencies increased with the passage of the years, but it was only after the World War that American imperialism came to maturity. Fattening upon the slain of that great slaughter, with the other imperialist countries paralysed by the murderous struggle, American imperialism was able to export capital (including the war loans) to the gigantic amount of 27 billion dollars. It has widely penetrated into a score of Latin American countries, reducing them to semi-colonies. Its influence in Canada is tremendous. It tries, with its Young Plan and other financial schemes of enslavement, to reduce Europe to its control. It has a hand in every imperialistic robbery in China and Africa. With its great navy and potentially tre-

[12] *Imperialism*, p. 66.

mendous military establishment, it has become the most powerful and ruthless of imperialist powers, aiming at hegemony over the world.

The development of world imperialism enormously sharpened all the contradictions of capitalism. The major economic contradiction between the producing and consuming powers of the masses was vastly deepened. The productive powers were increased, the exploitation of the workers in the industrial countries and the colonial masses was intensified. The class struggle became more acute, the war danger more menacing. The great powers began to fight more relentlessly to conquer the lagging world markets to dispose of their choking surpluses of commodities, to win new sources of supplies of raw materials for their industries and to re-divide the world to their respective advantage. Capitalism began definitely to show signs of the developing general crisis.

The World War was a great clash of the sharpening imperialist antagonisms, an acute expression of the growing general crisis of the capitalist economy. It was an attempt of the various powers to solve their deepening problems by eliminating each other as competitors in the world market and by re-dividing the colonial world. The capitalist nations, developing with uneven tempo, could not tolerate the pre-existing division of markets and colonies. The great capitalist crisis which was the World War naturally caused a tremendous intensification of the class struggle. Revolutionary upheavals took place in many countries. The outstanding result was the loss to capitalism of one-sixth of the globe, Russia, and what prevented its losing Germany, Italy and several other countries were the counter-revolutionary activities of the Socialist parties against the revolutionary workers, which defeated the revolution in these countries.

After the great war and these revolutionary upheavals, which nearly killed it, capitalism got a brief breathing spell. By 1924 it had achieved what the Communist International called a "partial and temporary stabilization," both economically, and politically. Economically this was based upon the replacement of the material destruction wrought by the war, catching up with the war-caused building shortage, and by investment of capital necessary to rationalize antiquated industries in various countries; and politically it was based on the defeat of the revolutionary attempts of the proletariat.

But this breathing spell for capitalism did not last long. The tendency for capitalist production to outrun the markets soon manifested itself stronger than ever. In a number of capitalist countries there has been an intense rationalization of industry. Thus in the United States, which is the extreme illustration, from 1923 to 1928 there was a total of 200,000 less workers required to pro-

duce 42% more in the industries.[13]   On the railroads a given quantity of freight is transported now
by 33% fewer workers than 20 years ago.[14]   Tugwell shows increases in efficiency in the various
industries, 1914 to 1925, of from 10% (meat packing) to 210% (automobiles).[15]   And in agriculture, 14% less farm workers produced 20% more
crops in 1925 than in 1910.[16]   Besides, in the
colonial and semi-colonial countries, such as India,
China, Africa, Australia, etc., there has been considerable industrialization in spite of the determined efforts of the imperialist countries to prevent
it and to retain these countries simply as markets
for their manufactured articles and as sources of
raw materials.

The purchasing power of the masses has in no
sense kept pace with this increased producing
capacity.   On the contrary, there has been a vast
crippling of the capitalist market through wholesale reductions in the real wages of workers and
the incomes of farmers the world over; that is, by
the widespread impoverishment and decline in the
living standards of the masses.   The result is a
great clogging of the world markets and the
present unprecedented economic crisis.

[13] A. F. of L., *Business Survey*, November, 1931.
[14] *Labor Fact Book*, p. 107.
[15] *Industry's Coming of Age*, p. 3.
[16] *Harvey Baum*, p. 73.

The Decaying Capitalist System

IN RECENT years, especially since the beginning of the present economic crisis, the process of the concentration of capital has been greatly speeded in all sections of capitalist economy and in all capitalist countries. In the United States this has been marked by the wholesale wiping out of small business, the mergers of banks, the liquidation of stock-holdings of the petty bourgeoisie, the confiscation of great areas of farm land by foreclosure, etc. This rapid concentration of capital intensifies all the contradictions of capitalism.

It has produced, together with the unparalleled depth and breadth of the economic crisis and mass starvation, previously discussed, many other manifestations which, in sum, constitute the general crisis and decay of capitalism in this, its final stage of monopoly and imperialism. Most of these decay factors were already in evidence, but the present economic crisis is greatly emphasizing and developing them. They sharpen the capitalist contradictions in every direction. They intensify the contradiction between the capitalist methods of production and exchange; they broaden and deepen the struggles between workers and capitalists, between the various capitalist countries, between the imperialist countries and the colonies, and between the two world systems represented by capitalism as a whole and the U.S.S.R. They are undermining

the foundations and breaking down the very fiber
of capitalism. They make more and more for industrial paralysis, mass starvation, war, revolution.

Some of the more outstanding of these manifestations of the growing general crisis are, without
analyzing in detail the specific gravity of each:

(a) *Over-expansion of Industry:* In view of
the limited capacities of the capitalist markets,
there is a large over-expansion of the industrial
plant in all the leading capitalist countries. This
constantly grows more pronounced. The United
States is a striking example of this condition. It
is typically illustrated by the automobile industry
with a capacity estimated at 10,000,000 cars yearly
and a record output of but 4,500,000; the bitumi-
nous coal mines with a capacity of 750,000,000 tons
yearly and an output (1929) of 535,000,000; the
steel industry with a capacity of 65,000,000 tons
and a maximum output (1929) of 56,000,000; textiles with 50% excess plant capacity, etc. Even
in the greatest boom periods these capacities cannot be fully utilized. Such conditions, common to
the most highly industrialized countries of capitalism, are not only basic causes of the economic
crisis but also prolific breeders of the ultra-reactionary practices of the destruction of commodities
and such dismantling of industry as the present
proposal to tear out 100,000 British looms and
10,000,000 spindles.

(b) *Chronic Industrial Stagnation:* In the growing general crisis of capitalism there is an intensification of the whole phenomenon of the economic crisis. As Varga says: "Crises now follow more speedily upon one another, attain a greater depth, and shake bourgeois rule more violently than before." Besides this, whole sections of the capitalist economy, even before the present crisis, had fallen into a state of more or less chronic depression. Thus England and Germany, the one with its foreign trade ruined and the other hamstrung by its imperialist rivals, had been in practically permanent crisis since the end of the war. Besides, the older industries (coal, textiles, shipbuilding, etc.) had suffered a similar stagnation in all industrial countries including the United States; only the newer industries (automobiles, chemicals, electrical, etc.) experiencing substantial growth and expansion. As for agriculture, it had been in a prolonged world-wide crisis of unprecedented dimensions, due primarily to a vast over-production of wheat, cotton, rubber, coffee, sugar, etc., caused by the lowered buying power of the world's toilers, improved methods of production, increased acreage, etc.

The present economic crisis, despite eventual recovery here and there, will unquestionably intensify and spread this condition of chronic industrial stagnation. At the same time that the purchasing capacity of the producing masses drops, the rationalization of industry is proceeding apace, at least on the stronger sectors of capitalism. A. T. Sloan says, for example: "As a result of the re-adjustment and refinement that is going on, our industrial machine is more efficient, more effective from every standpoint than ever before in its history." [17]   That is it exactly; more able than ever to flood the sickly market with a fresh mass of un-saleable commodities. We can be sure that the present economic crisis will involve the older indus-tries and weaker sections of capitalist economy into still deeper and more permanent stagnation.

(c) *Permanent Mass Unemployment:* Through-out the leading capitalist countries, as one of the most basic features of the growing crisis of capi-talism, is an ever-increasing army of unemployed. Capitalism, unable to provide work for the work-ers, faces permanent mass unemployment on a gigantic scale. This tendency was typically illus-trated by the large army of jobless in England ever since the end of the World War, and by the fact that in the United States, even during the boom period of 1929, there were at least 3,000,000 unemployed. In Germany and England it has reached the point where many youths graduate from school and reach manhood without ever hav-ing had a job, and with little prospect of getting one. In the present economic crisis this perma-nently jobless mass of workers, full of fatal por-

[17] *New York Times,* Jan. 7, 1932.

tent to capitalism, is being added to by many millions.[18]

(d) *The Choking of International Trade:* One of the sure signs of the decline of capitalism is the systematic strangling of international trade that is now taking place. This is being done principally by high tariffs and under slogans of "economic nationalism" and "autarchy." In their bitter fight for markets, the capitalist countries generally have adopted the double-phased policy of high tariffs and dumping. Tariffs everywhere are at unprecedented heights and constantly going higher. "Free trade" England has now become a leader in this reactionary movement. The general result is to greatly intensify the industrial paralysis and trade stagnation. The tendency is for each capitalist country to wall itself off from the commerce of the others. Mussolini says: "This blockading of the free flow of trade has caught hold of the world and the grip is placed like that of a powerful wrestler on his adversary. It cannot move its component parts and though it writhes and rebels it is helpless." [19] Then, to show what a constructive program Fascism has, he jacks up the Italian tariff a few notches and launches a "Buy Italian" campaign to match the "Buy British," "Buy

[18] Marx (*Capital,* Vol. I, p. 308) indicated the revolutionary significance of the rapidly growing army of unemployed when he said : "A development of the productive forces which would diminish the actual number of laborers . . . would cause a revolution, because it would put the majority of the population on the shelf."

[19] *New York American,* Dec. 27, 1931.

French," etc. movements. This "economic nationalism" cannot lessen, but must intensify the
general crisis of capitalism.

(e) *The Breakdown of the Medium of Exchange:* An important sign of the general weakening of capitalism is the breakdown of the medium
of exchange in the individual countries and internationally. More than half of the capitalist world
is now off the gold standard, and the percentage
constantly grows; in every capitalist country, including the United States (Finance Reconstruction
Corporation, etc.), various systems of inflating the
currency are in effect. Not only are the individual
capitalist countries of themselves unable to maintain a stable currency, but, in their brutal struggles
with each other, they are breaking down the capitalist exchange medium generally. They fight to
bankrupt each other. The raid on the mark early
in 1931 smashed the German and Austrian financial system, compelled the United States to grant
the moratorium, forced Germany and Austria to
their knees before French imperialism and almost
provoked a gigantic economic collapse in Central
Europe. The raid on the pound following soon
after drove Great Britain off the gold standard,
wrecked the Labor government and deposed London as the world's money center. Then came the
raid on the dollar, which cost the United States the
loss of $500,000,000 in 20 days and which menaces
the gold standard in this country. All this was

tied up with the internecine struggle over the question of the international war debts and reparations.

(f) *The Development of Fascism:* Another of the pronounced symptoms of the decline of capitalism is the growth of Fascism in various forms in all capitalist countries. The capitalists, faced with the task of drastically slashing the living standards of the workers and poor peasants and, where the political crisis is acute, the job of trying to save the capitalist system itself, no longer find adequate their bourgeois "democracy," of which the Social Democracy is a part, to hold the rebellious masses in check. Consequently, with the aid of the Social Democrats, or Social Fascists,[20] they are transforming the masked "democratic" capitalist dictatorship into open Fascist dictatorship, with its extreme demagogy and use of violence against the workers and poor peasants. Mussolini is not the symbol of a new era of capitalist development, but the sign of a decadent system of society vainly trying to hold back the clock of social progress.

(g) *The Birth of a New World Social System:* The most significant of all signs of the decline of capitalism is the rise of the Union of Socialist Soviet Republics. Capitalism no longer stands dominant in the world with its only rival the declining remnants of feudalism. Today it faces a new and deadly rival, the forerunner of the new

[20] Communists use the terms "Social Democrat," "Social Fascist" and "Social Reformist" practically interchangeably; why, we shall see in Chapter IV.

world social order. The rise of the Soviet Union enormously weakens the world capitalist system. Capitalism has thereby lost territorially one-sixth of the globe, and it is rapidly losing more to the Chinese Soviets; it has lost control of the great markets and raw materials of what was old Russia; it suffers enormously in loss of prestige in the comparison of its industrial crisis and generally decadent conditions with the great advance of the U.S.S.R.; it confronts the deadly menace of its workers inspired and organized by this great example of the success of Socialism. And all these losses and dangers for capitalism in the rise of the U.S.S.R. will increase as time goes on.

To the foregoing signs of the growing capitalist crisis and decline many more could be added, including the increase of the socially parasitic classes of mere bond clippers, the growth of artificial stimulants for the market such as instalment buying, the reversion to pre-capitalist forms of production and barter, the smothering of inventions and improved methods of production, etc. But most significant are the menacing danger of war and the world-wide revolutionary upsurge of the toiling masses.

The War Danger

WAR IS inevitable under the capitalist system. Imperialism is the era of great world wars. The capitalist imperialists consciously use war as a weapon for furthering their interests just as they do tariffs and dumping.   They cold-bloodedly send millions to slaughter in order to eliminate their imperialist competitors and to reduce whole populations to their programs of exploitation.   The general crisis of capitalism, with its vastly sharpening antagonisms, is fast driving capitalism to a new world war; in fact, war is already here, in Manchuria and China proper.   Only 14 years after the great "war to end all war" we stand on the brink of a still more frightful shambles.

How deliberately capitalists consider war as a necessary part of their business was shown by the New York correspondent of the London *Daily Telegraph* who, on Dec. 23, 1916, wrote: "The rumors of peace which were current during the last week caused alarm on the New York Exchange and a sharp drop in the value of bonds.   The price of wheat dropped heavily.   Everybody is talking about the disasters which will occur upon the conclusion of peace."   Now the capitalists of the world are just as cynically looking to war as the broad way out of the present crisis.   They see in mass murder on the battlefields the way to make business good with bonanza profits for themselves. They are circulating propaganda among the unemployed workers that war is the only way to restart the crippled industries, to do away with unemployment.   They prepare war to beat back the advancing world revolution, to overthrow the

Soviet Union. The cynical militarist, General William Mitchell, says: "Many nations think that at this time a foreign war would do them a great deal more good than domestic insurrection and revolution." [21]

But capitalism, characteristically, hides its war plans behind a mask of pacifism. This is to throw dust in the eyes of the masses who would rebel against a frank statement of imperialist war aims. As the war nears the capitalists multiply their camouflage peace conferences, disarmament meets, etc., behind which the preparations for war proceed ever faster. For modern warfare pacifism is just as necessary as airplanes. It is characteristic of capitalist pacifist hypocrisy that the principal architect of the militaristic French imperialism, Briand, is hailed as the great apostle of international peace.

The League of Nations is not a peace-striving institution, as the capitalists and their Social Fascist flunkeys would have us believe; it is a grouping of imperialist bandits intent only upon their own schemes of mass exploitation and war making. The Kellogg Pact, instead of being, as Nicholas M. Butler says, "the supreme act of the age in which we live," is a monstrous lure to blind the masses to the slaughter that is being prepared. In Manchuria, Japan, a member of the League and a signer of the Pact, wiped its feet on this "scrap of

21 *Liberty,* Jan. 30, 1932.

paper" and exposed the League of Nations' imperialist character. And what could be more bankrupt than the present "disarmament" conference of the League now being held in Geneva.

The Social Fascists and bourgeois pacifists who support the various "peace" plans of the capitalist governments (while at the same time they vote the war budgets) are only catspaws; they play the game of imperialism by creating illusions among the masses that the warlike capitalist governments actually want peace. Only by the mass resistance of the workers can the war plans of the capitalists be delayed; only when the toiling masses have defeated the world bourgeoisie can war be abolished altogether.

Behind the smoke-screen of pacifism war armaments pile up. Now they are greater than ever before in "peace" times. Over 10,000,000 men are now under arms and 35,000,000 are in reserve. The total world military expenditures are now 5 billion dollars yearly, against 2½ billion in 1913, with the United States expending far more for its armed forces than any other nation.[22] If the price index is taken as a basis it is found that since 1928 military expenditures of the principal powers have increased as follows: United States 48%, Japan 40%, France 43%, Italy 25%. The following figures show the large increases in the direct military

[22] "War and its by-products (pensions, etc.) cost the United States government $2,201,390,992 during the fiscal year that ended last June."— United Press dispatch, Feb. 3, 1932.

outlay of the five great powers, the United States, Great Britain, France, Japan and Italy:

1914..........$1,182,000,000
1923.......... 1,828,000,000
1928.......... 2,167,000,000
1930.......... 2,324,000,000

These huge expenditures are being accompanied by an unheard-of militarization and mobilization of the masses and the whole industrial system for war. New and hideous weapons are constantly being devised for mass murder; frightful poison gases and germ bombs; airplanes, tanks, submarines, etc., a hundred times more efficient at wholesale killing of human beings than during the World War. The decadent capitalist system, fighting to prolong its anti-social existence, menaces the very life of the peoples with its program of mass slaughter.

What these murderous war preparations mean is indicated by the jingo General Mitchell, who is trying to stir up a war against Japan. He says: "These (Japanese) towns, built largely of wood and paper, form the greatest aerial targets the world has ever seen. . . Incendiary projectiles would burn the cities to the ground in short order. An attack by gas, surging down through the valleys, would completely blot their population out." [23] And even as I write these lines, Japanese planes are bombarding and burning Shanghai, slaughter-

[23] *Liberty*, Jan. 30, 1932.

ing thousands of non-combatants. Stuart Chase, under the heading, "The Two-Hour War," gives a vivid picture of the new capitalist war-makers in action:

"War is declared. Nay, war is only threatened — for he who speaks first, speaks last. In Bremen, or Calais, a thousand men climb into the cockpits of a thousand aircraft, and under each is slung a bomb which the pressure of finger may release. A starting signal, an hour or two of flight — one muffled roar after another as the bombs are dropped per schedule — and so, the civilization which gave Bacon, Newton, and Watt to the world, comes, in something like half an hour, to a close. Finished and done. London, Liverpool, Manchester, Lancashire, Bristol, Birmingham, Leeds. Not even a rat, not even an ant, not even a roach, can survive the entire and thorough lack of habitability.[24]

The world stands in the most imminent danger of such a horrible blood bath. The whole capitalist system is a maze of acute war antagonisms, bred of and stoked by the increasing general capitalist crisis. The deeper the crisis, the more acute the war danger. Growing Fascism, with its intense nationalism, renders the danger all the sharper. The war antagonisms flare up between the various capitalist powers, between the imperialist countries and the colonial and semi-colonial countries, and especially between world imperialism and the Soviet Union. In order to preserve their system of exploitation the capitalists are proceeding direct

[24] *Men and Machines,* p. 310.

to a slaughter, beside which that of 1914-18 will seem pale, and which may well result in the destruction of the capitalist system. But, of this, more anon.

Among the great capitalist powers there exist many antagonisms, any of which may produce a devastating war, and these antagonisms constantly become more acute under the pressure of the deepening crisis of capitalism. Of them the more important are: the struggle between the United States and Great Britain for world imperialist hegemony; [25] the conflict between the United States and the rising system of French imperialism; the four-cornered fight between the United States, Japan, Great Britain and France for domination of the Far East; the struggle between Great Britain and France for financial supremacy and general leadership in Europe; the struggle of France and her vassal States (Poland, Rumania, Czecho-Slovakia, etc.) to choke Germany into submission and to hang on to their Versailles Treaty blood booty; the sharp antagonisms between France and Italy over control of the Mediterranean area; the tangle of potential war conflicts in the Balkans; and, of present special acuteness, the struggle between the United States and Japan for imperialist control in the Far East. In short, world capitalism presents the picture of a medley

[25] For the vast ramifications of this great struggle see Ludwell Denny's *America Conquers Britain*.

of hostile imperialist groupings preparing inevitably to cut each other's throats, and if they have not already done so it has been chiefly from fear of revolutionary upheavals of the workers.

The antagonisms between the imperialist countries and the colonial and semi-colonial countries likewise grow constantly more sharp. Stalin says: "The European bourgeoisie is in a state of war with 'its' colonies in India, Indo-China, Indonesia and Northern Africa." [26] One of the basic indications of the growing decline of world capitalism is the weakening of the hegemony of the imperialist powers over the colonial countries, the necessity of the imperialists to use more and more armed force against the colonies. These growing conflicts are caused primarily by the attempts of the imperialist countries to shift the burden of the crisis onto the colonial countries by means of intensified exploitation of the peasants and workers, tariffs, high taxes, the crippling of local industry, etc., all backed by imperialist troops, and by the rebellion of the colonial masses against this impoverishment. Great Britain, in increasing collision with its dominions, Canada, South Africa, Australia and Ireland, over the tariff and other questions, proceeds with armed force, under the leadership of the "Socialist" MacDonald, to crush rebellious India. France maintains its grip peri-

[26] Speech at the XVI Congress of the Communist Party of the Soviet Union.

lously upon Indo-China by "fiercest terror, mass shootings, the annihilation of whole villages by French occupational troops." Japan carries out its colonial policy by the armed conquest of Manchuria. And American imperialism, to hang onto its great Latin-American hinterland, finds necessary an ever-greater terrorism by its puppet governments in Cuba, Nicaragua, Chile, Salvador, the Philippines, etc. In all these situations lurks the danger of sudden and far-reaching war.

But the greatest and most imminent of war dangers is that between world imperialism and the Soviet Union. This antagonism is the most fundamental of all economic, political and social conflicts. The major political objective of world capitalism is to overthrow the Soviet government. The capitalists' central world strategy is to bridge over their own contradictions sufficiently to enable them to make a united front in war against the first Workers' Republic. Ingrained in the very fibre of world imperialism is the slogan, "Death to the Soviet Union." This is the struggle between two antagonistic world systems, capitalism and Socialism. It grows ever sharper with the deepening of the general capitalist crisis. Upon this central contradiction capitalism will eventually break its worthless neck.

In 1918-20, at the very birth of the Soviet government, France, Great Britain, United States, Germany, Japan, Czecho-Slovakia, Poland, etc.,

sent their armies against the revolutionary Russians. But these armed assaults were defeated by
the Soviet forces. The imperialist powers, faced
by dauntless revolutionary soldiers, fearing revolution at home and learning to their dismay that
their armies of workers and peasants often mu-
tinied rather than fight against the Russians (this
being the case also with the 310th United States
Infantry at Archangel), had to abandon for the
time being their program of violent overthrow of
the Soviets.

But the capitalist powers did not give up
their counter-revolutionary determination. With
French and American gold they built a steel
row of armed Fascist States along the Russian border; they established an economic, financial and political boycott against the Soviets; they
sabotaged the Russian industries from within; they
worked ceaselessly with their Social Fascist tools
to discredit the Soviet Union among the workers
of the world, as a preparation for a new armed
attack. With the manifest success of the Soviet
regime, especially the great victories of the Five-
Year Plan, the capitalists have redoubled the attacks against the Soviet government. They have
flooded the world with anti-Russian propaganda
— charges of red imperialism, dumping, forced labor, red plots, religious persecution, etc. France
has been the most militant in all this. Hardly less
active also is the United States, with its policy of

non-recognition, trade restriction, financial blockade, Fish committee propaganda, etc.; this country,
the world center of capitalism, has always viewed
with undisguised hatred the world center of Communism, the U.S.S.R.

In 1929 the imperialists made an effort to pro-
voke an anti-Soviet war by the seizure of the Chinese Eastern Railroad through subsidized Chinese
generals. But this was defeated by the prompt
and victorious action of the Red Army. And the
exposures made in the famous trials of the Industrial Party and the Mensheviks broke up the
plans for an armed intervention against the
U.S.S.R., scheduled to take place in the Spring
of 1931 under the leadership of the French General Staff. Doubtless, the great stores of wheat
assembled at that time by the Federal Farm Board
were to have been used to provision this war.

Now, in the Manchurian invasion by Japan,
world imperialism is developing a new and still
more dangerous attack against the Soviet Union.
In its present imperialist war against the Chinese,
Japan has clearly in mind the following objectives:
(1), the dismemberment of China and the capture
of its markets; (2), the crushing of the rapidly
spreading Chinese Soviets; (3), the establishment
of a strong base in Manchuria from which to
launch an early attack upon the Soviet Union.
The deliberation with which Japan is developing
this strategy against the U.S.S.R. is indicated by

the following quotation from a memorandum presented on July 25, 1927, by the then-Premier, Tanaka, to the Mikado:

"The Chinese Eastern Railway will become ours just as the South Manchurian Railway became ours, and we shall seize Kirin as we seized Dairen. It seems that the inevitability of crossing swords with Russia on the fields of Mongolia in order to gain possession of the wealth of North Manchuria is part of our program of national development."

While the general strategy of world imperialism is to develop the attack against the Soviet Union, this does not go forward on the basis of a solid bloc or united front of all its leaders with Japan, spearhead of imperialism, in China. This is because the violent antagonisms between the imperialist powers prevent such a firm unity. France, which actively prepares the offensive against the U.S.S.R. through Poland, etc., is solidly united with Japan and supports it. But England maneuvers against France and Japan and has its eye on its Chinese interests, especially in the Shanghai district. As for the United States, it views with alarm the strengthening of its traditional enemy in the Pacific, Japan.

But all these powers are violent enemies of the Soviet Union, and their mutual antagonisms do not prevent the development of the imperialist attack generally against the U.S.S.R. In the *In-*

ternational Press Correspondence, Mar. 10, 1932, a writer puts the situation thus:

"The sharpness of the imperialist antagonisms renders difficult the formation of new groupings of power. But — as the Japanese campaign in Manchuria and in the Yangtse valley shows — it not only does not form an insurmountable obstacle to the immediate war preparations but is also no obstacle preventing the world from creeping into the world war, into military intervention against the Soviet Union. As experience shows, these groupings are formed at the outbreak and partly even in the course of war, in the carrying out of military operations."

The danger of imperialist war against the U.S.S.R. is now most acute. The imperialist bandits are trying to force the Soviet Union into the Manchurian war. That is the purpose of Japan's studied insolence and provocation, its massing of troops on the Soviet border, its organization of the counter-revolutionary White Russians. And the significance of the attempted assassination of the Japanese ambassador in Moscow by Vanek, a Czecho-Slovakian diplomat, was that France tried to organize another Sarajevo. Only the steadfast peace policy of the Soviet Union has prevented its being enmeshed in war. But there is a limit to such provocation. As Molotov says: "We do not need an inch of any other country's land; but neither will we give up an inch of ours."

The capitalists clearly intend to thrust war upon the Soviet Union. Their offensive may easily come during 1932. The deepening general crisis of their own system and the growing successes of the U.S.S.R. inevitably drive them on to this war. It is a situation that should arouse every worker to fight against the robber war on China, and to rally in defense of the Soviet Union. When the capitalists, to save their bankrupt system, launch their armed attack upon the U.S.S.R. to destroy its new Socialism, they must be taught a revolutionary lesson from which their system of robbery and misery will never recover.

The World-Wide Revolutionary Upsurge.

THE MOST basic indication of the growing general crisis of capitalism and its decline as the social order is the increasing revolutionary upsurge throughout the world. The toiling millions, finding it impossible to live in the starvation conditions everywhere developing, are gradually getting ready to wipe out capitalism and to establish Socialism. In his profound analysis of capitalist society, Marx says:

"Along with the constantly diminishing number of the magnates of capital . . . grows the mass of misery, oppression, slavery, degradation, exploitation, but with this grows the revolt of the working class, a class always increasing in numbers, and disciplined, united, organized by the very mechanism of capitalist production itself." [27]

[27] *Capital,* Vol. I, p. 836.

Reformist Socialists have always violently attacked this conception of growing working class pauperization and revolt. They have put in its stead their own theory of the gradual rise in the standards of the workers and their progressive acceptance of capitalist evolution as the way to Socialism. For a period, during the rise of imperialism in the leading industrial countries, bringing about improved conditions for the labor aristocracy, largely at the expense of the exploited colonial masses, the workings of Marx's principle were somewhat obscured. The opportunist Socialists were able to lend an air of plausibility to their bourgeois theories about the advancing standards of the working class under capitalism.

But now, with the development of the general crisis of capitalism, the truth of Marx's formulation stands out with crystal clearness. Truly, as the *Communist Manifesto* says, "pauperism develops more rapidly than population and wealth," and "it becomes evident that the bourgeoisie is unfit any longer to be the ruling class in society . . . because it is incompetent to assure an existence to its slave in his slavery, because it cannot help letting him sink into such a state that it has to feed him, instead of being fed by him." That is, on the one hand, as we have already seen, there is mass impoverishment developing upon the most gigantic scale, and on the other, as we shall now indicate, there is the growing revolt of the workers, so clearly foreseen by Marx.

The revolutionary upsurge of the workers and peasants is worldwide. It varies in intensity, corresponding to the uneven development of capitalism in the several countries, from intensified strike movements to actual struggles for power. Its tempo is greatly increased by the deepening of the capitalist crisis. Hoover had a smell of its significance when, in his message to Congress on Dec. 8, 1931, he informs us that: "Within two years there have been revolutions or acute social disorders in 19 countries, embracing more than half the population of the world." The resolution of the XI Plenum of the Executive Committee of the Communist International, (April, 1931), thus analyses the situation:

"There has been a further increase in the revolutionary upsurge bound up with the sharp reduction in the standard of living of the working class, the monstrous development of unemployment, the ruination of the office workers and urban petty bourgeoisie, the mass robbery of the peasantry, the extreme impoverishment of the colonies and the growing revolutionizing role of the U.S.S.R.

"The growing revolutionary upsurge found expression in: (a) the further intensification of the strike struggle and the unemployment movement, (b), the development and strengthening of Soviets and of the Red Army over a considerable area in China, (c), the growth of the revolutionary movement in the colonies, (d), the development of the revolutionary peasant movement, (e), the growth of the political and organizational influence of a number of important Communist Parties (Germany, China, Czecho-Slovakia, Poland), (f), the sharp intensification of oppositional ferments within the Social Democracy, (g), the growth of an opposition among the petty bourgeois masses of the towns, office employees and civil servants."

In the months since the foregoing was written the revolutionary upsurge has been accelerated on every front. In the industrial countries of Europe the strike movement has been greatly broadened and intensified, in spite of the efforts of the powerfully intrenched Socialists to stifle all struggle. The strikes are more numerous, they include more workers and they are more militantly carried on. During this period one of the most striking events was the mutiny of the British Navy sailors against a wage-cut. This affair sent a shiver along the spine of the world bourgeoisie.

The United States is not exempt from the developing world-wide movement of struggle. American workers, faced by intolerable conditions, are also exhibiting the characteristic signs of radicalization. During 1931 the number of strikers doubled over the previous year. A series of important strikes have been carried on (coal miners in Western Pennsylvania, Ohio, West Virginia, Kentucky and the anthracite districts, textile workers in Lawrence, Allentown, Paterson, etc.) in spite of the rankest betrayal by the A. F. of L.

leadership, all these strikes being very militant in character. The unemployed are also showing increased radicalization, indicated by such important movements as the National Hunger March, the Ford Hunger March, the big demonstrations in Chicago, Cleveland, etc.; notwithstanding the extreme brutality of the police, nine workers having been killed in the three latter movements. The Negro workers, in strikes and unemployment movements, have been distinguished for their militancy, the Camp Hill and Scottsboro outrages being attempts of local authorities to terrify them. Among the skilled workers a striking demonstration of the radicalization taking place is the rank and file referendum of unemployment insurance in the A. F. of L., a movement involving hundreds of thousands of workers and going directly contrary to the policy of the reactionary leadership. These are only a few indications of the deep-going radicalization now taking place among the American working class. But, of this subject, more will be said in Chapter IV.

In Germany events are moving towards a revolutionary political crisis. The masses of workers, in spite of Socialist treachery and Fascist repression, are preparing to free themselves from the tyranny of the Versailles Treaty and its Young Plan, and with it, from the capitalist system itself. The Communist party, rapidly growing, now counts almost five million votes. The proletarian revolution advances irresistibly in Germany. It is in the vain hope of defeating it that the employers are building up Fascism through the Social Fascists, the Bruening government and the Hitler movement.

Poland is another country where the revolution begins to menace capitalism. The industrial and agrarian crises are acute. More than half the workers are either wholly or partly unemployed. One wave of wage-cuts follows another. The peasants are expropriated in masses for non-payment of rent. The country is burdened with militarism. The various national minorities are ruthlessly repressed. The country is stagnant from the loss of its former Russian markets. In this situation the Communist party, in spite of the ferocious terror of Pilsudski and Social Fascist treachery, steadily gains ground. The workers and peasants are becoming rapidly revolutionized. Great strikes, unemployment demonstrations and anti-tax and rent movements in the villages develop in rapid succession. There is a revolutionary storm brewing.

Spain is also a country where capitalism faces a developing revolutionary crisis. The producing masses suffer intolerable exploitation and misery from capitalist and semi-feudal conditions. The first phase of their revolt swept away the monarchy; now it turns sharply against capitalism itself. Social Fascist, Anarchist and Syndicalist illusions still act as a brake on the movement, but the revolutionary Communist party constantly becomes stronger.   The recent seizure of many towns and villages and the hoisting of the red flag are forerunners of the revolutionary struggle that is on its way.

Throughout the whole Asian colonial and semi-colonial world the revolutionary upsurge manifests itself upon a gigantic scale.   The basic trend of the hundreds of millions of toilers in these countries is towards Socialism, not capitalism.   The efforts of the national bourgeoisie, led by the Gandhis, Chang Kai Sheks, etc., to build up a powerful capitalism shatter themselves upon the rocks of the world industrial and agrarian crisis, the determination of the imperialists (to whom the native bourgeoisie always surrenders) to prevent the industrialization of the colonies, and the revolutionary struggles of the vast masses of incredibly exploited and impoverished workers and peasants. Under the increasing leadership of the Communist International, these revolutionary national struggles develop more and more, not only into fights again American, British, Japanese, French and Dutch imperialist domination, but against the whole capitalist system.   Asia is now undergoing profound revolutionary developments.

In China, 70,000,000 people are already living under the Provisional Chinese Soviet government, organized Nov. 7, 1931.   The Chinese Red Army

controls one-sixth of China and is constantly
spreading its influence. It is now hammering at
the gates of Hankow. Strikes and peasant movements develop in many other parts of China. The
prestige of the Kuomintang diminishes; that of the
Communist party rises. "Everywhere a decided
swing to the left is evident" said a *New York Times*
Chinese correspondent on Jan. 20, 1931. And 11
days later another said in the same paper: "Again
the Communists are making rapid progress in organizing town and country Soviets as rapidly as
they overrun new territory . . . the peasants and
common people are giving a hearty welcome to the
returning Communists. They say that after comparing their status under previous Communist rule
with the bad government and confiscatory taxation
enforced upon them after the arrival of the Nanking troops last Summer, they enjoyed greater liberty and a greater degree of prosperity under the
Reds than under Nanking." It was largely the
fear of the growing Chinese revolution, its tremendous effect upon the vast millions of Asia, the
danger of a great Russian-Chinese Soviet Union,
that determined the imperialists upon their present
war to partition China and to lay the basis for an
attack upon the Soviet Union.

In India the revolutionary struggle, while not
so advanced as in China, rapidly gains momentum.
The masses of peasants and workers are beginning
to break with the counter-revolutionary non-re-

sistance policies of Gandhi, which paralyze their struggle and enable a handful of British troops to rule the country. The failure of the London Round Table Conference is being followed by a great intensification of revolutionary activity in India. Over 50,000 "politicals" are in jail. The newly-organized Communist party consolidates itself and strengthens its position. Great strikes, militant peasant movements, etc., which sharpen to the point of armed clashes with the government, are the order of the day in India. And the revolutionary blaze will spread, despite the announced policy of the "Socialist" Ramsay MacDonald's government to "make a desert out of India." British imperialism and Indian capitalism have nothing to offer the Indian workers and peasants but starvation; and the inevitable reply of the latter will be revolution.

In Indo-China, controlled by French imperialism, a similar revolutionary foment exists. Despite terrific repression by French troops, there is a growing wave of strikes, mutinies, seizures of food supplies and local governments, leading to armed conflicts and guerilla warfare. In the North, where the influence of the Chinese revolution is strong, there has been the formation of local Soviets. This deepening revolutionary movement is mainly under the leadership of the Communist party.

In Latin America there is also to be seen the

growing revolutionary foment common to all colonial and semi-colonial countries, although not yet
in such acute form as in Asia.   The conditions of
the workers and peasants, in the deep industrial
and agrarian crises, go from bad to worse.   A
growth of revolutionary spirit is everywhere evident.   During the past three years many governments in South America have been overthrown by
coups d'etat.   While these "palace revolutions"
were largely engineered by American and British
imperialism in their struggles against each other,
they nevertheless had as a background the discontent of the masses.   This discontent, by undermining the strength and prestige of the existing
governments, made it easy for rival imperialist
agents to overthrow them.   In recent months, however, the struggles in Latin America assume a more
revolutionary character.   The working class and
radicalized peasantry are developing real mass
movements.   The Communist parties are becoming
more and more the leaders.   This development of
revolutionary struggle in Latin America is exemplified, among other events, by the Chilean Navy
mutiny and general strike, the Peruvian general
strikes and armed struggles, the big Cuban strikes
and the revolutionary struggles in Salvador.   In
the latter upheaval, for the first time in the Western Hemisphere, local Soviets were established.
We may expect further and still more important

revolutionary developments in Latin America in the near future.

The Revolutionary Perspective

THE GENERAL capitalist crisis heads inevitably, but not at the same speed in all countries, towards the revolutionary overthrow of the world capitalist system.   To the American with a bourgeois outlook, such a perspective will seem remote indeed. The American capitalism that he comes in contact with appears strong and no revolutionary danger seems to loom from the toiling masses.   But the perspective of revolution in general and in the United States in particular cannot be determined simply upon the basis of the present situation in this country.   American capitalism is part of the world capitalist system, subject to its general laws and bound up with its fate.   This is the first point to be borne in mind.

The second is Lenin's theory of the "weakest link."   The world capitalist system, as Marx has taught us, is not of uniform strength in all its parts. Hence, because of its uneven development in point of time, extent, etc., in the several countries, it is like a chain of stronger and weaker links.   The revolution advances, not by breaking the chain simultaneously everywhere, but by beginning the break at the weakest links.   Old Russia was such a weak link and the Russian revolution was such a break.

The capitalist chain, with the progress of the general capitalist crisis, is becoming full of weak links. The entire chain is weakening. As we have seen, among the especially weak links are Germany, Spain, Poland, China, India, etc. So far has the capitalist crisis developed in these countries that the toiling masses may make a revolutionary break through at any time, with disastrous results upon the whole chain. Such revolutionary breaks may come either as an accompaniment of imperialist war, or by the maturing gradually of the inner contradictions of capitalism in a given country, culminating in a struggle for power by the workers and toiling masses. And world capitalism is faced with imminent danger from both these directions, which are, of course, intimately related to each other.

The revolutionary danger to the capitalist system from the developing war situation is acute and menacing. If and when the imperialist powers launch a great war among themselves we may be sure that in many countries the workers and peasants, following the famous strategy of Lenin and under the leadership of the Communist International, will transform the imperialist war into a civil war against the capitalist system. The World War of 1914-18 resulted in the formation of the first Soviet Republic; another great war can well produce a Soviet Europe.

Capitalism will run no less a danger for its existence when it launches its eventual attack upon the Soviet Union. The Japanese were astounded at the brave resistance put up by the half-armed Chinese soldiers in Shanghai, fighting to defend their country from imperialist invasion. And the capitalist powers that attack the Soviet Union will be doubly and fatally surprised when they go against the Red Army. They will learn that their drafted masses of workers and peasants will have no taste to fight their Russian brothers; they will find out also that revolutionary soldiers fighting for Socialism are worth many times their number of toiler soldiers pressed into the service of capitalism. The capitalists will learn, finally, that they will have to face their aroused workers at home, for the defense of the Soviet Union will be carried out not only by the Red Army but by the militant working class all over the world. And the way this job will be done will bode ill for capitalism.

But the development of the revolution does not depend upon the initiation of imperialist war. As we have remarked, it also grows out of the sharpening of the economic and eventually political crisis within the given countries. This revolutionary process now goes ahead on a world scale with the deepening of the general crisis of capitalism.

We have seen how rapidly the revolution approaches in this way in Germany and other countries.

The proletarian revolution in Germany would be a deadly blow to the whole capitalist system throughout the world. Such a revolution would in all probability draw with it Poland and other countries on the Russian border. Thus, with the U.S.S.R., there would be created a gigantic Soviet bloc. This great Soviet Union, supported by the growing revolutionary movement in the remaining capitalist countries, would be well able to defend itself from the inevitable military attacks of the capitalist imperialists. More than that, it would certainly be in a dominant world position as against the decadent capitalist system. The center of gravity in the world relation of class forces would be shifted definitely on the side of the revolution. These far-reaching possibilities are now, with the sharpening of the crisis in Germany, already within the scope of practical political perspectives.

When the situation is thus looked at from the Marxist-Leninist conception of capitalism as a world economy, when it is realized that the capitalist system is like a chain of stronger and weaker links, and when it is seen how imminent a revolutionary break becomes in some of these links, and how disastrous to world capitalism such a break would be, then the perspective for the American revolution looms up in a quite different manner than though we kept our eyes fastened solely upon the immediate situation in this country. American capitalism, like capitalism in other countries, is travelling the same road to revolution. The chronological order of the United States' entry into the developing revolution is, as yet, a matter of speculation; but it would be sheer assumption to conclude that because this is the strongest capitalist country, it will be the last to go into revolution. One day, despite the disbelief of the capitalists and of their still more cynical Social Fascist lackeys, the American workers will demonstrate that they, like the Russians, have the intelligence, courage and organization to carry through the revolution. The American capitalist class, like that of other countries, is living on the brink of a volcano which, sooner than it dreams, is going to explode. George Bernard Shaw is right: the time will surely come when the victorious toilers will build a monument to Lenin in New York.

It is upon the background of this growing general crisis of capitalism that the present economic crisis develops. That is why it is of such unprecedented scope, depth and duration. Those who compare the prevailing crisis with the cyclical crises of the pre-war period are deluding themselves, living in a realm of false hopes. The pre-war economic crises developed during the period of the upward trend of capitalism; the present one, although retaining the cyclical character, occurs during the decline of capitalism. The former liquidated themselves into wider circles of capitalist growth; the latter leads to deepening crisis and decay.

In view of all this, the questions arise: can the capitalists secure even a temporary respite from the onward march of the revolution by a revival of industry ? Is the present one the last crisis of capitalism ? In answering these questions there must be borne in mind the considerations that, first, the present economic crisis is of a cyclical character, and, second, the question of the relation of forces between the working class and the capitalist class, with the possibility of breaks at weak links in the capitalist chain where the working class takes the revolutionary path. Where there is no strong revolutionary movement the capitalists will find a way out at the expense of the toiling masses; that is, the economic crisis, following the laws of cyclical crises, will eventually wear itself out by reducing production, slashing prices and wages and drastically reducing the living standards of the masses.

But that such a turn will come soon or extend far is doubtful. Already, as we have seen, in the deepening general capitalist crisis, whole sections of the capitalist economy have fallen into more or less chronic paralysis, and the tendency is for this paralysis to spread. The economic crises become more frequent, more widespread and more lasting. Varga points out, in illustrating the severity of the present crisis, that contrary to all previous experience: "so far there has been in general no diminution of visible (world) stocks; nay, some commodities even having increased in this respect."[28]   Any recovery, therefore, that may be registered from the present economic crisis can, at most, be only very partial and temporary in character.   It must soon be followed by another crash still more far-reaching and devastating to the capitalist system.

Capitalism is doomed.   The capitalist system of private ownership of industry and land, production for profit, and exploitation of the workers is reaching the end of its course.   It has outlived its historic mission.   In its earlier stages capitalism was a progressive system; it constituted an advance over feudalism, which preceded it.   Under capitalism there has been built an industrial system, at least in the imperialist countries; industrial technique has been developed; the proletariat has been created and disciplined.   But even the limited progress that capitalism has accomplished for humanity has been achieved at the cost of incredible misery, poverty, ignorance and slaughter of the working class.

Capitalism has created the objective conditions for Socialism.   But it can go no further.   It can-

[28] *International Press Correspondence,* Mar. 10, 1932.

not carry society to higher stages of development, to Socialism and Communism; it has become an obstacle in the upward path of humanity, a means of condemning hundreds of millions of people to mass starvation and death. History will soon sweep aside this obsolete system. Capitalism has provided its own executioners and grave diggers, the proletariat. The workers and peasants of the world are getting ready for their great social task of abolishing capitalism and establishing Socialism. They are freeing themselves from the illusion that capitalism provides the way to prosperity; they are gradually breaking the leadership of the MacDonalds, Gandhis, and other similar misleaders; under the banner of the Communist International they are securing revolutionary organization and program. In due season they will break through the Social Fascist and Fascist trickery and violence with which decadent capitalism sustains itself. World capitalist society is heading irresistibly towards the proletarian revolution.

CHAPTER II

THE RISE OF SOCIALISM

Now LET us turn away from the decaying, declining capitalist system, with its mounting mass misery, exploitation, war and Fascist terrorism, and look at the new rising system of Socialism in the Union of Socialist Soviet Republics. No longer is Socialism, which is the first stage of Communism, only a theory; no longer is it simply the aspiration of an oppressed working class. Now it is a living, growing reality. Operating simultaneously in the world with capitalism, it is showing in the everyday demonstration of life its immense superiority in every field over the obsolete capitalist system. The very existence of the Soviet Union has a profoundly revolutionizing effect upon the working class. It is the growing hope and strong leader of a working world preparing to strike off the shackles of the murderous capitalist system.

The workers and peasants of the Soviet Union have overthrown the capitalist State and have set up their Soviet government. They have abolished capitalist ownership of industry and land and are

building a great system of socialized industry and
agriculture. They have done away completely
with all exploitation of the toiling masses by owning, ruling classes. These fundamental political
and economic measures are the substance of the
revolution. They solve the many contradictions
of capitalism and they open the door to an era of
general prosperity, freedom and cultural advance
hitherto completely unknown to the world.

In the Soviet Union, where the economic and
political foundations of Socialism have been laid,
production is carried on for the social good, not for
the profit of an exploiting class. What determines the character and volume of production is
not whether capitalists can sell it at a profit for
themselves in a clogged market, but the needs of
the masses of people. Socialism thus liquidates
the basic contradiction — that is, the production of
social necessities for private profit — out of
which originates all the miseries and chaos of capitalism. Socialism thus revolutionizes the aim of
production from production for profitable sale to
production for social use. In so doing it frees
humanity from the narrow limits of capitalist
economy and embarks upon a totally new era of
social development.

This social advance is made in an orderly and
intelligent way. Socialism abolishes the chaos and
anarchy of capitalist production and social organization; it does away with the dog-eat-dog com-

petition of capitalist industry, breeder of industrial crises and war. It sets up instead a planned system of economy in harmony with the national and international character of modern industry and social relationships. Only under Socialism, with its great nationalized industries and collectivized agriculture, is such a scientific planned economy possible and inevitable.

In the Soviet Union this systematic advance on every social front is proceeding under the famous Five-Year Plan. In a world thrown into deepening disorder and demoralization by its growing general crisis, the superiority of the system of planned Socialist economy stands out like a great mountain. Even the capitalists themselves are compelled to recognize it and they try vainly to adapt it to the capitalist system. The correspondent of the *New York Times* only voices an almost universal opinion when he says: "The Soviet leaders know precisely what they want and are doing it, in sharp contrast to the rest of the world where leadership seems to be a lost art."

The Five-Year Plan constitutes a gigantic mobilization of the social forces of a great nation for an organized general forward movement. It covers the most diverse phases of social activity, stimulating them all into expansion and systematic development. Ilin says of it:

"The Five-Year Plan is a project: not of one factory, but of two thousand four hundred factories. And not only of factories, but also of cities, of electric stations, of bridges, of ships, of railroads, of mines, of state farms, of rural communes, of schools, of our libraries. It is a project for the rebuilding of our whole country, and was prepared, not by one man or by two men, but by thousands of trained persons. To the work of building came not tens, but millions of workers. All of us will help to build the Five-Year Plan." [1]

The Five-Year Plan deals with industry, agriculture and the transportation and communication systems, calculating the resources of these branches of economy, and providing for their development in every direction. It deals with the questions of housing, with the building of hospitals, etc. It provides for the maximum production and distribution of foodstuffs, expanding the new food industries in every part of the country. It figures out the number of workers required for production and plans their mobilization. It determines the total wage funds, including those for the cultural needs of the workers, for social insurance, etc. It makes provision for an organized development of science backed by the resources of the government. It calculates the national income and bases its whole program thereon. Besides the general Five-Year Plan, or rather within the framework of it, every city and every factory also has its own plan of organized work and development. The great Five-Year Plan is not simply an expedient for the

1 *The New Russian Primer*, p. 5.

present building of the Soviet economy; it represents the basic, planned method native to Socialist society and foreseen by Marx two generations ago. Planned economy is one of the great contributions of Socialism to humanity.

Flourishing Bolshevik Industries

IN THE Soviet Union there is taking place an unparalleled growth in production. As Louis Fischer says: "The Soviet frontier is like a charmed circle which the world economic crisis cannot cross. While banks crash, while production falls and trade languishes abroad, the Soviet Union continues in an orgy of construction and national development. The scale and speed of its progress are unprecedented." [2] This huge and rapid development, this immunity from the devastating world economic crisis, is possible because Socialism by its very nature provides the basis for a steady and enormous expansion of the productive forces.

Capitalism, as we have seen, robs the toilers of a large share of what they produce. This cripples their purchasing power, making the markets lag behind the more rapidly expanding productive forces, and thereby causing over-production and economic crisis. It also, finally, puts positive restrictions upon the development of the productive forces themselves.

[2] *The Nation*, Nov. 25, 1931.

But under Socialism there is no exploitation and the masses as a whole get the full value of what they produce — after the deduction, of course, of what is necessary for the maintenance of the government and the further extension of industry — consequently, their purchasing power cannot fall behind production, but, on the contrary, tends constantly to stimulate it by the ever-increasing demand due to the rising standards of living. There can be no clogging of the social economy with unsaleable surpluses of commodities. The way is wide open for continuous industrial growth. The economic crisis is a capitalist thing foreign to Socialist society. The experience in the U.S.S.R. proves this beyond question. Not even the fact that the Soviet Union has to trade with capitalist countries, and therefore feels the heavy downpull of their sagging industries and declining prices, has been able to disrupt its fundamentally sound Socialist economy.

The existence in the Soviet Union of this constant and huge impulse for the development of the productive forces explains why it has no unemployment and why its industries are developing at a pace totally unequalled in the whole world history of industry. Stalin thus indicates the fundamental superiority of Socialism over capitalism in the development of the productive forces:

"Here in the U.S.S.R., the growth of consumption (purchasing capacity) of the masses constantly outruns the growth of production and stimulates it, while there, under the capitalists, on the contrary, the growth of consumption of the masses (purchasing capacity) never keeps pace with the growth of production and constantly lags behind it, again and again condemning production to crises." [8]

When the Soviet government launched the Five-Year Plan, which proposed to triple pre-war industrial production and to make huge advances on every social front, it was greeted with a world chorus of ridicule by the capitalists and their retainers. It was one grand laughing stock. "The Bolsheviks," the argument went, "are losing their grip upon the masses, so now, to hold on a bit longer, they come forward with this fantastic project." Especially the Social Democrats distinguished themselves in "proving" the "absurdity" of the Five-Year Plan. Kramer, President of the Union of German Industrialists, typically expressed capitalist world opinion when he said: "If the Five-Year Plan could be realized in 50 years, it would be a magnificent achievement. But that is utopian."

The Russian Communist Party replied to this barrage of ridicule and cynicism by putting out the slogan, "The Five-Year Plan in Four Years," and mobilized all possible forces to achieve this herculean task. At the end of the third, "decisive" year, Dec., 1931, the record stood, in percentages

[8] Speech at XVI Congress of the Communist Party of the Soviet Union.

of accomplishment yearly of the Plan's proposed quotas of industrial output: 1929 — 106%, 1930 — 107%, 1931 — 113%. Hence, taking into account the progress in agriculture and all other factors, and in spite of a lag in several industries (coal mining, metal, railroads, etc.) in 1931, chiefly because of transportation difficulties, Kubyshev, President of the State Planning Commission, could correctly say: "The 36% increase (for 1932) of the output of planned industry means the complete realization of the proposals of the Five-Year Plan in 1932"— that is, in four years. The "absurd" and "fantastic" is being accomplished.

Ossinsky, a Russian economist, says: "Before us is one more year of Bolshevik attack, of decisive struggle for the Socialist industrialization of the country. When we shall sum up next year what has been done, out of the removed scaffoldings, on the cleared building sites, there will arise before your eyes, in harmonious perspective, the mighty edifice of the completed Five-Year Plan — a new Socialist country, reconstructed by the indomitable will and inexhaustible strength of the proletariat, headed by its Bolshevist vanguard."

In 1932, as in the past three years, the main stress is being laid upon the heavy industries — metal, coal, chemicals, engineering, transport, etc. Also the utmost attention will be paid to consolidating the gains made, by the application of

Stalin's celebrated "six points" for the organization of the labor supply, the reorganization of the wage scales, the establishment of greater personal responsibility, the creation of a working class technical intelligentsia, better working relations with the old bourgeois specialists and better accountancy systems. Reporting on the first three months of 1932, the *New York Times* Moscow correspondent states (Mar. 21): "Preliminary figures for the first quarter produced yesterday at a meeting of the State Planning Commission show a startling advance over the same period last year."

"Japan, westernizing and industrializing itself 50 years ago, was doing child's play compared to what the Soviet Union is doing today," says Frazier Hunt.[4] Already, almost overnight, the U.S.S.R has become an industrial country. In 1931 the value of the products of industry exceeded those of agriculture, as 60 to 40. And that the development is going into the direction of Socialism, (which the Social Democrats also said was impossible), is decisively shown by the fact that the output of the Socialist sector of the general economy, including agriculture, amounted in 1931 to 91% of all production, as against 52% in 1928.

Not only is the output of industry being increased, but the industrial base also constantly broadens. A solid foundation of heavy industry has already been laid, including the big tractor,

[4] *New York American*, Jan. 14, 1930.

automobile, chemical, electro-technical and other industries, which have been built from the ground up. Daily new products, never before made in the U.S.S.R., are being turned out, from watches and cameras to gigantic blooming mills and great electrical machines. This year there will be produced $500,000,000 worth of commodities formerly imported. A year ago the construction of a turbo-generator of 10,000 kilowatts was hailed as a great victory; now several of 77,000 kilowatts are being built. The U.S.S.R. is rapidly becoming a great industrial unit practically independent economically of the capitalist world.

The great speed with which this industrial development is taking place is quite without precedent. Russian industrial production leaps ahead at an average increase of 22% to 25% per year; whereas the best average achieved by the United States, from 1870 to 1890, was 8.3%. The *New York Herald,* of Jan., 1930 (Paris edition), says: "The Plan aims to accomplish in half a decade an amount of industrialization which other nations — even one so richly endowed by nature as the United States — took a generation or two to achieve." Brand says: "There was a time when Europe was astounded at American speed, at the rapid growth of towns, construction of large enterprises and skyscrapers. The U.S.S.R. has left American speed behind." E. Lyons says in *Current His-*

tory, Nov., 1931: "The colossal economic program on which the Soviet government is now engaged amounts to the telescoping of half a century of progress into a decade or less."

In 1931 capital investment in Russian heavy industry equalled that of the three previous years; there was a 40% increase in the production of electric power; 518 new factories of all kinds were opened. The value of electrical products in 1930 was 580,000,000 rubles, in 1931 it amounted to 1,000,000,000, and in 1932 it will be 1,850,000,000.[5] In 1931 the food industries increased 36% over 1930. In 1932 the total new capital investment in all spheres will increase from 16 billion to 21½ billion rubles. The State budget will advance from 20½ billion in 1931 to 27½ billion in 1932, with a surplus of 500,000,000 rubles, as compared with the gigantic government deficits in the capitalist countries. The value of industrial production since 1929 has increased 50%. Many industries and factories (oil, tractors, machine-building, electro-technical, etc.) have completed the "impossible" Five-Year Plan in two to three years. Leningrad, the greatest of all Russian industrial cities, had already finished the Five-Year Plan at the end of 1931. In three years the productivity of labor in the U.S.S.R. has increased 34%. On many jobs (Dnieperstroy, Stalingrad,

[5] A ruble is worth approximately 51 cents.

etc.) world construction records were broken, etc., etc.[6]

As against these great achievements, the Communists, with dynamic "self-criticism," point out many shortcomings. Thus Molotov says: "We did not fulfill our estimate for the raising of the productivity of labor in industry. . . We have also not carried out the proposals of the Five-Year Plan in regard to increasing the harvest yields. . . We have not fulfilled the tasks in regard to the reconstruction of transport, in particular of railroad transport." These weak spots are now the center of special attack.

What the present tremendous growth of Russian industry means over a period of years is expressed by *Pravda,* Feb. 2, 1932:

Annual Production

	1925		1931
Coal	17,600,000	(tons)	56,000,000
Coke	1,600,000	"	6,700,000
Oil	7,200,000	"	22,300,000
Peat	2,500,000	"	9,400,000
Pig Iron	1,500,000	"	4,900,000
Steel	2,100,000	"	5,300,000
Copper	12,000	"	48,800
Cement	872,000	"	3,300,000
Superphosphates	67,800	"	521,000
Machine construction	730,000,000	(rubles)	5,700,000,000
Tractors	469	(units)	41,200
Electrical power	3 billion	(kwhrs.)	10½ billion

[6] The daily press just announces, March 30th, that the great Dnieperstroy dam has been completed six months ahead of schedule.

This terrific speed is the famous "Bolshevik tempo" of development. It is made possible by the sound economics of the Socialist system, which makes for a rapid growth of the productive forces, by the determination of the workers to build Socialism (and thus prosperity) as quickly as possible, by the pressure of the swiftly rising living standards and demands of the toilers, by the revolutionary enthusiasm of the masses in building the industries, by the burning necessity to render the U.S.S.R. economically independent of the capitalist world at the earliest possible period and to enable it to defend itself against the developing capitalist war attack, by the determination to show the workers of the world the superiority of Socialism over capitalism.

One of the basic factors, as we have indicated, in the stormy advance of Russian industry is the blazing enthusiasm of the workers. They have this enthusiasm because they realize they are building the great industrial system for their own benefit, not for a small clique of capitalist exploiters. Thus they have developed the celebrated "Socialist competition," by which factory and factory, industry and industry, city and city, compete with each other in comradely rivalry to carry through sooner and better their production plans. Besides, the well-established plants "lend" large numbers of their better-trained workers to localities where mass production is just being introduced. They also have their "shock brigades" of workers to push forward difficult tasks, and "self-control" committees to check up on the work. There are 200,000 shock brigades, with 3,500,000 worker members, and a great mass of the self-control committees. The workers submit their "counter-plans" of production against those formulated by the industry heads. Examples: In the "Electric Apparat" plant in Leningrad the management planned a 72,000,000 ruble output for this year, whereupon the workers presented their counter-plan to increase the output to 94,500,000 rubles; the great Saratov agricultural machine plant was officially scheduled to begin operations by Jan. 1, 1932, but the workers' counter-plan called for a production of 200 machines daily by that date.

Shock brigades, self-control committees and Socialist competition lead to great improvements in industrial technique and labor efficiency. Rubenstein says: "The number of suggestions and inventions by workers has increased one-hundred-fold during the past year. Frequently one finds factories receiving thousands of suggestions of the workers in the course of the year."[7] How futile are the American B. & O. plan, "pep talk" methods in comparison. The young workers are the prime movers and organizers of this great shock-brigade, Socialist-competition, self-control movement the

[7] *Science at the Crossroads,* p. 20.

like of which is totally unknown in capitalist countries.

Swift though the present speed of development in the U.S.S.R. may be, the Russians would and could go still faster. Were credits available they would double or triple their orders for machinery in the capitalist countries. But most of these countries, especially the United States, systematically place hindrances in the way of such credits, hoping thereby to wreck the Five-Year Plan, or at least to slow down the, to them, very dangerous speed of Russian industrial growth. American imperialism, to the glee of Matthew Woll and Hamilton Fish, prefers to shut down its plants and throw the workers out on the streets to starve than to let them work on Russian industrial orders.

The new Russian industries are being built upon a scientific basis, not haphazard as in capitalist countries. The railroads, with great feeder lines of auto-trucks, canals, etc., are being built by plan, not with the endless waste, duplication and general anarchy to be found, for example, in the United States. The steel mills, chemical plants, etc., are constructed according to the last word in industrial technique, located at the most strategic points and coordinated with each other and with the whole industrial system. It is all one vast industrial machine, all the parts of which fit into and work with each other.

Naturally, the plants and the industrialization as

a whole are on an immense scale.   No combination
of capitalists anywhere could organize such gigantic projects.   This can be done only by a Socialist
State.   With only one or two exceptions, the great
plants here cited are by far the largest in the world.
A few of the new industrial giants, either just finished or in course of construction, are: the well-
known Stalingrad, Leningrad and Kharkov tractor
plants, with a capacity of 100,000 tractors yearly;
the great Amo and Nizhni-Novgorod automotive
plants, the latter exceeded in size only by the Ford
River Rouge plant; the huge power plant and industrial combine on the Dnieper, costing 840,000,-
000 rubles and employing 35,000 builders; the
gigantic Volga and Angara river hydro-electric
plants and industrial combines, both larger than
any in the world, the Volga plant, starting in 1932,
to cost 1,200,000,000 rubles, and its combine of
local copper, chemical, aluminum, etc., plants to
cost 3,000,000,000 rubles, or about as much as all
the plants together of the United States Steel Corporation; the monster steel mills on a similar scale
at Magnitogorsk, Kuznetz, Zaporozhie, Noginsk,
etc.; the great Kamensk-Sinarsk plant alone to have
a capacity of 2,000,000 tons of pig iron yearly.
The gigantic Novo-Sibirsk agricultural machine
plants — two years ago there were only two combined harvesting machines in all Siberia, now this
plant will build 15,000 annually, in addition to
35,000 tractor seed drills, 30,000 tractor hay mow-

ers, etc.; the new Kashira electric locomotive
works, capacity 1600 large American-type engines
yearly; the Yaroslavl rubber-asbestos combine, unequalled in size anywhere, employing 22,000 workers and operating upon local-grown rubber (the
newly-found "towsagis"); the vast new textile
combine in Siberia; the monster electrical machine
building combine in the Urals, to begin early in
1932 and to have an output valued at 2,000,000,000
rubles yearly; the monster Leningrad clothing factory with 18,000 workers, the great copper mining
and reduction plant, larger than any in the United
States, near Lake Balkash, to turn out 400,000
tons of copper annually, or more than eight times
as much as the total Soviet copper production for
1931, etc., etc.

Just a few further details in this wholly unparalleled industrialization are the building of a
modern national meat packing industry, the setting up of the most powerful radio station in the
world, the construction of the "Turk-Sib" railroad,
the digging of the Volga-Don and Volga-Moscow
canals, the latter to cost 100,000,000 rubles, the
opening of 10,000 new retail stores in 1932, the
completion of 138 airlines with 100,000 miles of
airways by the end of 1932, the Moscow subway,
to cost nearly a billion rubles, the great Palace of
Soviets, 6,000 new motion picture installations,
etc., etc.

On such a scale and with such speed and planfulness, are the Russian workers building their industries. And the joke of it all is that only a year or two ago the Communists were universally condemned by capitalist wiseacres as hopeless tyros industrially. Now they are teaching the whole world an entirely new perspective of industrial possibilities.

The Revolution in Agriculture

IF SOCIALISM proceeds with great speed in industry, it goes still faster in agriculture. The vast development of the productive forces and the reorganization generally that is taking place with almost lightning speed in Russian agriculture is something altogether new in the world. During the 30 days from Jan. 20 to Feb. 20, 1930, one-third of all the peasants entered the collective farms in the monster organization campaign, raising the total of collectivized homesteads from 4,300,000 to 14,000,000 at one stroke. Anna Louise Strong thus describes this tremendous movement: "Can one give a smooth account of an earthquake? The storm of collectivization that I found on the Lower Volga in late November, 1929, was as elemental as an earthquake, as a tidal wave, as a whirlwind." [8]

The Five-Year Plan was completed in two years in the collectivized farms, in three years in the

[8] *The Soviets Conquer Wheat*, p. 24.

State farms. The Plan called for 20% of all farms to be collectivized by the end of 1933; already there are 62% and this year will raise it to 75%, which will practically complete the most important districts. There were 1,000,000 collectivized farms in 1929, now there are 22,000,000 organized into 200,000 collectives; there were 143 State farms in 1930, now there are 4,000, or far in excess of the quota called for by the Five-Year Plan. Duranty says (*N. Y. Times,* Jan. 2, 1932) that nine-tenths of the chief grain centers are already collectivized.

These new farms are huge in size. In 1927 the average size of Russian farms was 11 acres, now it is 973. The State farms range as large as 100,-000 to 200,000 acres; the collectives are still more gigantic, some running as great as 500,000 acres of cultivated land, exceeding thus in size by four or five times the biggest farms in any other country in the world. Whole districts have become practically single farms, worked in common by the organized farmers.

Russian farming is fairly leaping ahead from a condition of almost medieval primitiveness to the most advanced in the world. In many parts of the Soviet Union farming methods of 2,000 years ago were still in use up till the great drive for collectivization. Even close to Moscow things were not much better. Says A. L. Strong: "In the district of Koshira, only three hours by rail from

Moscow, a survey made in 1930 of farm equipment showed a population of 62,000 souls and some 6,200 plows, of which 2,659 were of the home-made wooden style." But so swift is the pace of development that Kalinin could say on Mar. 6, 1931, at the Sixth Congress of Soviets: "In industry great may be the advance in comparison with our backward past, we are still only striving to overtake the technical development of more advanced countries. But in farming we are leaders on a new road. *Here we go before all nations"*

The farms are being rapidly and scientifically mechanized. Lenin said: "If 100,000 first class tractors could be produced and supplied with gasoline and tractorists tomorrow (and you know that this is still but a fantasy), the middle peasant would say: 'Yes, I am for the commune,' that is, for Communism." Well, the tractors are now in the fields, 150,000 of them, and the middle peasants are practically won for Socialism, as Lenin foresaw. One of the revolutionary features of the new mechanization is the "tractor stations." These are centers that furnish machinery and repairs, instruction, recreation, etc., to the peasants. In Dec., 1931, there were 1400 of them; in 1932, 1700 more are being organized, thus covering the entire country with a network of farm machine local centers, radiation points of all that is needed to build the new farming and Socialism. With this mechanization goes a fundamental improvement of methods in all directions, the development of scientific fertilization, the building of great irrigation projects, the beginning of the electrification in farming, etc. They are now even sowing wheat by airplane.

Already, although the general movement is just getting under way, vast improvements are to be registered in farming results. In three years there has been a 21% increase in the total cultivated area. The cotton acreage now amounts to three times pre-war, and other industrial crops show accordingly. Despite a still great lack of machinery and fertilizer, the yield on the collectives runs from 25% to 50% better than on the old individual farms. The year 1931 was a drought period; formerly it would have produced a famine, but with collectivized farming the general output equalled the previous year.

In 1932 there will be a further stimulation of the whole movement. The total new capital investment in the Socialist sector of agriculture will be 4,360,000,000 rubles instead of the 3,600,000,000 in 1931. There will be increases of the State cattle ranches of 40%, State piggeries 200%, State sheep ranches 40%, cotton sowing 14%, sugar beets 13%, spring wheat 5%, and a myriad of other developments of agricultural production. The world agrarian crisis does not bear down upon the Soviet Union; while in other countries they are burning coffee, wheat, etc., and the very farmers themselves are starving, in the U.S.S.R. every effort is being made to increase production, and the conditions of the rural population rapidly improve.

The revolution in Russian agriculture is of profound economic, political and social significance. The farmers are being proletarianized and revolutionized. The collectivized farms lay a solid Socialist basis in the country. The remnants of competitive, individualist farming are being liquidated, and the rich kulaks with them. The farms are being mechanized and industrialized, the unity of city and country established. The workers in the cities and on the farms are being knitted into one solid working class. Light and prosperity are being brought into the dark Russian villages. The whole social basis of the Soviet government is being enormously strengthened. The winning of the "fundamentally anti-Socialist" middle peasants to Socialism has been practically accomplished.

Outstripping the Capitalist Countries

WHEN Lenin called upon the Russian workers to "overtake and outstrip the most advanced capitalist countries" industrially, this historic appeal was greeted with hilarious guffaws all over the capitalist world, especially in Social-Democratic circles. How could the "impractical" Bolsheviks ever do that? Preposterous! But now capitalism's laugh is on the other side of its face. It is compelled to see that the Soviet Union, advancing with giant strides, is fairly running past the industrially stagnant and declining capitalist countries.

"In the U.S.S.R.," says Premier Molotov, "24 new blast furnaces were started in 1931, while 29 were closed down in the United States from January to September of the same year." "In the U.S.S.R.," states Brand, "we are building workshops, in Europe and the United States they are closing them down; the U.S.S.R. is launching new ships, in Hamburg, London and New York ships are being converted into scrap iron." In 1931, while the Soviet Union was advancing its general industrial production 21%, that of the capitalist countries declined on an average of 25%. Since 1928 Russian industrial production has increased 86%, and that of the capitalist world has fallen 29%.[9] While the national income of the U.S.S.R. increased 14% in 1931, the general drop in capitalist countries ran from 15% to 20%.

In the production of oil the Soviet Union now stands second among the nations, in coal mining and heavy machine building fourth. In 1927, it stood seventh in the production of electrical equipment; in 1931 fourth, in 1932 it will be second, standing behind only the United States. In the making of automobiles, 1932 will put the Soviet

[9] Data from League of Nations' sources and German Economic Institute.

Union ahead of both Germany and Italy. In the steel industry it is overtaking one capitalist country after another; in 1929 Belgium was passed, in 1931 England was outdistanced, only three countries now being ahead of the Soviet Union in steel, and they also are being rapidly overhauled.

In the matter of total national income the U.S.S.R. now stands second in the world, its figure of 38 billions for 1931 being twice that of 1913 and exceeding the pre-crisis figures for Germany, Great Britain and France.

In total volume of industrial production the U.S.S.R. also occupies second place. The *Economic Review of the Soviet Union* (Apr. 1, 1932) informs us: "By August (1931) industrial production of the Soviet Union already exceeded that of Germany and was second only to the United States. While in 1928 the share of the United States in world industrial output was nearly ten times that of the U.S.S.R., by October of last year it was only about three times." Few, if any, of the capitalist countries, now stricken by economic crisis, that are being so rapidly passed by the Soviet Union, will ever catch up with it again, even temporarily.

The second Five-Year Plan, recently announced and which will go into effect at the end of this year when the present Five-Year Plan is completed, provides a gigantic program of industrial and agricultural development that will further advance the position of the U.S.S.R. in world economy. The XVII Party Conference of the C.P.S.U. says in its resolution: "In the second Five-Year Plan the Soviet Union will advance to the first place in Europe in regard to technique." The purpose of the new plan is to "transform the whole national economy and to create the most modern technical basis of all branches of national economy." The first Five-Year Plan greatly frightened the capitalist world; the second increases its demoralization.

The tremendous scope of the second Five-Year Plan may be realized from the fact that it provides for a total new capital investment of 150 billion rubles, or about 78 billion dollars. What this gigantic sum means in the way of development is indicated by the comparison that it is equal to three times the I.C.C. valuation of the total railroad mileage of the United States — 26 billion dollars, a figure which includes one-third to one-half of watered values.

Some of the details of the immense second Five-Year Plan are the following: the development of six times as much electrical power in 1937 as in 1932, extension of the machine building industry $3\frac{1}{2}$ times, increase of coal production from 90 million tons in 1932 to 250 million in 1937, 300% increase in the production of oil, the yearly production of 22 million tons of pig iron, (requiring a tempo of development twice as fast as that of the United States and Germany in their best days), an output of 170,000 tractors per year, the building of 30,000 kilometers of railroads, accompanied with a complete reorganization, including the establishment of the block system, automatic couplers, bigger locomotives and cars, new bridges, extensive electrification, etc. The main aim will be to build the heavy industries and power base, but the light industries will also be developed 200% to 300%. In agriculture similar great advances will be made, including a large extension of the sown area (cotton and flax 100%, sugar beets 200%, etc.), complete collectivization of the land, complete mechanization of the main branches of agriculture and the beginnings of electrification, including the electrical stimulation of plant growth, a huge increase of livestock, a large expansion of wheat production to insure against drought years, the construction of automobile roads on a vast scale, etc., etc. The Party resolution expresses "the firm conviction that the main tasks of the second Five-Year Plan will not only be fulfilled, but even surpassed."

The accomplishment of this stupendous plan of development will put the U.S.S.R. within hailing distance of the United States in the matter of industrial output. In one fundamental (not to mention many lesser ones), that of the production of electrical power, the Russian figure in 1937 will exceed that of the United States in 1929. Engineer C. A. Gill of the B. & O. Railroad, just returned from the Soviet Union, says of the railroads: "Russia is today already second only to the United States in tonnage carried. In the next five years she will equal this country." [10] At its present rate of development the U.S.S.R. will be the world's leader in industrial production within 10 years. By that time Lenin's famous slogan, "to overtake and surpass the most advanced capitalist countries," will be fully realized.

Real Prosperity for the Toilers

But the Soviet Union is not only rapidly increasing its industrial and agricultural production; it is at the same time building an industrial (and social) system superior in structure and function to that of capitalism. Instead of a hodge-podge of competitive and unprogressive industry and agriculture, it is creating a great, modern, progressive industrial-agricultural machine; instead of a profit-making apparatus to fatten a few while millions starve, it is building its industries for the benefit of the producing masses. That is why the Soviet Union is a land of no strikes. That is why the Russian workers and peasants are toiling so resolutely to build their new industrial system, undeterred by either the appalling difficulties of an undeveloped economy or the endless obstacles placed in their way by the world capitalist enemy.

The growth of Socialism marks the birth of the

10 *New York Times*, Feb. 19, 1932.

first era of prosperity for the workers. Under capitalism everywhere wealth piles up automatically in the hands of the parasitic owners of the industries, while the masses of actual producers live at the bare subsistence line. But in the Socialist Soviet Union all this is fundamentally changed. There production is carried on for the benefit of those who actually work. There are no artificial limits placed upon production by the need to sell in a clogged market. Hence productive forces develop freely and rapidly, and as production increases the added output inevitably translates itself into higher wages, shorter hours, better working conditions, more elaborate cultural institutions, etc., for the toilers. "There are no beggars or lines of unemployed in Soviet streets — no rent evictions, no ragged despair," says Duranty. One of the most infamous and ridiculous capitalist lies against the Soviet Union is that the Russian workers are "exploited." How can they possibly be "exploited" when there is no ruling, owning class, no class to get a rake-off from the worker's production ? [11]

It is a revolutionary fact of first importance that only in the Soviet Union, of all the world, are the conditions of the toilers now being improved. In every respect they are advancing, while in all capitalist countries, the United States included, the

[11] A typically absurd argument against Socialism is made in *The Forum*, Nov., 1931, by Andre Maurois that, "a permanent betterment of standards will again build up a bourgeoisie."

standards of the workers have catastrophically declined, until mass starvation is a common phenomenon. The workers everywhere, penetrating the lies of capitalism, are beginning to understand the significance of this rise of workers' standards under Socialism and their decline under capitalism. That is the reason millions of them want to go to the Soviet Union; it explains why the working class everywhere is more and more looking to the Soviet Union as the guide it must follow in its fight for freedom and prosperity.

The main task of all capitalist governments is the suppression and exploitation of the toiling masses; but the very reason-for-being of the revolutionary Soviet government is the fundamental improvement of the conditions of these masses. This, characteristically, the Soviet government does according to plan. Not only is the development of industry and agriculture the object of the State planning, but also the systematic improvement of wages, hours, living and cultural conditions, etc. Up till now, in order to lay a solid Socialist foundation for real worker prosperity, the government has had to apply every possible energy and resource to the development of industry. Nevertheless, it has been able to accomplish profound betterments in the workers' conditions. Let us briefly review some of them:

Unemployment, that terror of the capitalist system, has no place in a Socialist system. The consuming power of the masses keeps pace with and outstrips their producing power. Hence, unemployment has been wiped out in the Soviet Union. The right to work, alien and unknown to capitalist society, has been fully established. While millions of hungry workers desperately seek employment in capitalist countries, in the Soviet Union every worker has a job. And it will so remain. From 1922 to 1928 there was considerable unemployment in the Soviet Union, despite the steady growth of industry and increase in the number of workers employed, this being caused by large numbers of workers coming from the villages to the cities. Originally, the Five-Year Plan did not contemplate the complete elimination of unemployment by 1932. Nevertheless, this has been accomplished. Moreover, there is a huge shortage of workers in every industry. The working class, the most basic element in the productive forces of society, either stagnant or actually declining in numbers in capitalist countries, is rapidly on the increase in the Soviet Union. In 1927, there were (except agricultural) 8,866,000 workers and in 1930, 12,429,000. The last year of the Five-Year Plan, 1933, called for a grand total of 15,800,000 workers, but this year the number has already reached 18,700,000. In 1932 another 3 millions will be added, raising the total to over 21 millions or 133% of the Plan. Thus the very basis of the revolution, the working class, is being enormously strengthened, and that, too, by plan.

Under Socialism wages are as high as the total economy will permit; under capitalism they are as low as the workers can be compelled to accept. Hence, with the rapidly expanding economy in the U.S.S.R., wages are swiftly on the increase, in contrast to rapid wage declines in all capitalist countries. In the U.S.S.R. average yearly wages (except in agriculture) were; 1927 — 729 rubles, 1930 — 956 rubles, 1931 — 1010 rubles. Calculating upon the principles of purchasing power and socialized wages, (which include social insurance, vacations, etc.), the wages of Russian workers are now about double what they were before the revolution. And the tempo of wage advance becomes ever faster in the Soviet Union, as the general economy expands, even as the rate of wage decline increases in the industrially decaying capitalist lands. Last year the Russian average wage increase was 18%, in 1932 it is planned to be 27%.[12] The final year of the Five-Year Plan called for a total wage fund of 15,700,000,000 rubles; but in 1931 it had already reached 21,000,000,000 and in 1932 it will be 26,800,000,000, or 171% fulfillment of the Plan. In the question of wages the principle of "overtaking and surpassing" the capitalist countries also applies. The Russians in this re-

[12] Associated Press dispatches of Mar. 31, 1932, announce a general wage increase of 11% to 20% in all the light and heavy industries of the U.S.S.R.

spect have already passed many countries; undoubtedly they are even ahead of many categories
of American workers, including miners and textile
workers, and with wages advancing so rapidly in
the Soviet Union and falling so fast in all capitalist countries, they will soon pass the rest.   In all
likelihood, considering the incomes of the working
class as a whole, the second Five-Year Plan, which
will at least double the wages of the workers, will
put the Russian workers in the lead of the whole
world.

In the question of the short working period, the
Russian workers already are in the forefront of
the world's working class.   In the U.S.S.R. the
average workday is 7.02 hours, with a five-day
week, as against an average of 8.50 hours per day
in the United States, for an average 5¾-day
week.   In the U.S.S.R the maximum workday is
8 hours, with the 6-hour day for the youth and
workers in dangerous and unhealthy trades
(mines, chemicals, etc.,); in the United States the
sky is the limit for hours, with the 10-hour day
widespread, 53% of the workers in the steel industry working 10 to 12 hours daily and 27%
working the 7-day week,[13] little or no limitations
upon the hours of youth and women workers, etc.
The Five-Year Plan contemplated completing the
introduction of the 7-hour day by the end of 1933,
but this also will be accomplished in four years, at

13 *Labor Fact Book*, p. 87.

present about 90% of the industrial workers being upon the 7-hour day basis or less. In the capitalist countries, despite the huge unemployment, there is actually a tendency to increase the length of the working day; whereas, of course, in the Socialist Soviet Union the working day is constantly being cut. The second Five-Year Plan will make the 6-hour day practically universal in the Soviet Union.

The social insurance of the Russian workers, already the most comprehensive in the world, also is being rapidly developed. It covers every form of disability — sickness, accident, unemployment, old age, child-birth, etc., etc.,— and is fast reaching the stage of full wages under all conditions of disemployment. In the capitalist countries, as part of the program of thrusting the burden of the crisis upon the shoulders of the working class, the workers' benefits under State social legislation are being drastically reduced. In the Soviet Union, of course, the reverse is the case. Even the radical provisions of the Five-Year Plan in this field are being greatly exceeded in accomplishment; the Plan provided that the social insurance budget for 1933 should be 1,900,000,000 rubles; as a matter of fact, however, it had reached 2,500,-000,000 already in 1931, and will mount to 3,400,000,000 in 1932, or about double the original Plan figure. "Russia," says Rep. Sirovich, (Dem. N. Y.) (*New York Journal,* Dec. 10, 1931), "is the only place in the world where charity and philanthropy have been abolished." The Russian workers and farmers, with their elaborate social insurance, have no need for such miserable handouts.

The health and safety of the workers, in industry and in social life generally, is in the very nature of Socialism a first concern of the Soviet government. Tremendous progress is being made in these fields. In the same series of articles, Sirovich says, "Russia has a widespread and thorough health program. The Commissariat of Health gathers the best medical knowledge in the world and places it free of charge at the disposal of the Russian people." While in capitalist countries, under the pressure of the speed-up system in industry, unemployment, low wages, undernourishment, etc., accidents pile up in industry and the health of the working class is undermined; in the Soviet Union just the reverse tendencies are manifest. The old-time plagues of cholera and typhus are now only terrible memories; the health of the masses is being scientifically cultivated. Industry is being made safe and healthy. No workers in the world have the vacations with pay, free rest homes and sanatoria, free medical services, etc., that the Russian workers have. In 1929 the Soviet government spent 54,500,000 rubles for safety and sanitation in industry; in 1931 this work absorbed 124,000,000 rubles, and further huge improvements are planned. For the general health services, including sport, the national budget for 1932 calls for 1,737,000,000 rubles. Such figures, of course, do not include the hundreds of millions more spent by the local Soviets.

The housing problem in the Soviet Union is a severe one, what with the heterogeneous collection of miserable shacks left over from the Czarist regime and the terrific growth of urban population. But this problem is also being solved rapidly. The national government housing program, which does not include innumerable large local projects, increases in volume from year to year: in 1926 it amounted to 292,000,000 rubles; in 1931, 1,117,-000,000; and in 1932 it will be 2,892,000,000. Whole new cities are being built from the ground up, and the old ones rebuilt, on Socialist lines. Under the State Institute for City Planning 100 of such gigantic building projects are being pushed. Never was planned city building carried out upon such a huge scale. Such places as Leningrad and Nizhni-Novgorod are being rebuilt into model Socialist cities, with great systems of schools, theatres, clubs, municipal baths, libraries, athletic fields, factory kitchens, laundries, crematoriums, stadiums, hospitals, refrigeration plants, etc. Besides, Socialist cities are also being built in the country, the most striking of these being the already famous "Socialist Farm City" of Filanova. This city, to be completed by 1934, will contain a population of 60,000, now scattered in 127 villages, and it will have all modern facilities. The whole district will be one great farm, the toilers living in the city and going to their work in automobiles. This revolutionary city is being built in a district where the peasants are just emerging from the darkness of the middle ages.

The improved living standards of the workers are paralleled by similar advances in the peasants' conditions. The whole village life is being transformed. More food, better clothing, better housing, a raised standard of living generally is the order of the day in the country. The collective farm movement is freeing the peasants from the hopeless drudgery of the past; it is giving them a much greater return for their work; it brings education and a new culture; it makes a huge saving in labor power which is being used to rebuild and modernize the whole life in the country. The Russian peasants are now taking the most gigantic and swiftest steps forward in culture and well-being ever made in any country in the history of the world.

The general rise in Russian living standards is manifested by a large increase in consumption of the more nutritious foods. The consumption of meat, for example, has increased 25% in four years, with a further heavy increase planned for in 1932. The production of eggs and potatoes, exceeded last year by 20% to 50%; the produc-

tion of meat, butter, sunflower seeds and linseed by
50% to 100%; that of poultry and tobacco 100%.
Whereas government experts in the United States
are now teaching the workers how to live on a few
cents a week, while masses of foodstuffs rot in the
warehouses, the Soviet government is bending
every effort to increase food production — which
automatically means to increase consumption. In
10 years it is planned to quadruple the present
number of cattle, sheep and hogs. The resolution
of the Central Executive Committee of the Soviet
government says: "In the year 1932, the fund
allotted to goods intended for mass consumption
will be greatly increased. This fund is rising
(computed according to the retail prices of last
year) from 27,200,000,000 rubles to 35,000,000,-
000. That is to say, the retail turnover of the
Socialist sector increases 30%." What government other than that of the U.S.S.R., would thus
plan the betterment of the toilers' conditions ?

The second Five-Year Plan will greatly accel-
erate the rise in Russian living standards. This
will be possible with the more developed industrial
base. Wages will be doubled or tripled. The six-
hour day will become almost universal. The
social insurance system will reach the stage of full
wages for every form of disability. Production
of consumption goods will be enormously increased.
Vast housing plans will be completed. The resolution of the XVII conference of the Communist

Party of the Soviet Union provides: "In the light industries and in the food industries production is to be extended and a three-fold increase in the standard of consumption of the population is to be secured."

The Russian workers and peasants, it is true, are still poor. This poverty is their heritage from Czarism and capitalism. But with control of the industries and the land, with capitalist exploitation and robbery stopped, with rapidly developing Socialist industries and farms, they have the solid basis for such a prosperity as no working class in the world has ever even remotely approached. The rapidity with which this prosperity will develop and its great depth and breadth will soon astound the world. Capitalists everywhere understand this. They sense the revolutionizing effect it will have upon the millions of workers in their countries who, in the growing crisis of the capitalist system, are falling deeper and deeper into poverty and starvation. This is the basic reason why the capitalists are redoubling their efforts to develop war against the Soviet Union.

The Cultural Revolution

THE PROLETARIAN revolution ushered a new era of social culture into what was old Russia. Culture, instead of being the monopoly of the few exploiters and a tool to maintain their class rule, has now become the boon of the broad masses, and a means for their emancipation. Instead of being designed to make intellectual slaves of the toilers, as is always the aim of the capitalist "culture," the new culture in the Soviet Union is free and scientific. For the first time in history the working masses have a chance to understand life and to enjoy the intellectual treasures that modern conditions are able to produce. It is a veritable cultural revolution which, in the next few years, by drawing out the repressed intellectual capacities of the masses under the conditions of Socialism, will profoundly transform every feature and phase of human thought and intellectual activity. The Russian revolution is giving the greatest stimulation to science, literature, music, the theatre, etc., that the world has ever known.

In the Soviet Union the foundations of the new culture are being laid by a huge campaign of popular education. This is also being conducted according to the principles of Socialist planning. In providing for the building of great factories, the Five-Year Plan also utilizes the new industrialization for the education of the masses. Mass education in the Soviet Union assumes the aspect of a great "cultural offensive" which also develops with "Bolshevik tempo." Even foreign capitalistic observers must remark the breadth and depth of this unprecedented movement. Duranty correctly says, (*New York Times,* Dec. 1, 1931):

"There seems to be no parallel in history to the drive for learning in all branches of knowledge, from reading and writing to the abstruse sciences, now in progress in the Soviet Union."

Before the revolution only about 7,000,000 children attended school; now there are 23,000,000. The whole school system is growing by leaps and bounds; the teaching is according to the most scientific methods, it is carried on in 70 languages, there being over 100 peoples going to make up the Soviet Union. A system of compulsory schooling has been adopted and everywhere applied. In the secondary schools there are now eight times as many pupils as in pre-war days. All told, 46,000,-000 people, one-third of the population, are attending educational institutions. In 1932 the national government budget calls for an expenditure of 9,200,000,000 rubles for social-cultural enterprises. This is aside from a veritable network of educational institutions of the Communist party, the Communist Youth League, the trade unions, cooperatives, factories, the Red Army, etc. There is a whole deluge of books pouring from the printing presses, the Soviet Union being already the world leader as a publisher of books — not to speak of their superior quality. The theatre, the swiftly-growing radio and motion pictures, are also tremendous educational instruments.

One of the great achievements of this vast work is the rapid wiping out of illiteracy. In 1913 only

25% above the age of 10 could read; 90% of women were illiterate. Illiteracy has now been practically eliminated from the industrial centers and it will also soon go from the villages. By the end of 1932 illiteracy is to be liquidated completely. The fight against illiteracy is not simply a matter of the regular educational institutions; a real assault is being made upon it by the more educated sections of the masses under the historic slogan, "Literate, Teach the Illiterate." The struggle against illiteracy and for education in general keeps pace with the growth of industry and the collectivization of the farms. Thus in those districts where the collectivization is well advanced the whole body of illiterates are undergoing instruction.

But the cultural revolution, as we have already indicated, is much more than merely giving the masses an elementary education. It is also more significant than simply a rapid extension of schools, scientific institutes, theatres, etc., that is now taking place in the Soviet Union. It is a profound revolution in all culture. A whole new cultural system is being born.

Under capitalism science is a slave to the class interests of the bourgeoisie. Thus biology justifies the mad class struggle and war; economics puts an unqualified blessing upon wage slavery; history proves that capitalism is society perfected; psychology explains away poverty on the basis of inferior beings, etc. Capitalist science is also a veritable fortress of metaphysical concepts of every kind. But Socialism strikes all these fetters from science. The working class exploits no subject class. Therefore, it has no interest to degrade science into a subtle system of propaganda, but on the contrary to give it the freest possible development. Marxian dialectical materialism destroys the metaphysics that paralyzes bourgeois science.

Capitalist science is planless and anarchic, the hit-or-miss task of whoever may be. But Socialism organizes science. In the Soviet Union scientific work is being done on a planned basis, with full government support. There is a special Scientific Research Sector of the Supreme Economic Council. Bukharin says: "The plan of Socialist construction is not only a plan of *economy;* the process of the *rationalization of life,* beginning with the suppression of irrationality in the economic sphere, wins away from it one position after another; the principle of planning invades the realm of mental production, the sphere of science, the sphere of theory." [14]

Capitalist science sets up a metaphysical separation of theory and practice, and a corresponding arbitrary division of intellectual from manual labor. It is based upon a caste theory and does not develop the creative abilities of the masses. But Socialism liquidates this reactionary system. In

[14] *Science at the Crossroads,* p. 20.

the U.S.S.R. scientific theory and practice are being linked up; science is being brought to the masses and in so doing is revolutionized; a great mass development in science is going on such as exists in no other country; the basis is being laid for the eventual wiping out of the difference between so-called "mental" and "physical" labor.

In the U.S.S.R., as part of the general cultural revolution, religion is being liquidated. Religion, which Marx called, "the opium of the people," has been a basic part of every system of exploitation that has afflicted humanity — chattel slavery, feudalism, capitalism. It has sanctified every war and every tyrant, no matter how murderous and reactionary. Its glib phrases about morality, brotherly love and immortality are the covers behind which the most terrible deeds in history have been done. Religion is the sworn enemy of liberty, education, science.

Such a monstrous system of dupery and exploitation is totally foreign to a Socialist society; firstly, because there is no exploited class to be demoralized by religion; secondly, because its childish tissue of superstition is impossible in a society founded upon Marxian materialism; and thirdly, because its slavish moral system is out of place, the new Communist moral code developing naturally upon the basis of the new modes of production and exchange.

Religion is now in deep crisis throughout the

capitalist world. The quarrels between "modernists" and "fundamentalists" in American churches are one form of this crisis. Religion, born in a primitive world, finds it extremely difficult to survive in a world of industry and great cities. When capitalism was young and strong its great scientists, the Darwins, Spencers and Huxleys, were Atheists; but capitalism, grown decrepit and in crisis, tries to preserve religion in order to check the rebellion of the workers. This is why Einstein ("cosmic religion"), Millikan, Eddington, and other bourgeois scientists now are trying so diligently to "harmonize science and religion." In the U.S.S.R., as it must be in any Socialist country, religion dies out in the midst of the growing culture. As the factories and schools open the churches close. But stories of religious persecution in the U.S.S.R. are utterly false, being part of the anti-Soviet campaign. Freedom of worship exists unrestricted for all those who desire to practice. Religious liberty is guaranteed by the Soviet Constitution, which declares:

"In order to guarantee to all workers real freedom of conscience, the church is separated from the State and the school from the church, and freedom of religious and anti-religious propaganda is bestowed on all citizens."

In the realms of art, literature, music, etc., the cultural revolution also proceeds at a rapid pace. New standards, freed from the stultifying profit-motive, conventionalism and general reactionary spirit of capitalism, are being developed in all these spheres. In this great field, as in all others, the Russian revolution is carrying humanity on to new and higher stages. The capitalist world as yet has not even an inkling of the profound changes involved in the cultural revolution in the U.S.S.R.

Accomplishing the "Impossible"

IN CARRYING the revolution on to success the Russian toilers have faced difficulties without parallel in history. They have had to deal with a whole series of problems quite unique in human experience. But under the leadership of the Communist party, with a clear Marxist-Leninist program, and with the irresistible power of the revolutionary masses, they have been able to batter their way through all of them and to fight on to victory after victory. At every step in their hard-won progress, they have had to face, as part of the world capitalist attack, a persistent chorus of "It cannot be done." And when the Russian workers have solved one set of problems their capitalist enemy has ignored or grossly misrepresented their victory and at once developed a whole group of new reasons why the Russian "experiment" could not possibly succeed.

No defenders of capitalism have been more energetic in these counter-revolutionary attempts to discredit the Soviet Union in the eyes of the toiling masses than the Social Democrats of the world and their American brothers, the A. F. of L. leaders, the Gompers, Wolls, Greens, etc. It has been the special task of the Social Democrats to lend an air of Marxism to these capitalist anti-Soviet lies. To this end they have macerated, juggled and distorted Marx to "prove" that the Socialist revolution must come first in the countries most advanced industrially and that it is impossible in a country so backward industrially as old Russia. Every capitalist lie against the Soviet Union has been fitted into this counter-revolutionary thesis and peddled to the masses of workers through the big organizations controlled by the Social Democrats. Even now, although he becomes ridiculous to the whole world, Kautsky, the leading Socialist theoretician, denies that any progress has been made towards Socialism in the Soviet Union.[15] He says: "Since 1918 the Russian proletariat has sunk ever deeper from year to year from the height it reached. It is not approaching Socialism but is receding farther and farther away from it."

According to these capitalistic Socialist pessimists, first it was impossible for the Bolsheviki to seize the power, and then it was doubly impossible to defend the new government against the armed attacks of world capitalism; next the U.S.S.R. could not possibly exist in the face of

15 *Bolshevism at a Deadlock,* and other writings.

the capitalist economic and political blockade; then all was surely lost when the great famine of 1921 came; and as for the introduction of the New Economic Policy, which temporarily made some concessions to private production and trading while the foundations of the Socialist industries were being laid, this was hailed as the beginning of the end by the gradual re-growth of capitalism; and, of course, it was also quite "impossible" to set in order the chaotic financial system by stabilizing the ruble, balancing the State budget, etc.

All these grave problems, and many more that could be cited, were indeed extremely difficult. Defeat in any one of them would have been a major and possibly fatal disaster for the revolution. But the heroic Russian workers and peasants with the Communist party at their head, solved them all. Consequently, one after another, the capitalist arguments against the revolution have been bankrupted in the face of reality. But no matter, the capitalists have never failed quickly to cook up a new mess of "impossibilities" for the Russian revolution, all of which were widely advertised among the working class by their Socialist and A. F. of L. tools.

Especially in the realms of industry were the problems of the revolution "insoluble." First it was said that never could the "impractical" Bolsheviks put again into operation the industries ruined in the long years of world war and civil war

— in 1921 industrial production averaging about
20% of pre-war, and in the metal industry it was
as low as 2%. Lenin's plans at this time for electrification were typically scoffed at as impossible
by H. G. Wells,[16] who had imagined so many
utopias and bizarre worlds, but whose mind could
not encompass the hard realities of Leninist policy.
The Communists, so it was said, could never set
up a voluntary labor discipline in industry, nor
hold in line the then semi-starved workers. They
could not defeat the counter-revolutionary strikes
and sabotage of the engineers, nor could they produce a new supply of technicians and skilled workers. Later on, when these earlier problems were
either completely solved or well on the way to
solution, then the capitalist argument had it that
the Bolsheviks, although they could restart the old
industries, never could build new ones; especially
was the Five-Year Plan absurd, etc. And finally,
when the great new plants were built and their
existence impossible to ignore, the capitalist apologists, with a myriad voices, declared that the workers never could learn to operate these modern
industries.

But the workers have overcome all these "impossibilities." One of the most stubborn of all the
problems they have had to meet is that of securing
an adequate supply of reliable managers, engineers, technicians and skilled workers, of building

16 *Russia in the Shadows.*

up whole new industrial cadres. This problem has been attacked in various ways; the old engineers have been disciplined and paid highly, foreign specialists have been brought in, including many Americans; but the basic approach to the problem is the education of new cadres of industrial technicians. This is being done on a huge scale. In 1931 there were 21,000 engineers and technicians graduated; in 1932 there will be 38,000. In 1932 it is planned to graduate from technical colleges and schools of all kinds 175,000, from "rabfaks" (workers' faculties) 121,000, from factory schools 364,000. By the end of 1932 there will be a grand total of 4,000,000 students in technical colleges, rabfaks, factory schools, etc., as against 2,700,000 in 1931. One of the most striking developments in this direction is the Society of Worker Inventors, with 700,000 members, at the recent Congress of which the slogan was put forward of, "Save one billion rubles for the U.S.S.R. in 1932."

In the second Five-Year Plan it is planned to train 1,500,000 technicians and specialists and to give technical instruction to from six to seven million workers. Such measures have cracked the backbone of this gigantic problem. But the need for skilled technical help in the Soviet Union is still a burning one. The Americans and other foreign engineers will play an important role for some time to come; but the Russians themselves, with their gigantic educational program, are settling definitely the "totally insoluble" problem of the industrial technician by the creation of a full supply of Red factory administrators and engineers, skilled workers, etc., out of the Russian working class.

In Feb., 1931, Stalin, at a great national workers' production congress, declared:

"The Bolsheviks must become masters of technique! It is said that technique is difficult. Untrue! There are no fortresses that Bolsheviks cannot capture. We have solved a series of most formidable problems. We have overthrown capitalism. We have seized power. We have built up a mighty Socialist industry. We have turned the middle peasant towards Socialism. The most important task of our construction we have accomplished. Not much is left to do; to gain technique, to master science. And when this is achieved, our pace shall become such as we dare not even dream of at present."

Events are proving Stalin right and the pessimists wrong. The workers are refuting in practice the capitalist assertions that they cannot operate the new plants being built under the Five-Year Plan. The huge problem of taking raw peasants from the fields and putting them to operate the latest type of modern industry clearly is being solved. Likewise that of combining democracy and efficiency in the industries. The productivity of Russian workers is rapidly rising, a 34% increase in three years. Small wonder indeed, with the newness of mass production in the U.S.S.R., that there were initial difficulties in putting into full production such great plants as that in Stalingrad.

The *New York Times,* Dec. 1, 1931, declares: "The Stalingrad plant began work with 10,000 hands, a great majority of whom were peasants, mostly illiterate, many of whom had never seen a machine." It is in the face of such unparalleled difficulties that the Russian workers are building Socialism. And what has since happened in this plant, the "failure" of which was gleefully hailed all over the capitalist world? Duranty says further: "In Stalingrad today the latest American machinery is being handled by girls of 20 no less efficiently than by men in the factories of Detroit." The official production records show for the latter months of 1931: Aug. 1866 tractors, Sept. 2151, Dec. 2735, Feb. 2875, thus bringing the plant to a full program basis. Ford recently praised the quality of these tractors.

"According to the Plan, the Azneft oil fields were supposed to reach American rapidity of drilling only at the end of the Five-Year Plan (1933). Several shock-fields, however, caught up to the American rates in the latter quarter of 1930," says the *USSR in Construction,* No. 12.

In the other great industries and modern works the same record is to be found. Many difficulties are still encountered, as for example recently in the Nizhni-Novgorod automobile plant, but these are chiefly local in character and are soon overcome. Duranty says (*New York Times,* Jan. 2, 1932), "1931 did for the first time demonstrate that the Soviet Union not only could build great producing units but could operate them success-fully." And lo, another great capitalist "impos-sibility" has gone to smash in the face of the revolution. Almost overnight the Russian work-ers have mastered mass production. The whole history of capitalist development cannot register an equal achievement.

But the extra-special, grand "impossibility" confronting the revolution was to win the peas-antry to Socialism. This, indeed, it was said, was utterly out of the question. The great masses of farmers, making up an overwhelming majority of the population, were hopelessly attached to the institutions of private property and bred-in-the-bone enemies of Socialism. Sooner or later they were bound to organize and drown out the Com-munist party and all its works.

How the world capitalists and their Socialist allies gloated over this prospect; how they depended upon the peasants as their great ace-in-the-hole. But alas, it was not to be; the Russian workers and peasants also found the answer to this terrific problem in the gigantic growth of collectivized farming. This has not only won the masses of middle peasants for Socialism but has enabled the practical liquidation of the rich kulaks as a class.

Driven from one propaganda "impossibility" to

another by the achievements of the revolution, capitalist apologists are now hard-pressed to find new "arguments." An example of their bankruptcy was given by Isaac Don Levine in a recent series of sensationalized articles in the *New York American*. The thesis of Levine is that the capitalists should not worry over the successes of the Five-Year Plan because the Soviet Union has no basic natural resources anyhow and the whole business is hollow and unimportant. Levine, after a reckless twisting, misrepresenting and distorting of official Soviet reports, says: "Singularly poor in iron, copper, gold and silver, the Soviet Union lacks the four essential metals for the attainment of the goals set by Stalin's jazzed edition of the Five-Year Plan." He says further: "The iron found above ground in America in the form of machinery, buildings and equipment, exceeds all the reserves, visible and possible, in the immense territory of the Soviet Union." Then he goes on to negate the supply of coal and water power in the Soviet Union, to belittle its oil and timber reserves, etc., reducing the U.S.S.R. to a beggarly country indeed in point of resources.

Now what are the facts? First of all, it must be borne in mind that the U.S.S.R. has been as yet but sketchily prospected for its mineral wealth. It is only now that this work is being systematically undertaken, and almost daily reports arrive of the discovery of new resources. Already, with vast regions still practically unexplored, the U.S.S.R. has known raw materials resources of gigantic, if not unequalled proportions. It has a super-abundance of practically all the basic materials necessary for the building of a great industrial system.

(1) Coal: by 1930 the known coal deposits of the U.S.S.R. were conservatively estimated at 700 billion tons, putting it fourth as a coal country. Besides this, however, there are rich, undeveloped deposits in Siberia, stretching over an area as large as Belgium. (2) Oil: the U.S.S.R. is the first country with regard to oil reserves, containing 35% of known world supplies and with new fields being discovered from time to time. (3) Water power: already, as we have seen, the second Five-Year Plan definitely provides for a greater electrical power development than that of the United States, the most of it from water projects, and with much still undeveloped. The Angara River power possibilities are 30 times as much as the great Dnieperstroy. (4) Iron: the largest iron ore deposits in the world are the new Kursk fields; Prof. Gubkin (*Soviet Yearbook,* 1930), estimates these at 40 billion tons of high class ore, and says, "Preliminary computations permit us to conjecture that the Kursk iron ores will probably double the known world resources of iron ore." (5) Copper: until recently the known supplies were limited; but large deposits have lately been found in

Kazakstan, and in Feb., 1932, a great new field was reported from the Okhostk-Udsk region, with deposits of rich quality and extending over 20 square kilometers. (6) Manganese: of this metal the U.S.S.R. contains the world's greatest deposits. (7) Platinum: same as in case of manganese. (9) Gold: important new fields have been found which will make U.S.S.R. a chief world producer. (10) Silver: a weak spot but new developments are extending production. (11) Timber: the U.S.S.R. has the greatest body of standing timber in the world. The bourgeoisie, seeking reasons why "it cannot be done," will have to look in some other direction than that of supplies of raw materials.

The capitalist arguments that "it is impossible" also found their echoes within the Communist party of the Soviet Union, where they reflected the despair of the defeated and declining capitalist remnants in the U.S.S.R. Their outspoken representative was Trotzky. He formulated theories that it was impossible to build Socialism in one country — that first the world revolution was necessary; that the Party was degenerating and surrendering to a rapid growth of capitalist elements in city and country; that the Socialist industry development was destined to go on in a declining curve of new production; that the Soviet Union had abandoned the world revolution, etc. The logic of his position would have led to the precipitation of abortive and fatal Communist revolts abroad and disastrous civil war at home against the great middle masses of peasants. All this would have surely defeated the revolution.

Such, in brief, was the "left" deviation, which was Menshevism in thin disguise, an opportunist retreat from the hard struggle under cover of "left" phrases. Then there was the openly right deviation, led by Bukharin, Rykov and Tomsky. The rights were alarmed at the rapid speed of industrialization; they were frightened at the sharp class struggle against the kulaks; they feared the workers would not stand the strain of carrying out the Five-Year Plan; they believed it impossible to raise the gigantic amounts of necessary capital in the face of the world capitalist financial blockade against the Soviet Union; they scoffed at the prospect of building the State farms and collectives. As a result of their wrong analysis, they wanted to make concessions to the kulaks and to slow down the fast tempo of industrialization. This, like Trotzky's plans, would have been a fatal error. It would have strengthened the capitalist elements in the U.S.S.R. and disastrously checked the growth of Socialism.

The capitalist world was filled with great hope by the development of these deviations, which were the subject of wide discussion in the Russian Communist party from 1926-29. Surely now, it was said, the Party will be split and the Soviet government disastrously weakened, if not overthrown. But again their hopes came to naught. Under the leadership of the Central Committee so ably headed by Stalin, the Party masses, supported by the working class generally, rejected and completely crushed first Trotzkyism and then the openly right deviation. Trotzky later developed a definitely counter-revolutionary position; he is now capitalism's chief maligner and slanderer of the Soviet Union, the whole bourgeois press being open and willing to pay for his attacks upon the Party and the U.S.S.R.

Life has fully justified the position of the Party in these historic controversies. The final answer to both the "left" and right deviations is the tremendous success of the Five-Year Plan, with its gigantic growth of Socialist industry and collectivized farming, burning enthusiasm of the workers, rising living standards of the toiling masses, the winning of the middle peasants for Socialism, the practical liquidation of the kulaks and nepmen, the great perspectives opened up by the second Five-Year Plan, the growing world prestige and revolutionizing effect of the Soviet Union upon the enslaved masses in all countries, and, in consequence of all this, the greatest degree of unity that the Russian Communist party has ever known.

The building of Socialism in the Soviet Union still confronts many great problems. And the Socialist system there will continue to face grave dangers and difficulties until the world power of the bourgeoisie is broken by the world's workers. But its inner problems are those of a successful, growing new social order. Socialism in the U.S. S.R. has definitely proved its soundness. At the XVI Party Congress Stalin thus put the question:

"When we speak of our difficulties, we have in view not decline and not stagnation in our development, but the *growth* of our forces, the *surging upwards* of our forces, the *forward march*, of our economy. How many points *to advance* by a given date, by what percentage to *increase* our output, how many *more* million hectares to sow, how many months *earlier* than the plan to build a works, a factory, a railway — our difficulties, in contradistinction to the difficulties of, say, America or Britain, are difficulties of *growth*, difficulties of *progress*."

Socialism and Communism

THE FINAL aim of the Communist International is to overthrow world capitalism and replace it by world Communism, "the basis for which has been laid by the whole course of historical development." On this the *Program of the Communist International* says:

"Communist society will abolish the class division of society, i.e., simultaneously with the anarchy in production, it will abolish all forces of exploitation and oppression of man by man. Society will no longer consist of antagonistic classes in conflict with each other, but will represent a united commonwealth of labor. For the first time in its history mankind will take its fate into its own hands. Instead of destroying innumerable human lives and incalculable wealth in struggles between classes and nations, mankind will devote all its energies to the struggle against the forces of nature, to the development and strengthening of its own collective might."

The future Communist society will be Stateless. With private property in industry and land abolished (but, of course, not in articles of personal use), with exploitation of the toilers ended, and with the capitalist class finally defeated and all classes liquidated, there will then be no further need for the State, which in its essence, is an organ of class repression. The revolutionary State of the period of transition from capitalism to Communism, the dictatorship of the proletariat, will, in the words of Engels, "wither away" and be replaced by a scientific technical "administration of things." The present planning boards in the Soviet Union are forerunners of such a Stateless society.

Under Communism the guiding principle will be: "From each according to his ability, to each according to his needs." That is, the distribution of life necessities — food, clothing, shelter, education, etc. — will be free, without let or hindrance. Communist production, carried out upon the most efficient basis and freed from the drains of capitalist exploiters, will provide such an abundance of necessary commodities that there will be plenty for all with a minimum of effort. There will then be no need for pinch-penny measuring and weighing. Proletarian discipline and solidarity will be quite sufficient to prevent possible idlers from taking advantage of this free regime of distribution by either refusing to work or by unsocial wasting.

The Communist system will bring the greatest advance in culture and general well-being of the masses in the history of the human race. The present progress in the Soviet Union in this respect is only a bare indication of the tremendous developments to come. Industry, freed from capitalist anarchy and exploitation, will develop a high efficiency and lay the basis for genuine mass prosperity. Culture, emancipated from bourgeois class ends, will become the property of the masses and pass to new and higher levels.

The road to this social development can only be opened by revolution. This is because the question of power is involved. The capitalist class, like an insatiable blood-sucker, hangs to the body of the toiling masses and can be dislodged only by force. But when the workers have conquered power, however, then the way is clear for an orderly development of society by a process of evolution. Naturally, even after capitalism has been overthrown and the power taken by the workers, society cannot simply leap to a complete Communist system. There are stages of development to be gone through. The first of these is the transition period from the overthrow of capitalism to the establishment of Socialism; then there is the period of Socialism, which is the first phase of Communism. The complete realization of Socialism and Communism in any country implies the defeat of the world bourgeoisie.

The Soviet Union has been passing through the transition period from the overthrow of capitalism to the establishment of Socialism. It has been laying the economic and social foundations of Socialism by the building of a great system of socialized industry and agriculture, by raising the living and cultural standards of the toiling masses, by decisively defeating the nepmen and kulaks, remnants of the old exploiting classes. The foundations of the Socialist economy are being completed with the carrying out of the Five-Year Plan. Capitalism has been decisively defeated in the Soviet Union. Molotov says: "The fundamental Leninist question 'who will beat whom' has been decided against capitalism and in favor of Socialism."

The second Five-Year Plan carries the Soviet Union definitely into the period of Socialism; the resolution of the XVII conference of the Communist party of the Soviet Union says: "The fundamental political task of the second Five-Year Plan is the final liquidation of the capitalist class and of classes in general, the complete removal of the causes which produce class differences and exploitation, the overcoming of the remnants of capitalism in economy and in the minds of the people, the conversion of the whole of the working population of the country into conscious and active builders of the classless Socialist society." But, says Molotov, the stage of Socialism, "will not by a long way be ended in the second five-year period."

On the general characteristics of the Socialist stage of development and its relation to Communism, the *Program of the Communist International* says:

"This higher stage of Communism, the stage in which Communist society has already developed on its own foundations, in which an enormous growth of social productive forces has accompanied the manifold development of man — pre-supposes, as an historical condition precedent, a lower stage of development, the stage of Socialism. At this lower stage Communist society only just emerges from capitalist society and bears all the economic, ethical and intellectual birthmarks it has inherited from the society from whose womb it is just emerging. The productive forces of Socialism are not yet sufficiently developed to assure a distribution of products of labor according to needs; these are distributed according to the amount of labor expended. Division of labor, i.e., the system whereby certain groups perform certain labor functions, and especially the distinction between mental and manual labor, still exists. Although classes are abolished, traces of the old class divisions of society, and, consequently, remnants of the proletarian State power, coercion, laws, still exist. Consequently, certain traces of inequality which have not yet managed to die out altogether, still remain. The antagonism between town and country has not yet been entirely removed. But none of these survivals of former society is protected or defended by any social force. Being the product of a definite level of productive forces, they will disappear as rapidly as mankind, freed from the fetters of the capitalist system, subjugates the forces of nature, reeducates itself in the spirit of Communism, and passes from Socialism to complete Communism."

The Dictatorship of the Proletariat

THE PROLETARIAN revolution marks the birth of real democracy. For the first time the toiling masses become free. Under chattel slavery, feudalism and capitalism they were oppressed and enslaved, merely the forms of this slavery changing with the varying modes of exploitation. All the capitalist "democracies," the United States included, are only the dictatorship of the bourgeoisie, masked with hypocritical democratic pretenses. But the proletarian revolution, by doing away with private ownership of the social means of production and distribution and by abolishing the exploitation of the toilers, destroys the very foundations of enslavement and lays the groundwork for the establishment of a true democracy in which there are neither oppressors nor oppressed.

The first form of the new toilers' democracy after the overthrow of capitalism is the dictatorship of the proletariat. Of this type of State Marx said, with wonderful penetration, over two generations ago:

"Between capitalist and Communist society there lies a period of revolutionary transformation from the former to the latter. A stage of political transition corresponds to this period, and the State during this period can be no other than the revolutionary dictatorship of the proletariat."

The dictatorship of the proletariat, unlike the capitalist dictatorship, makes no pretenses of being an all-class democracy, a democracy of both exploiters and exploited. It is frankly a democracy of the toiling masses, directed against the exploiters. Its freedom is only for useful producers, not for social parasites. Lenin, writing before the Russian revolution, says: "Together with an immense expansion of democracy — for the first time becoming democracy of the poor, democracy of the people and not democracy of the rich folk — the dictatorship of the proletariat will produce a whole series of restrictions of liberty in the case of the oppressors, exploiters and capitalists." [17]

The dictatorship of the proletariat, or the Workers' and Farmers' government, is a kind of State. Lenin thus defines a State: "The State is a particular form of organization of force; it is the organization of violence for the holding down of some class." Thus the capitalist State, strong right arm of the bourgeoisie, has as its basic function, the

[17] *The State and Revolution,* p. 90.

holding by force of the working class under capitalist exploitation. But, Lenin goes on to explain: "What is the class which the proletariat must hold down? It can only be, naturally, the exploiting class, i.e., the bourgeoisie." The fundamental difference between the capitalist State and the dictatorship of the proletariat, however, is that the former is the rule of a small, exploiting minority, and it perpetuates this rule by force and demagogy; while the latter is the rule of the great toiling majority and it directs its power towards abolishing every form of exploitation and the liquidation of the exploiting classes. The *Program of the Communist International* says:

"The dictatorship of the proletariat is a continuation of the class struggle under new conditions. The dictatorship of the proletariat is a stubborn fight — bloody and bloodless, violent and peaceful, military and economic, pedagogical and administrative — against the remnants of the exploiting classes within the country, against the upshoots of the new bourgeoisie that spring up on the basis of the still prevailing commodity production."

To establish the dictatorship of the proletariat it is not merely a question of making over the defeated capitalist government. Engels states in his 1888 preface to the *Communist Manifesto:* "One thing especially was proved by the (Paris) Commune, viz., that the working class cannot simply lay hold of the ready-made State machinery and wield it for its own purposes." The capitalist State must be broken down and the Workers' State built from the ground up on entirely different principles, and this was done in the U.S.S.R.   In doing so it has been necessary to set up a powerful Red Army and the well-known O.G.P.U. to defend the revolution against the capitalist attacks from within and without.

The dictatorship of the proletariat is the democratic rule of the toiling masses, with the working class in the lead, developing the revolutionary program and forming the core of the revolutionary organization.   The *Program of the Communist International* says:

"The dictatorship of the proletariat implies that the industrial workers alone are capable of leading the entire mass of the toilers.   On the other hand, while representing the dictatorship of a single class, the dictatorship of the proletariat at the same time represents a special form of class alliance between the proletariat, as the vanguard of the toiling masses, and the numerous non-proletarian sections of the toiling masses, or the majority of them. It represents an alliance for the complete overthrow of capital, for the complete suppression of the opposition of the bourgeoisie and its attempts at restoration, an alliance aiming at the complete building up and consolidation of Socialism."

Only when the capitalist class is decisively beaten on a national and international scale and class lines finally broken down will the workers' need for a State die out and the proletarian dictatorship "wither away."   Under the classless, Stateless regime of Communism there will exist a broad and genuine freedom such as the world heretofore has not even remotely approached.   Lenin says in his *The State and Revolution,* p. 91:

"Only then will be possible and will be realized a really full democracy, a democracy without any exceptions. And only then will democracy itself begin to wither away in virtue of the simple fact that, freed from capitalist slavery, from the innumerable horrors, savagery, absurdities, and infamies of capitalist exploitation, people will gradually *become accustomed* to the observance of the elementary rules of social life, known for centuries, repeated for thousands of years in all sermons.   They will become accustomed to their observance without force, without constraint, without subjection, without the *special apparatus* for compulsion which is called the State."

The government of the Soviet Union is a dictatorship of the proletariat, or rule of the workers. For the toiling masses of factory and farm it establishes a genuine democracy, a democracy totally different from and incomparably in advance of the so-called democracy of the capitalist countries. But, as we have remarked, this democracy does not extend to the exploiting classes, or rather what is left of them.   The Soviet government, as a Workers' State, is liquidating these classes and the whole system of robbery upon which their rule was based. The economic and political power of the big capitalists and landlords has been completely shattered and they no longer exist as a class; now the kulaks (rich farmers) and nepmen (petty traders) are going the same way into social oblivion as classes. All this has not been accomplished without the sharpest struggle which, in its early stages, amounted to civil war. But the current blood-curdling stories of violence and persecution are gross fabrications, circulated by capitalist agents to discredit the Soviet Union in the eyes of the world's toilers.

Citizenship in the Soviet democracy is based upon work, only those doing useful labor being allowed to vote. The parasitic remnants, such as ex-nobles, Czarist officers, landlords, capitalists, clericals, etc., are disfranchised. There are no qualifications of sex, nationality, residence, etc.; whoever works can vote. The Soviets are made up of representatives coming directly from the toiling masses, from the factories and the villages. Not wealth, as in all the capitalist countries, but actual service to society, is the foundation of citizenship in the U.S.S.R.

Not only in politics do the toiling masses exercise their democracy, but also in every field of social organization and activity. The trade unions, based upon factory committees, establish an industrial democracy completely without parallel in any other part of the world. Even in the realms of art and science and literature, the influence, direct and indirect, of the working masses in the factories and fields is felt. For example, the formulation of the second Five-Year Plan is being made on the basis of the broadest mass discussion. Duranty says, (*New York Times,* Mar. 5, 1932): "Every stage of the work is subjected to full discussion by workers, party members, executives and government officials." In no country in the world do the toilers enjoy such free speech, right of organization and general participation in every social institution as in the Soviet Union. Tales about the personal dictatorship of Stalin, about "forced labor," about the suppression of the freedom of the masses, are, like the earlier stories about the "nationalization of women," etc., plain lies. Charges by enemies that the Soviet system is an oppressive autocracy conflict fatally with their other charges that there is so much democracy in industry that it interferes with efficiency.

Lenin says: "The Soviet democracy consists of workers organized so informally that for the first time the people as a whole are learning to govern." [18] To carry out their democratic activities in all social fields, the Russian workers and peasants have built up the most gigantic mass organizations in human history. These stretch over all phases of the economic, political and social life, and are of decisive influence. Among the more important of them are the Communist organizations proper (the Party, the Youth and the Pioneers) with about 15,000,000 members all told, the trade unions with 17,000,000, and the consumers' co-

[18] *The Soviets at Work.*

operatives with 70,000,000. Besides, there are many more vast organizations for culture, defense, sport, aviation, etc., containing scores of millions of members. The Soviet electorate, numbering 85,000,000 voters, is by far the largest in the world. These tremendous mass organizations of toilers, entirely without comparison in capitalist countries, are the very backbone of the whole Soviet system. They are all growing very rapidly, an example being the Party, which has increased seven-fold, from 440,000 members to 2,800,000, since the death of Lenin.

While the workers in all capitalist countries face ever-increasing tendencies towards Fascism and the denial of their most elementary rights, in the Soviet Union the workers and peasants are building a great new freedom. In the comparison, fatal to the world capitalist system, of the decaying capitalism as against the rising Socialism, this fact has a vital significance that the oppressed toilers of the world will not fail to understand. It is one of the revolutionary nails that are being driven into the coffin of moribund capitalism.

The Communist Party of the Soviet Union

THE LEADER and organizer of the proletarian dictatorship is the Communist party. In a Socialist society, based upon the workers and farmers and where the aim of the government is to advance solely the interests of these toiling masses, there is room for only one Party, the Communist Party. Of course, in the capitalist countries the Socialists and other defenders of the pseudo-democracy of capitalism protest against this situation and demand the right of political organization for the remnants of the old exploiting classes. But what stupidity it would be for the victorious workers, whose aim it is to liquidate all classes, to permit these counter-revolutionary elements to organize themselves into political parties and thus enable them to sabotage the new regime, to fight for the re-establishment of their system of robbing the workers and generally to act as a barrier to the progress of the new society.

It is a capitalist lie that pictures the Russian Communist party as a sort of clique ruling over the masses. On the contrary, the doors of the Party, although they are closed against the remnants of the former ruling classes, are wide open to all earnest workers and poor farmers who accept its full program and are willing to perform the hard tasks which it demands of its members. A great mass organization itself and growing by leaps and bounds, the Communist party gives all possible stimulation to the other vast mass organizations which, under its general leadership, are the foundations of the proletarian democracy. The toiling masses of the Soviet Union know that the Communist party is their great leader and they give it their enthusiastic support. They have learned from long years of the bitterest struggle any people has ever passed through that the Party of Lenin is the only Party of the revolution.

The Russian Communist party is unique in function and structure. As the Party of the toilers it has the responsibility of facing and solving every major problem of the revolution. It is the Communist party that works out the basic line of action in all spheres of the economic and political life. As the crystallization of the most class conscious elements of the toiling masses, it gives the revolutionary lead in every direction. For this purpose its structure is especially adapted, being based upon nuclei (units) in the shops, villages, army, trade unions, cooperatives, schools, Soviets and every other institution. It is thus part of the very flesh and bone of the toilers everywhere. Without a doubt, the Russian Communist party, with its manifold tasks and roots deep into the masses, is by far the most complicated and highest type of organization ever developed by mankind in all its history.

The Communist party is the brain and heart and nerves of the Russian revolution, and so it must be in any proletarian revolution. It makes the most severe demands upon its membership. They must be models of proletarian courage, initiative, energy and resourcefulness. They are the leaven that lightens the whole lump. In the bitter civil war they were the leaders and inspirers at the fighting front. In the dark period of the great hunger and famine it was the Communists who set the example of self-denial and encouragement for the masses. And now, in the building of Socialism, it is they, who, in the face of incredible obstacles, are carrying through the great Five-Year Plan to success, to the amazement of the whole capitalist world. In every crisis it is the Communists who fling themselves into the breach; for every great problem it is they who come forward with the solution and militantly apply it. That is why the Party of Lenin stands unchallenged as the leader of the masses in the Soviet Union.

The Communist party of the U.S.S.R. is based upon the principles of democratic centralism, developed by Lenin. That is, first the decision is democratically arrived at by the widest mass discussion and then, the discussion closed, the policy is executed with strong discipline and the mobilization of all possible forces. This is an irresistible combination. The mass discussion lays the basis not only for a correct decision but also for the discipline necessary to carry it through effectively. The Communist party of the Soviet Union is incomparably more democratic than the Socialist parties, the A. F. of L. and other conservative trade unions of the world. These organizations, with their hard bureaucratic ruling cliques and their contempt for the masses, are true expressions of the autocratic capitalist system of which they are such loyal defenders. The Communist party is the bearer of the first real democracy in the modern world.

A recent example of the workings of Communist democratic centralism was seen in connection with the struggle against Trotzkyism and the right deviation. These issues were the subjects of the broadest mass discussions, no other country or organization in the world has seen the like. Not only the Party membership but millions of other workers were involved. The results were briefly: a fundamental and mass analysis of every angle of the industrialization and other problems confronting the U.S.S.R.; the crystallization of a clear policy, backed by a solid mass opinion united and clarified in the great discussion; the overwhelming defeat of Trotzky and Bukharin, both ideologically and by the almost unanimous vote of the workers; the achievement of an unparalleled unification of the Party; and finally, the building up of a militant and intelligent mass discipline and mobilization of forces which is the basis of the terrific pace in carrying through the Five-Year Plan. Democratic centralism, the expression of the fundamental democracy of the workers and their natural discipline, bodes ill for the capitalist system.

The proof of the effectiveness of the Russian Communist party and its program stands amply demonstrated by life itself. It is the Communist party that has led and organized the toiling masses to the accomplishment of all the "impossibilities" of building Socialism in the Soviet Union. It is the Communist parties in the other countries, led by the Communist International and supported by the masses, that will strike the death-blow to world capitalism and build Socialism universally. The Soviet Union, the crystallization of the Communist program in life, and the shock-brigade of the world proletariat, rising and flourishing with its great revolutionary strength in the midst of a decaying, declining capitalist system, is the hope and guarantee of a new life for the starved and exploited of the earth.

CHAPTER III

CAPITALIST ATTEMPTS TO LIQUIDATE THE CRISIS

(a) *Quack Capitalist Economic Remedies*

IN CHAPTER I we have seen that the capitalists all over the world try to find a way out of the crisis for themselves by throwing the burden of the crisis upon the workers and poor farmers through wage-cuts, reductions in social insurance, speed-up in industry, lengthening of working hours, tax laws directed against the producers, inflation of the currency, etc., by intensifying their competition against each other through tariffs, dumping, rate wars, etc., and by preparing to deluge the world with a new blood-bath of war.

This is the main line of capitalist policy. Besides, and in connection with it, the capitalists have developed a whole series of additional "remedies" to cure the economic weaknesses of capitalism and to shield the capitalists from their effects. It is with these measures especially that we shall now deal. They have to do with both of the major contradictions of capitalism; the economic gap between the producing and consuming powers of the masses, and the class conflict between the capitalists and the exploited masses of workers and farmers. First let us deal with those of an economic character.

The Rationalization of Industry

IN THE years following the World War the capitalist countries, under stress of the growing economic crisis, developed a world-wide movement for the rationalization of industry. In this the United States took the lead. Mass production, the speed-up in industry, became the cure-all for capitalism. Ford was worshipped as the patron saint of the capitalists everywhere. American speed-up methods spread themselves throughout the capitalist world. The League of Nations officially supported rationalization.

True to their role as "agents of the bourgeoisie," the Socialist parties in the various countries took up the program of the rationalization of industry and made a fetish of it. They even became more enthusiastic than the capitalists themselves. They put it forward to the masses not only as the way to capitalist prosperity, but also the golden road to the gradual establishment of Socialism. The British Labor Party and trade unions became a tail to the speed-up plans of Mond and other industrialists, endorsing the League of Nations' rationalization program, the first provision of which is "to secure the maximum efficiency of labor with the minimum of effort." The German Social Democracy was no whit behind, its unions declaring that: "In full agreement with the memorandum of the German industrialists, we consider that rationalization is the most important condition for the well-being of the nation." The Socialist party of the United States, including the Muste "left" group, grew no less enthusiastic over this bosses' plan to still more sharply exploit the workers.

The leaders of the American Federation of Labor, of course, fell into step with the bosses for the rationalization of industry. Their main policy, variously expressed as the B. & O. Plan, the "higher strategy of labor," and the "new wage policy," was collaboration with the bosses to increase production. Industrial efficiency became the tin god of trade unionism. Wm. Green said, *American Federationist,* (Jan., 1928) : "The Union is the workers' business agency for industrial efficiency." The trade union leaders made a strong plea to the capitalists to let them organize their workers for joint exploitation. They declared that the labor movement had come to maturity; the class struggle was over; class consciousness was out-of-date; now nothing remained to do but cooperate with the capitalists for the industrial speed-up, which would automatically benefit everybody. They hired efficiency engineers for the unions and set out arm-in-arm with the employers to drive the workers ever faster in industry.

But now the whole rationalization of industry movement is ideologically bankrupt. While the bosses, of course, seek to increase the speed-up in the plants that are operating, it is patent for all who have eyes to see that it offers no solution for the crisis. The entire rationalization of industry philosophy was based upon the illusion that capitalist markets automatically extend themselves to absorb capitalist production. But in reality the rationalization movement, by hugely developing the productivity of labor while the consuming power of the masses lagged far behind, greatly sharpened the major contradiction between capitalist production and markets, and it was one of the main factors in bringing about the present world-wide economic collapse. That which was to save capitalism just about ruined it.

The American "New Capitalism"

THE RATIONALIZATION movement reached its highest pitch in the United States. Here it was based on the principles of mass production and "high" wages, "protection" and inflation of the home market by sky-high tariffs and installment buying, and a militant imperialistic drive all over the world to conquer markets for capital and other commodities. This was the so-called new capitalism.

This "new capitalism" was hailed as ushering in a new era. Its proponents declared that it provided the way to liquidate the conflict between capitalist production and exchange, and that, consequently, it had solved the tormenting cyclical crisis. The "new capitalism" was to abolish poverty, to do away with the class struggle and to open up an endless perspective of industrial development. Its champions boastfully shouted that Ford had hopelessly beaten Marx and that there never could be a revolution in the United States. And all the capitalist world, harassed by the ever-encroaching general crisis, looked to the American capitalist heaven with wonder and hope, patterning after it as best they could. The Social Fascists of the world hailed the movement as the savior of capitalism. Even in the ranks of the American Communist party the theory found expression; Lovestone, later expelled, developing the notion that American capitalism provided an exception to the general laws of capitalism.

But what a sad awakening was in store. The American capitalist dream has turned into a dreadful nightmare. The terrible economic crisis is upon us again and with more devastating effects than ever before. It is exactly in the United States where the drop in production has been most catastrophic, where the army of the unemployed is the largest. Mass production has flooded the limited markets with a tidal wave of unsaleable commodities; "high" wages have turned out to be a tragic joke in the face of the gigantic unemploy-

ment and wholesale wage-cuts. The "new capitalism" has proved itself to be very much a part
of the old capitalism of the rest of the world. The
savior very badly needs saving. And the purse-
proud American businessman is humiliated in the
eyes of the whole capitalist world. Indeed, his
erstwhile admirer, Mussolini, was unkind enough
recently even to blame the world economic crisis
upon exactly the boasted American mass production. After all, Marxism has triumphed over
Fordism.

In the "new capitalism" the thing counted upon
to cure the basic economic weakness of capitalism
was "high" wages. Its advocates, with Ford at
their head, had a glimmering of the menacing contradiction between the producing and consuming
powers of the masses, of the folly of going ahead
developing production on the simple theory of
unlimited markets. In words at least they recognized the necessity of increasing the low purchasing power of the masses. Their whole conception
was best developed by Foster and Catchings in
their books, *Business Without a Buyer* and *The
Road to Plenty*. They argued, with their theory
of "financing the buyer," that economic crises
could be averted if, at the first sign of such, the
declining purchasing power of the masses was
promptly bolstered up by the initiation of broad
building programs. President Hoover, as is
known, was an advocate of this theory.

But it was all a sham and a delusion. The so-called "financing of the buyer" never took place under the "new capitalism," nor could it. To suppose otherwise is to assume the possibility of the capitalists progressively giving up their profits. The alleged high wages during the heyday of this theory were confined almost entirely to the skilled workers. The gains to the buying power of the masses in this respect were more than offset by the accompanying huge increases in industrial and agricultural productivity. The whole thing was only an elaborate method of intensified rationalization of industry. The exploitation of the workers was increased, not diminished. The mass of surplus value taken by the employers was relatively and actually greater, not less. The basic economic effect was to still further widen the gap between the producing and consuming powers of the masses. This deepening of the economic contradiction is graphically illustrated by the following figures, taken from Tugwell's *Industry's Coming of Age* and the 1927 U. S. Census of Manufactures:

	Wages paid	Value added by manufacture
1914—	$ 4,009,000,000	$ 9,224,000,000
1923—	11,000,000,000	25,832,000,000
1927—	10,800,000,000	27,500,000,000

During the Coolidge period American capitalism was able to make a great show of prosperity, not because it had overcome the major economic contradiction of capitalism, but because of a whole series of temporarily advantageous factors. Among these were the huge loans to war-stricken Europe, which translated themselves largely into exports of manufactured goods; the easy conquest of world markets by powerful American imperialism, unscathed by the war, in the face of the broken-down European competitors; the growth of the automobile industry; the development of installment buying, which for a time artificially stimulated the market, etc.

But these erstwhile favorable factors have now radically altered. The automobile industry has become more than saturated; the installment system has exploded; exports have fallen off, with the European capitalist powers constantly meeting the United States with a sharper competition, etc. Hence, the inner contradictions of American imperialism are able to manifest themselves with full force and they are doing so with a vengeance. When Hoover blames Europe and the war for the crisis he is only a shallow apologist for capitalism. The fact is that American capitalism, like world capitalism in general, is rotten at the heart. The present great economic world crisis began in the United States.

The crisis has shown conclusively just how feeble and artificial was the American plan of "financing the buyer." At the outset of the crisis President Hoover made many spectacular gestures in line with this theory.   He called national conferences of industrialists, bankers, and "labor leaders." Then he filled the country with rosy prophecies that the crisis would be promptly liquidated by the gigantic building, no-wage-cut program outlined by his conferences.

But the whole thing turned out an inglorious fizzle.   The "financing of the buyer" degenerated into an attempt by Hoover to exorcize the crisis by pollyanna prosperity ballyhoo.   The "great" construction program developed into the biggest sag the building industry has ever known.   Even the government building program failed to materialize, the *New York American,* (Mar. 16, 1932), stating, "The total expended on public works (national, state, local) was actually less in 1931 than in 1929."   And as for keeping up wage scales, hardly were the Hoover conferences concluded than the wage-cuts began, and since then sweeping slashes have taken place in the railroad, mining, steel, textile and many other industries.   The Grand Lama of the "high" wage theory, Ford himself, has also put through general wage-cuts. Likewise, the government, locally and nationally, is reducing wages in every direction.

But the most graphic repudiation of the scheme of "financing the buyer" is to be found in the starvation unemployment relief system of the Hoover government.   The throwing of 12,000,-000 workers into unemployment gave the market an awful jolt because of the reduction in the general purchasing power of the masses. Here was a good chance to "finance the buyer" by giving the unemployed a system of government insurance. But instead they have been given only the most miserable charity dole. To do otherwise would touch the sacred profits of the bosses. The only elements to which the Hoover government has extended assistance in the crisis are the banks, the railroads, the big taxpayers.

Thus the fire of the economic crisis exposes the fact that the results of the "new capitalism" are the same basically as those of capitalist imperialism generally, only more ruthless and devastating. The American capitalist class is as deep in the mud as its European rivals are in the mire, and like them, it throws the burdens of the crisis upon the working class, it rationalizes its industries, enters more desperately than ever into the struggle for international markets, and takes the world lead in preparing war as a way out of the crisis. The "new capitalism" has not cured the contradictions of capitalism, but has enormously sharpened them.

Trusts and Cartels

In his work, *Imperialism*, (p. 12), Lenin says, "Half a century ago when Marx wrote *Capital* free competition was considered by the majority of economists as one of Nature's laws." But the development of imperialism and the intensification of competition on every front has ended such notions. Now capitalism everywhere strives to eliminate competition and to establish monopoly. Thus the maze of trusts and cartels on a local, national and international scale. The aims of these monopolistic organizations is to screw up prices, to cut labor costs, to control markets, etc. One of their major objectives is to restrict production, to cramp the expansive productive forces within the confines of the narrow markets. To this end every reactionary practice has been used, from suppression of important inventions to wholesale destruction of commodities and means of production. This is typical of the anti-social, parasitic character of decadent monopolistic capitalism, to attempt to limit production for the benefit of a few idle owners in a world where the overwhelming majority of the people are lacking the necessities of life. In *Solidarity,* (Nov., 1931), P. Boyden gives a number of examples of such commodity destruction, from which the following items are culled:

"A few months ago, in Oakland, Cal., 100,000 gallons of milk were dumped into the river. At about the same time, 40,000 salmon were destroyed in Ketchikan Bay, Alaska. In Los Angeles 120 carloads of cabbages were plowed under in the fields. Not long ago in California a Rotary Club played baseball with 60,000 eggs that were destroyed to keep them out of the market. And it is the same in other parts of the world; in Brazil 2,000,000 sacks of coffee were thrown into the sea, in Australia vast herds of sheep are simply massacred to keep the price of lamb high.   Corn is poisoned so that it will be unfit for human consumption."[1]

But trusts and cartels have not proved a cure for the economic crisis, any more than has the American "new capitalism."   This is true, both for capitalism as a whole and for the respective industries.   Instead of "stabilizing" industry, as their proponents say, these organizations are, on the contrary, feeding the crisis with their policies of rationalization of industry, mass lay-offs, wage-cuts and intensified exploitation of the workers. Even their very resistance to price declines prolongs and intensifies the crisis.   As Stalin said in a recent speech, "The capitalists are chopping off the branch that supports them.   Instead of escaping the crisis, they are aggravating it, piling up new causes for a still more severe crisis."

Consider the plight of the United States, home of the trusts.   Here 24 banks hold assets worth more than those of 20,000 small banks; four great financial interests control 95% of the total output of electrical power; the entire railroad system is dominated by a half dozen New York banks.   Yet the whole industrial-financial machine is prostrate in deepest crisis.   Nor have the individual trusti-

[1] Press dispatches announce that the Brazilian government has decided to burn 12,000,000 sacks of coffee and to cut down 400,000,000 coffee trees in the State of Sao Paulo.

fied industries been able to shield themselves. The great automobile industry, erstwhile boast of American industrialists, in which three of each four cars are constructed by either Ford or General Motors, is working, as I write these lines, at only 20% of capacity. Or take steel, with two big corporations controlling 52% of the industry, operating at only 20%. The oil industry, home of great combinations, is likewise a picture of anarchy, over-production and paralysis. The other industries, whether trustified or not — coal, textiles, chemicals, etc.— are in a similar pickle. Also the railroads, government-regulated and most highly-monopolized of all American industries, experience the general economic crisis, with two-thirds of their workers either totally unemployed or working only part-time and with bankruptcy knocking at the doors of many companies.

It is exactly in the most trustified countries— the United States, Germany, Great Britain, Japan — that the crisis bears down most heavily.

The trusts do not escape the laws of capitalist society. They cannot get away from competition. They compete against the untrustified sections of their own industries; against other industries (coal against oil and waterpower, railroads against auto-trucks, etc.) and against the industries of other countries. Besides, their whole position is undermined by the crisis in backward, hopelessly competitive agriculture. But more important than all this is the fact that the whole trend of the trusts is to increase the exploitation of the workers and poor farmers and thus to render these masses still less able to buy back what they produce. The trusts unavoidably widen the fatal gap between capitalist production and distribution, the basic cause of the crisis.

The cartel movement has had no better success than the trusts in checking the economic crisis, either in general or in individual industries. The cartels have the same major objectives as the trusts, to curtail production, boost prices, etc., but their inner organization is more frail, even when headed by "dictators" like Will Hayes and Dudley Field Malone. In the present crisis the cartels, so hopefully welcomed by capitalism generally, are breaking under the strain. It is no contradiction for the capitalists of the various countries to drastically rationalize their industries so that they can the more effectively compete with each other, and at the same time set up international cartels presumably for the purpose of limiting competition and production. This is because these international cartels, in reality, are only new battlegrounds for the competitors; the fight for markets goes on inside their limits, with the stronger groups pushing the weaker ones to the wall, forcing them to accept smaller production quotas, poorer markets, etc.

This is clearly reflected in the experience of the

famous European Steel and Iron Agreement, signed in 1926. This organization faced not only ruinous competition from without, from the steel barons of Great Britain, Poland, etc., but also from within. The *New York Times,* (Sept. 9, 1931), says that the members of the cartel "engaged in a free-for-all scramble for orders, cartel regulations and prices being entirely disregarded." It is not surprising therefore that this great cartel has collapsed. Chadbourne's international sugar cartel is fast going the same road because of the same disease. The *New York Times,* (Mar. 19, 1932), states that the Chadbourne plan is now "practically abandoned" because of incurable dissensions among the sugar producers.

Mr. Chadbourne attaches very great importance to his cartel. He has declared that in this attempt to limit the world production of sugar and to boost prices "the capitalist system itself is on trial." If so, then capitalism will surely be found guilty and sentenced to death, for the cartel movement cannot overcome the over-production that causes the capitalist crisis. On the contrary, as I. Lippincott says, the cartel "is a great stimulant to further production, and it thus aggravates the problem which it is designed to solve."[2]   Summarizing the experiences of the cartel movement, a dispatch to the Scripps-Howard papers (Mar. 3, 1931) says: "European cartels in steel, rayon,

2 *Economic Resources and Industries of the World,* p. 55.

cement, aluminum and coal, and international agreements in nitrates, sugar and coffee were studied by the U. S. Government trade experts in their examination of world price-fixing arrangements. In no case was the objective of the cartel attained in full and, in several instances, the entire project was abandoned."

Viewing the general capitalist economic collapse and the failure of all trust and cartel remedies to cure it, *The Course and Phases of the World Economic Depression,* a League of Nations publication, is forced to this lugubrious conclusion:

"When we consider the magnitude of the losses from which the world suffers during a period of economic stagnation similar to that through which the world is now passing it is impossible not to be impressed by the almost absolute failure of society up to the present to devise any means by which such disasters may be averted."

The Movement for Capitalist Planned Economy

ALARMED on the one hand at the breakdown of the chaotic capitalistic economy in the crisis and on the other at the forging ahead of the Soviet Union with its planned Socialist economy, defenders of capitalism, especially in the United States, are raising a great clamor for a planned capitalist economy. "Give us a plan," they cry in every key and in manifest confusion. Many of them frankly state that it is a case of either a planned capitalist economy or Communism. Prof. W. B. Donham says in the *New York Times* of Mar. 15, 1931, "Unless greater stability is achieved, it is doubtful whether capitalist civilization can long endure." The frightened Nicholas Murray Butler declares in the *New York Times* of July 12, 1931 . . . "the world today is in the grasp of the greatest economic, financial, social and political series of problems which have ever faced it in history. . . The period through which we are passing is a period like the fall of the Roman Empire, like the Renaissance, like the beginning of the political and social revolution in England and France; it is different from them all, is more powerful than them all and holds the world more in its grasp than any of them." Mr. Butler then cries out somewhat hysterically for "an international plan designed to show that capitalism is a superior system to Communism."

Such clamor has resulted in a whole series of "plans" being devised to stabilize the anarchistic capitalist economy. The country is infested with a plague of 5- and 10-year plans, and the deepening crisis will bring more. Among them are the projects of Swope (General Electric), U. S. Chamber of Commerce, Associated General Contractors of America, Civic Federation, A. F. of L., La-Follette, Stuart Chase, Norman Thomas, *The Forum*, Beard, Donham, etc., etc. These schemes range from mere statistics-gathering and advice-giving to drastic general reorganizations of industry.

What these "plans" usually have in common is a demand for more active participation of the government in the trustification and control of industry. Capitalist "planning" is a step still further into State capitalism. The capitalist government, as the instrument of the ruling class, always has as its main function the furtherance of capitalist industry and the increase of profits at the expense of the workers, and it more and more directly intervenes in industry, but never was this intervention so direct and far-reaching as the capitalist "planners" now propose. The movement for capitalist "planning" is an effort to hasten the process of monopolization with still more vigorous aid of the government. It also tends in the general direction of Fascism.

It is characteristic that the Social Fascist and Fascist leaders of the Socialist party and A.F. of L., together with many liberals, are advocates of capitalist "planning." They try to prove that the revolution is not necessary for an ordered economy and prosperity for the workers. As agents of finance capitalism, these elements always manage to find "progress" in every new step that the capitalists find necessary for the exploitation of the workers. The A.F. of L. leaders' demand now for "planning" and the abrogation of the anti-trust laws is just as much in the service of the

employers as their support of the tariff, the rationalization of industry, the present wage-cut drive,
etc.

But these capitalistic economic "plans" must and
do fail. They are wrecked on the same reefs as
the trusts and cartels: viz., the inability of capitalism, whether "planned" or not, to sell its commodities in a market that lacks the wherewithal to buy
them; and the hopelessly competitive character of
the capitalist system. Capitalism "cannot eat its
cake and have it." "Planned" capitalist economy
cannot bridge over the basic economic and political
contradictions of capitalism. It is as fruitless as
capitalist "efforts" to end war.

In fact, capitalist economic "plans" are not
plans at all, in the sense of a fundamental control
of the whole resources and production of society, as
the Russians practice it. At most they are only
a crude sort of government regulation. Private
ownership of industry, exploitation of the workers, production for profit, competitive scramble
for markets — all foundation stones of capitalist
economy — make totally impossible the orderly
balance between production and exchange and the
thorough mobilization of all economic forces, either
by agreement or compulsion, that is fundamentally
necessary for real social planning. In such
"plans" as that of Charles A. Beard in, *America
Faces the Future,* which is an example of modern
industrial utopianism, such basic objections to capi-

talist "planning" as profit-making and competition are glossed over with a glib phrase or two and the whole problem is considered merely as a technical one, instead of primarily as one of class struggle.

By going in for "planned" production, capitalism would steal a leaf from the Soviet book, despite the frenzied denials of Matthew Woll. Stuart Chase says: "The American problem is to 'plan' without revolution." But this will not work; it is a case of the whole Soviet book or nothing. Planned economy and capitalism are mutually exclusive. Rubenstein correctly declares: "A plan is in contradiction to the very structure of capitalism." [3] As Milyutin says: "Planned economy presupposes the dictatorship of the proletariat, the abolition of private property in the means of production, the socialization of the means of production — in other words: the victory of Socialism." [4] Only when the industries are socialized, when exploitation has ceased, when production and the markets, freed of the profit motive, automatically balance each other — that is, under Socialism — is a genuine planned economy possible. The central principle of Socialist planning cannot be grafted onto the alien capitalist system. Socialism in the Soviet Union works with a plan, because its whole nature calls for planfulness and system. Capitalism has never developed a plan in any country,

[3] *Science at the Crossroads*, p. 21.
[4] *International Press Correspondence*, Nov. 5, 1931.

because it is in its very substance planless, competitive, chaotic.

All the capitalist "planners" enthusiastically cite the experience of the War Industries Board as a glowing example of the success of their principle. But they overlook one fundamental fact which wrecks all their calculations. This is that during the war period the question of finding a market for the products of industry presented no problem. Capitalism's task now is not to improve production, which was all the War Industries Board did, but to find markets for its commodities. The movement now for capitalist "planning" will come to a no better end than the even more enthusiastic movement for the famous slogan, "Mass production and high wages," in the "new capitalism" era.

But the capitalist "planners" have also passed from the word to the deed. Only calamitous failure has been the result. In the United States capitalist "planning" has proved no more effective in checking the crisis than have the Economic Councils of Germany and France. We have already remarked the sad fate of Hoover's "planned" building boom and his "planned" maintenance of high wages, but the most outstanding examples of Hoover's "planning" are the adventures of the Federal Farm Board in wheat and cotton. These are comparable only to the exploits of Jack, the giant-killer, or Sindbad, the sailor.

With wheat and cotton in deep crisis from

over-production, the Hoover government set out blithely to "stabilize" these great crops, of course. in the interests of the capitalist elements in agriculture. The government's confidence was equalled only by its arrogance and stupidity. It set up the Federal Farm Board and gave it $500,000,000 with which to begin its great work of capitalist "planning" by cutting production, regulating sales and boosting prices.

Let us first see what happened to wheat: the Farm Board bought some 330,000,000 bushels of wheat and carried on a wide propaganda for reduced acreage, backed up by refusals of the banks to make loans to small farmers. The general result was that the price of wheat dropped about 40 cents a bushel, production was 35,000,000 bushels more in 1931 than in 1930, the unmarketable surplus of wheat is larger than ever and the Farm Board has thrown away vast sums of money. Quoting Stone, the head of the Farm Board, the *New York Times,* (Nov., 1931), says, "The Farm Board's holdings of wheat on Oct. 31, totalling 189,656,187 bushels, represented an investment of $1.17 a bushel . . . about $222,000,000. It was worth on Oct. 31 about (57 cts. a bushel, WZF) $120,000,000 or $102,000,000 less than cost."

Capitalist "planning," Hoover brand, made a no less brilliant showing in cotton. Again, as in the case of wheat, the market price of cotton has fallen about 60%, many millions of dollars have been squandered, and production, despite the Farm Board's notorious slogan, "Plow under each third row of cotton," has been increased 700,000 bales over last year. Says the *New York Times,* further quoting the "planner," Mr. Stone: "In cotton the Farm Board on Oct. 31, held 1,310,789 bales, representing on the same basis as wheat, an investment of 18 cents a pound, or about $120,000,-000. The value of the cotton at quotations on Oct. 31, was about (6 cents a pound, WZF) $45,-000,000, or a loss of $75,000,000."

These official figures of the Farm Board show a loss to the government of $177,000,000. But this by no means covers all; it accounts only for the devaluation of the stocks now on hand. There should be added another $100,000,000 or so on account of the vast quantities of wheat and cotton sold for less than the purchase price. Besides, there are the many hundreds of millions lost by the farmers themselves.

Thus operates capitalist "planning" even under powerful American imperialism. The wheat and cotton farmers have been impoverished to the point of pauperization; the crisis of over-production has been intensified; hundreds of millions of dollars have been handed over to the bankers and speculators in wheat and cotton. And meanwhile, as the storehouses are bursting with the unsaleable wheat and cotton, millions of unemployed workers and their families clamor in vain for bread and clothes.   All this is a clear example of the suicide economics of capitalism, of the forces that impel the workers and poor farmers towards the establishment of a Soviet United States.

The Question of an Organized Capitalism

THE DEVELOPMENT of the movement for capitalist "planning" raises afresh the question of whether or not an organized capitalist system is possible, for proposals of a "planned" capitalist economy are proposals of an "organized capitalism."   Here the Social Fascists come forward in full panoply. They are the special champions of the theory of organized capitalism, although the present crisis has given them a sad jolt.   Hilferding, (*Arbeiter Zeitung,* Vienna, Jan. 1, 1930), says: "The year of 1928 was a year of powerful development of organized capitalism.   A new capitalist era commenced in 1929.   Modern capitalism is overcoming and removing everything which made for the anarchy of capitalist production."

The theory of organized capitalism is found best developed in Hilferding's and Kautsky's conception of super-imperialism, and it is a foundation premise of Social Fascism in general.   Kautsky and other Social Fascist theoreticians hold that the process of capitalist trustification is overcoming and will continue to overcome the contradictions of capitalism.   That is, eventually trustification will become world-wide, thus at once liquidating the economic crisis, abolishing the class struggle, and dissolving the war conflicts between the rival imperialist nations into an organized and monopolized world system of production and distribution. Meanwhile, as this develops, capitalism will at the same time, by a process of purchase by the ever-more democratic State, be gradually turned into a system of Socialism. This is the theory of the peaceful evolution of capitalism into Socialism.

But this whole theory of organized capitalism goes contrary to the most basic development of capitalism. The capitalist system cannot be "organized"; it is fundamentally competitive and chaotic. An ordered, balanced social system is incompatible with the private ownership of the industries and land and with production for profit. Monopolization, instead of diminishing the contradictions of the capitalist system, is increasing and deepening them. While trustification undoubtedly brings a modicum of regulation and system within the confines of its direct organization, it at the same time, aggravates the conflicts within capitalism as a whole. With the development of monopolization, in this period of imperialism, of the decline of capitalism and of the rise of Socialism, the collisions increase in severity between trusts and untrustified industry, between the trusts themselves, between industries as such, between the various imperialist nations, between the producers and the exploiters, and between the decaying capitalist system and the advancing Soviet Union. This process of growing conflict and struggle is thus stated in the *Program of the Communist International:*

"The development of capitalism, and particularly the imperialist epoch of its development, reproduces the fundamental contradictions of capitalism upon an increasingly magnified scale. Competition among small capitalists ceases, only to make way for competition between big capitalists; where competition between big capitalists subsides, it flares up between gigantic combinations of capitalist magnates and their governments; local and national crises become transformed into world crises affecting a number of countries and, subsequently, into world crises; local wars give way to wars between coalitions of states and world wars; the class struggle changes from isolated actions of single groups of workers into nation-wide conflicts and subsequently, into an international struggle of the world proletariat against the world bourgeoisie. Finally, two main forces are organizing against the organized might of finance capital — on the one hand *the workers in the capitalist states*, on the other hand, the victims of oppression of foreign capital, *the masses of the people in the colonies*, marching under the leadership and hegemony of the international revolutionary movement."

The decisive trend in capitalism is towards the sharpening of its contradictions. Nor will this be overcome by the process of trustification. As the tendency develops to "organize," that is, to trustify sections of capitalist economy, this tendency is outrun by the counter-tendency to sharpen and deepen the antagonisms within the capitalist system and between it and the new Socialist system of the Soviet Union. In short, the very process of capitalist monopolization speeds capitalist society ever faster along the road to imperialist war and proletarian revolution. Lenin thus analyses capitalist development:

"There is no doubt that the development is going *in the direction* of a single world trust that will swallow up all enterprises and all States without exception. But the development in this direction is proceeding under such stress, with such a tempo, with such contradictions, conflicts, and convulsions — not only economical, but also political, national, etc., etc.— that before a single world trust will be reached, before the respective national finance capitalist will have formed a world union of 'ultra-imperialism,' imperialism will inevitably explode, capitalism will turn into its opposite." [5]

(b) *Futile Efforts to Quench the Class Struggle*

THE MAJOR social contradiction of the capitalist system is the conflict in interest between the owning capitalist class and the producing working class. This gives rise to class struggle, the capitalists always seeking to more intensely exploit the workers, and the workers struggling to retain the products of their labor. The class struggle, as we have already seen, becomes ever sharper with the

[5] Preface to Bukharin's *Imperialism and World Economy*, p. 14.

intensification of the general crisis of capitalism, and it eventually culminates in the proletarian revolution.

Necessarily, the capitalist class has always had as a fundamental objective the liquidation or softening of this revolutionary contradiction. But the facts demonstrate that it is proving no more successful in accomplishing this than it is in its efforts to wipe out the basic economic contradiction of capitalism, the conflict between the capitalist modes of production and distribution. In spite of all the efforts of the capitalists to quench the class struggle, by damping down or beating out the workers' opposition, it flares up ever broader, more vigorously and more menacing to capitalism.

Throughout the capitalist world the trend of the exploiters is towards Fascism; that is, to push through their offensive against the working class by policies of extreme demagogy and violence. The speed of the development of Fascism and the forms that it takes in the various countries depend upon the extent to which the capitalist crisis has progressed. Fascism develops along two main channels; that is, open Fascism and Social Fascism.

In Italy and some of the Balkan countries, where the revolutionary crisis early became acute, Fascism came into power by the violent seizure of the State power, followed by the wholesale smashing of workers' unions, cooperatives, political parties, the complete liquidation of bourgeois democracy, the setting up of government trade unions, etc.   In other countries the capitalists, approaching the crisis at a somewhat slower pace, follow, at least at the outset, the "dry road" or "legal" way to Fascism.   By this process of fasciszation the Bruening government in Germany is gradually developing the Fascist dictatorship; the MacDonald government in Great Britain is going in the same direction; Japan is openly menaced by Fascism; and in the United States many Fascist tendencies are in evidence, as exampled by the dictatorial methods of Hoover in the question of unemployment relief, etc.; by the decline in prestige of parliamentary government and the demand for a "strong man" dictator; by the demand of the American Legion convention for a "peace-time National Council of Defense"; by the appearance of many Fascist "planning" schemes (Swope, Woll, etc.), and by the wave of unpunished lynchings, wholesale arrest and deportation of militant workers, etc.   One of the most basic features of this trend of world capitalism towards Fascism is the gradual fasciszation of the conservative trade unions and Socialist parties.

From Social Reformism to Social Fascism

It has always been a policy of the capitalist class, especially in the imperialist countries, to split and

weaken the working class by making certain concessions to the skilled workers.   This provided the
base of Social Reformism.   The Socialist parties
of the world and such trade unions as the American Federation of Labor fitted themselves into this
bosses' strategy, seeking to develop the skilled
workers as a privileged aristocracy of labor.   They
based their organization, economic and political,
upon the skilled workers, ignoring or openly be-
traying the unskilled workers, as a thousand
sold-out strikes testify.   They cultivated illusions
among the skilled workers that their interests lie
in collaboration with the bourgeoisie rather than
in class struggle of the workers.   Social Reformism was and is a tool of the capitalist class in its
struggle against the working class.   The Social
Reformists are in reality, as Lenin called them,
"agents of the bourgeoisie in the ranks of the
workers."

The hey-day of Social Reformism was during
the early, "peaceful" stage of capitalist development and in the first phase of imperialism.   This
general period may be said to have closed with the
beginning of the World War.   In this period,
with the world capitalist system generally on the
upgrade, the capitalists, especially in United
States, England and Germany, could and did
make many concessions to the skilled workers.
Few of these, however, seeped down to the unskilled and semi-skilled, who remained in a state

of poverty. Upon this economic foundation Social Reformism built for itself a strong mass following among the workers.

But the development of the general crisis of
capitalism has changed the complexion though not
the basic role of the Social Reformistic "lieutenants of capital." The employers, trying to find a
way out of their difficulties and to preserve their
profits at the expense of the workers, intensify
their wage-cut drive, reduction of unemployment
benefits, etc.; not even the skilled workers, although they are partly shielded, escaping the rapid
downward trend. The old system of concessions
to the skilled workers, the basis of Social Reformism, becomes increasingly narrowed down and is
succeeded by more direct and rigorous methods of
repression.

Adapting themselves to the needs of the employers, the reformist Socialist and trade union
leaders have developed their movement into an
organ of the bosses for the Fascist repression
and intensified exploitation of the working class.
They have practically grafted the Social Democracy and the conservative unions onto the capitalist
State and the employers' exploitation machinery.
They devote to capitalism their long-established
prestige as workers' leaders, their strong organizational control over the masses, and their unquestioned demagogic skill in covering up their services
to capitalism with pleas that it is all necessary in

the building of Socialism. Where necessary they do not hesitate to use open violence against the revolutionary toilers. The policy of the Social Democracy is basically that of Fascism; the beating back of the proletarian revolution, the saving of capitalism and the profits of the employers at the expense of the workers. The principal difference is that Social Democracy hides its Fascism under a mask of Marxian Socialism. Thus, in the period of the decline of capitalism, Social Reformism becomes Social Fascism.

The Fasciszation of the American Federation of Labor

In the A.F. of L. the process of fasciszation is far advanced. In fact, the top leadership of this organization, the Greens, Wolls, Lewises, etc., are already practically open-Fascist. They are brazen defenders of capitalism. They have become the chief strike-breaking agency of the employers. To this end they work hand-in-glove with the Hoover government, the American Legion, the Ku Klux Klan, the National Civic Federation, the Chambers of Commerce, the churches, and all and sundry other institutions of the employers for the exploitation of the workers. Their policy is to make the trade unions more company-union-like than the company unions themselves. Politically illiterate and with the sycophancy typical of para-

sites, these leaders take their "opinions" ready-
made from the most reactionary sections of the
bourgeoisie. They greedily lap up every mess of
capitalist economics and politics that their masters
set before them. Developing Fascism in the United
States has a main foundation in the leadership of
the American Federation of Labor. Their system of craft unionism, maintained as against industrial unionism to prevent unity of action by the
workers and to furnish additional jobs to officials,
is a shameless method of union scabbery. Their
endorsement of election candidates of the capitalist parties, or "reward-your-friends" policy, is a
plain sell-out of the working class. Their support
of the rationalization of industry is part of the
speed-up program of the bosses. Their systematic
betrayal of the Negroes, women and young workers dovetails into the employers' special exploitation of these sections of the workers. Their long
years of peddling the interests of the unskilled
workers and their breaking up of attempts of these
workers to organize constitutes the greatest of all
their crimes against the working class. They are
saturated with graft — racketeering was born in
the A.F. of L. With their huge salaries, ranging
from $10,000 to $20,000 yearly or as much as those
of United States governors, senators, etc., they
have nothing in common with the workers in their
way of living and thinking. So faithful a servant
of capitalism is the A.F. of L. leadership that, if

one wants to know its policy in any field of politics or economics, all that is necessary is to find out the policy of the bosses and you have the answer.

The present tasks of the A.F. of L. leadership, dictated by the employers, are to defeat the demand of the workers for unemployment insurance and relief, to push through the employers' wage-cutting campaign, to advance the preparations for imperialist war, to beat back the advance of the Trade Union Unity League and the revolutionary minorities in the reformist unions.

In the question of unemployment the A.F. of L. leadership sinks to the greatest depths of cynical betrayal of the workers. The Vancouver, 1931, convention of the A.F. of L., re-affirming the existing policy, said: "Compulsory unemployment insurance legislation such as is now in effect in Great Britain and Germany would be unsuited to our economic and political requirements and are unsatisfactory to American workmen." When Green, Woll and Co. say this they speak for their capitalist masters, not for the workers. The A.F. of L. convention which could adopt such a decision was made up of 90% high-paid officials; the workers had no voice or representation. The A.F. of L. membership, who favor unemployment insurance, have never in any way been consulted or given an opportunity to express their opinion on the question. The A.F. of L. leadership, either openly or by their silence, have endorsed every

attack of the police upon unemployed demonstrations. The millions of unemployed workers,
destitute of unemployment insurance and in a condition of semi-starvation, have the A.F. of L. very
much to thank for their present plight. It may
be that under the growing mass pressure many
A.F. of L. leaders will be forced to tip their hat
to "unemployment insurance" of the Groves Law
type, (half a dozen governors having endorsed it),
but this demagogy will not change their real opposition. The A.F. of L. leaders are a central pillar
of the Hoover program of starving the unemployed.

The A.F. of L. leaders are also a principal instrument of the bosses for cutting the workers'
wages. During the past two years, despite the
Hoover-Green no-wage-cut agreement, the wages
of the workers in practically every industry have
been slashed and the A.F. of L. has not waged a
single major strike against this offensive. Where
the militancy of the workers has forced strikes,
(Ohio miners, needle trades, etc.), these have been
betrayed into means for accomplishing wage-cuts.
Agreeing with the bosses that the standards of
the workers must come down, the A.F. of L. leaders
have adopted a policy of "voluntary" wage-cuts.
They are accepting cuts off-hand in the building,
textile, printing, clothing and other industries all
over the country, and glorying in them as victories.
Matthew Woll called the recent "voluntary"

cut of the railroad workers, which was a most shameful sell-out, "an achievement such as we have never before witnessed in the United States." In their wage-cutting program the A.F. of L. leaders do not hesitate to cut the wages of organized workers even below those of the unorganized. In the Colorado mines of the Rocky Mountain Fuel Co. the U.M.W. of A. leaders "voluntarily" gave up 50% of the workers' pay in order to enable that company to out-compete its competitors. In West Virginia, the U.M.W. of A. leader Van Bittner declared that he would "outscab the scabs," and signed an agreement with the Pursglove Company, cutting the already starvation wages of its 1600 workers from 30 to 22 cents per ton, thereby reducing them far below the unorganized miners of the vicinity. The American Federation of Full Fashioned Hosiery Workers, (U.T.W.), in the Fall of 1931, accepted a cut of 35% to 45%, shamelessly announcing that its purpose was to undercut the production costs of the non-union mills and to drive them out of business. In all this wage-cutting campaign no unions have been more active than the Socialist-controlled needle trades organizations.

Not only does the A.F. of L. take the initiative in forcing through wage-cuts, but it also actively breaks the resistance of the workers, the unorganized or those united in the Trade Union Unity League, when they strike against reductions of their standards, examples of this being the recent strikes in Western Pennsylvania, Kentucky, Lawrence, Paterson, New York, etc. It used to be that when the employers broke strikes of their workers they called in such professional scab-herders as Farley, Pinkerton, the Feltz-Baldwins, etc., but now they use the Greens, Lewises, Doaks, Schlessingers, Hillmans, etc.

Notoriously, the A.F. of L. leaders are militaristic jingoes, and support every phase of the imperialists' war program. They are rabid enemies of the Soviet Union. The A.F. of L. convention poisonously declared: "We regard the Soviet regime in Russia as the most unscrupulous, most anti-social institution in the world today. Between it and our form of political and social organization, there can be no compromise of any kind." Their hatred of the U.S.S.R. is a class hatred, as is that of the employers. They fear the revolution like all other exploiters of labor, usually more acutely than even the capitalists themselves.

Naturally, to enforce in the unions the policies of wage-cuts, starvation of the unemployed, speed-up, etc., more and more use has to be made of Fascist methods of control of these organizations. Democracy, never vigorous in the A.F. of L. and railroad Brotherhoods, has now been practically wiped out. The organizations are dominated from top to bottom by bureaucrats and gangsters; including the "Socialist" unions. The rank and file have little or nothing to say on vital questions of policy. Union elections are a farce, the ruling cliques stealing as many votes as they may require. Often they even refuse to put the opposition candidates on the ballot. Conventions are packed with administration henchmen. The union journals are closed to all serious discussion. And when the workers object to this growing Fascist regime they face gangsterism and expulsion from the organizations.

The employers directly assist the reactionaries in controlling the unions. Rebellious workers in the unions are, upon the proposal of the union leaders, blacklisted from the industries. More than ever the check-off is used to hold the workers in the organizations by force (anthracite, needle trades, textiles, etc.). In Illinois, for example, the miners have led several revolts against the U.M.W.A. but are still compelled, by the check-off, to remain members.

Fascism everywhere seeks to amalgamate the trade unions with the State, so that the workers may be the more effectively controlled, Mussolini's "trade unions" being actual State organs. Gradually the A.F. of L. and railroad unions are becoming Statized, being already practically the official government unions. Their foreign policy dovetails completely with that of American imperialism and obediently follows all the windings of the State Department. Significantly, Mr. Hoover, together with a flock of governors, senators, mayors, generals, etc., went to the Boston, (1930), convention to tell the A.F. of L. leaders to fight against unemployment insurance. And during the 1931 coal strike of the National Miners Union in Western Pennsylvania, President Hoover, Secretary Doak, and Governors Pinchot and White actively interfered to break the strike, assisting and often calling upon the coal operators to rebuild the U.M.W.A. and arranging conferences to this effect.

Between the police and the A.F. of L. bureaucrats there is a close working arrangement. At the top Matthew Woll and the Department of Justice cooperate in the issuance of their periodic joint "red scares"; at the bottom, the lesser officials turn the names of revolutionary workers over to the police. The Department of Labor, when 35 members of Local 28 of the Sheet Metal Workers got out an injunction against their crooked officials, sent its agents to terrorize these workers as "Reds," (*New York World-Telegram*, Apr. 1, 1932) this being a direct support of A.F. of L. racketeer leaders by the Federal government. Nor do the courts fail in protecting the A.F. of L. officials against attacks by the workers. They issue injunctions against the TUUL unions on behalf of the A.F. of L. And in Southern Illinois, Gebert, Tash, Frankfeld, et al., were indicted for criminal syndicalism, being charged by the State with "maliciously, unlawfully and knowingly combining, federating," etc., "to injure the character of the United Mine Workers of America."

The Fasciszation of the Socialist Party

TRAVELING to Fascism, the Social Democrats, internationally as well as in this country, are fulfilling every task assigned them by the employers. In summing up their intellectual fasciszation, the *Program of the Communist International,* says:

"In the sphere of *theory,* Social Democracy has utterly and completely betrayed Marxism, having traversed the road from revision to complete liberal bourgeois reformism and avowed social-imperialism; it has substituted in place of the Marxian theory of the contradictions of capitalism, the bourgeois theory of its harmonious development; it has pigeon-holed the theory of crises and of the pauperization of the proletariat; it has turned the flaming and menacing theory of class struggle into prosaic advocacy of class peace; it has exchanged the theory of growing class antagonisms for the petty bourgeois fairy tale about the 'democratization' of capital; in place of the theory of the inevitability of war under capitalism it has substituted the bourgeois deceit of pacifism and the lying propaganda of 'ultra-imperialism'; it has changed the theory of the revolutionary downfall of capitalism for the counterfeit coinage of 'sound' capitalism transforming itself peacefully into Socialism; it has replaced revolution by evolution; the destruction of the bourgeois State by its active upbuilding, the theory

of proletarian dictatorship by the theory of coalition
with the bourgeoisie, the doctrine of international solidarity — by preaching defense of the imperialist father-
land; for Marxian dialectical materialism it has substituted the idealist philosophy and is now engaged in
picking up the crumbs of religion that fall from the
table of the bourgeoisie."

The practice of the Socialist parties and trade
unions conforms to this Fascist theoretical degeneration. There have been no demands made upon
them by capitalism in crisis which they have not
obeyed. When the capitalists of the various countries called upon them to organize the great World
War they responded by identifying everywhere
their interests with those of their national bourgeoisie and by mobilizing the workers for the
slaughter. And ever since they have worked with
their capitalist masters to help them prepare the
next war. In Great Britain the MacDonald "Socialist" government maintained intact the great
war machine of British imperialism; in Germany
the Social Fascists voted for the rebuilding of the
German navy; in France they prepared the infamous universal military service law now in force;
in Poland, Czecho-Slovakia and many other countries they vote the war budgets. Everywhere they
are the special decoy ducks of capitalist pacifism,
the shield of imperialist war.

In the war plans of the capitalist nations against
the Soviet Union the Social Democrats play a lead-

ing role. They scoff at the danger of capitalist war against the Soviet Union and thus disarm the workers' defense; they make the capitalist war appear as a fight against autocracy in the U.S.S.R. The Social Fascists hate the Soviet Union because they see in it the living refutation of their whole policy, a menacing threat to the capitalist system of which they are the most profound theoretical and practical defenders. They have never hesitated, (in Georgia and elsewhere), to take up arms against the Soviet Union. The exposures in the recent political trials in Moscow showed that the Second International is working hand-in-glove with the French imperialists in preparing armed intervention against the U.S.S.R. As a recent resolution of the Communist International says: "The Social Democracy has turned itself into a shock-brigade of world imperialism which is preparing for war against the U.S.S.R."

The special task of the Social Fascists is to discredit the Soviet Union among the workers. As we have seen, they are the most skilled in building up arguments against the Soviet Union, covering their sophistries with a cloak of pseudo-Marxism. They take up every capitalist anti-Soviet lie and assiduously propagate it among the workers. These they alternate with hypocritical pretensions of friendship, knowing that the masses are sympathetic to the U.S.S.R. A few quotations will show their malignant attacks upon the Russian revolution and their true attitude towards it:

"Russian Soviet imperialism, which has robbed a whole series of non-Russian peoples of their rights and principles, is striving to extend its rule still further and to cause trouble between other countries. *This is the greatest danger of war.*" [6]

"The Soviet Government has been the greatest disaster and calamity that has ever occurred to the Socialist movement. Let us dissociate ourselves from the Soviet government." [7]

"I agree in the main with Prof. Beard's vigorous statement: 'One thing, however, is certain; the Russian government rules by tyranny and terror, with secret police, espionage and arbitrary executions.'" [8]

In the great revolutionary upheavals following the World War the Social Fascists saved European capitalism. In Italy they betrayed the revolution into the hands of Mussolini. In Germany, in their efforts to preserve the capitalist system, they shot down thousands of revolutionary workers. All this was done in the name of fighting for Socialism. The MacDonald "Socialist" government simply displayed its true Social Fascist character by shooting and jailing thousands of revolutionary workers and peasants in India. The Social Fascists were the main force in the speed-

[6] *Vorwearts*, official organ of the German Social Democratic Party.
[7] Morris Hillquit, American Socialist leader, *New Leader*, Feb. 4, 1928.
[8] Norman Thomas, *As I See It*, p. 93.

up, rationalization movement, their real leader being Henry Ford, not Karl Marx.

Now again, when capitalism is trying to find a way out of its deep crisis by reducing the standards of the workers, its main allies are the Social Fascists. The world Social Democracy is not better than a strike-breaking, wage-cutting, dole-slashing tool of the employers. In every capitalist country the Social Fascists are cooperating closely with the capitalists, accepting as their working principle that in the crisis the workers' living conditions must come down. In the United States J. P. Morgan speaks over the radio for the starvation, "block-aid" system, and so does Norman Thomas. In Great Britain, with the aid of the Labor government, the bosses have deeply cut the wages in every industry, besides making sharp reductions in the State unemployment insurance. In Germany the Bruening and other capitalist governments, all the while receiving the active support of the Social Democratic party, have cut the wages of the workers and the benefits of the jobless to starvation levels.

The Socialist parties of the world are the third parties of capitalism. They do not fight for even the most elementary demands of the workers. They are a part of the capitalist machinery for taking the bread out of the mouths of the workers and their families, the principal barrier to the revolution. That is why in Great Britain, Germany and other countries the capitalists have supported Social Fascists to head their governments. In every case their record has been one of subservience to the program of the exploiters. In practice their policy of the gradual building of Socialism has resolved itself simply into a desperate effort to keep the breath of life in capitalism. Their so-called nationalization of industry is only a covert aid to capitalist trustification. In no country have they achieved the slightest progress towards Socialism, or even made serious proposals looking in that direction. The Liberal English writer, Ratcliffe, says in *Current History*, (Dec., 1931) : "The first nominally Socialist Prime Minister of England has at no time proposed a single Socialist measure." The same may be said with equal truth of every "Socialist" Prime Minister in every country. Even Norman Thomas has to grudgingly admit that "the record of parliamentary governments by Socialist parties in Europe is no record of thrilling achievement." [9] Manuilsky states the case correctly when he calls the Social Democracy, "a party more reactionary and counter-revolutionary than the bourgeois parties were in the past when capitalism was still on the upgrade."

The Social Democracy not only increasingly applies more Fascist methods itself against the workers, but it further serves its capitalist masters by preparing the ground for open Fascism. In Italy

[9] *America's Way Out*, p. 181.

the betrayal of the great metal strike by the Socialists opened the door to Mussolini. In Austria the Social Democracy disarms the workers before the advancing Fascism. In Great Britain, by their betrayal of the great general strike and by the debacle of the Labor government, the Social Fascists threw demoralization into the ranks of the workers and petty bourgeois sympathizers, giving direct encouragement to Fascism. In Germany the Social Fascist leaders are clearing the way for Fascism through their theory and practice of "the lesser evil." With the argument that the starvation capitalist system is a "lesser evil" than the dictatorship of the proletariat they support the Bruening government, with its wholesale wage-cuts, suppression of the workers' rights and program of gradual fasciszation. Under the name of Socialism they call upon the workers to vote for the monarchist, von Hindenburg. In many places they join hands with the Hitlerites and police for armed attacks on the Communists. To the Social Fascists the major danger is the Communist revolution; to defeat this the end justifies the means.

The "fight" between Social Fascism and Fascism is so much "sound and fury signifying nothing." The two movements are blood-brothers. Manuilsky says: "Fascism and Social Fascism are two aspects of one and the same bulwark of bourgeois dictatorship," and Stalin says: "Fascism is a militant organization of the bourgeoisie resting

upon the active support of Social Democracy."
Their quarrel is only a case of friction between two
methods of repressing the workers, between two
sets of capitalist agents fighting for the fleshpots
of office and control.   The Social Fascists would
maintain the semblance of capitalist democracy as
the best means of forestalling the revolution and
they would be its administrators; whereas the Fascists would sweep aside this fake democracy and
its champions and proceed to more direct methods
of repression.   But an accommodation of these
conflicting ideas and interests is being arrived at
by the gradual fasciszation of the State and of the
mass organizations of the Social Democrats.   In
due season the Social Fascist leaders, in the name
of Socialism, will join with the Hitlerites in shooting down the revolutionary workers.   It is because
of the essential unity of Fascism and Social Fascism that Hamilton Fish, one of the most conscious
Fascists in this country, could enthusiastically endorse Norman Thomas for office in the 1931
elections.[10]   The Mussolinis, Pilsudskis, Briands,
and MacDonalds are only fully-matured Social
Democrats.

The record of the Socialist Party of the United
States is altogether in line with that of its brother
parties in Europe. It has undergone the same
ideological degeneration in the direction of Fascism.   It supported the imperialist program of

10 *New York Herald-Tribune,* Nov. 2, 1931.

MacDonald and the endorsement of the Bruening government. It advocated the whole capitalist rationalization of industry, and class collaboration, removing from its program all reference to the class struggle. Now, naturally, it comes forward for capitalist "planning." In Reading and Milwaukee, Socialist strongholds and long notorious for their low wages and open-shop conditions, the same starvation program for the unemployed prevails, the same jailing of unemployed demonstrators as in Mayor Walker's New York. The Socialist party has cemented its alliance with the A.F. of L. leadership and carries out the same line of wage-cutting and strike-breaking against the revolutionary unions, but with more skillful strategy and demagogy. The Socialist-controlled New York needle trades unions, saturated with corruption and gangsterism, are just as much at the service of the employers as any unions in the whole A.F. of L. Wherever it is to be found, the Socialist party, under its false-face of working class phrases, is a maid-of-all-work for the capitalist class.

The "Left" Social Fascists

THE DEEPENING of the crisis and the growing revolutionization of the masses is accompanied by a strong development of radical phrase-mongering on the part of many groups of open and covert defenders of capitalism. This demagogy is part of the capitalist offensive against the workers. Its aim is to delude the workers with promises of drastic relief, while at the same time holding them tied in practical policy to the basic capitalist program of exploitation. It is a means to prevent the masses from following the leadership of the Communists.

Of such demagogues the Fascists are outstanding examples. Before Mussolini seized power his program was extremely "radical," containing demands for a republic, suppression of all chambers of commerce and stock companies, confiscation of church properties, nationalization of the war industries, etc., all of which he completely repudiated in practice. At the present time Hitler is trying to carry out the same Mussolini strategy, to deceive the German masses with pretenses of radicalism as a screen for the naked capitalist dictatorship and exploitation he has in store for them. The new-found radicalism of the Roosevelts, Pinchots, LaFollettes, Murphys, Father Coxes, etc., is of essentially the same stripe in this country, so much empty demagogy to win a mass following of the discontented.

The Social Fascists are still more dangerous masters at this demagogic art. As we have seen they have, under pretense of fighting for Socialism, backed up every plan that capitalism has put forward for saving itself and more intensely exploiting the toilers. Under the fig-leaf of Socialism they supported the World War, the Versailles Treaty, the Dawes and Young Plans, the Kellogg Pact, the Chinese butcher, Chang Kai Shek, and the Indian faker, Gandhi. Even as these lines are being written, they are working together with the Spanish coalition government to shoot down the heroic revolt of the Spanish workers, (*Daily Worker,* Jan. 23, 1932). Nor are the Greens and Wolls anything lacking in demagogic ability, with their blather about the 5-hour day, their vague talk of "revolution if something is not done," etc.

But the most insidious and dangerous to the workers of all this crop of demagogues are the so-called "left" Social Fascists. The substance of their activities is, while giving practical support to the right Social Fascists, to criticize them in the name of the revolution. They are the radical phrase-mongers par excellence. Their objective task is the confusion of the most advanced elements of the workers and therefore the breaking up of serious movements against the capitalists and their reactionary labor henchmen. Throughout the Second International there are such groupings, including the Maxtonites in Great Britain, the "left" Social Democrats in Germany, the various renegade Communist grouplets, etc. Trotzky belongs to this general category. The harm of such elements is typically illustrated by Trotzky's present denial of an immediate war danger between

Japan and the U.S.S.R., while at the same time he poses as an ultra-revolutionist.

During the post-war revolutionary upheavals in Germany and other countries such pseudo-left elements sprang up, forming a separate world organization, the so-called 2½ International. These "lefts," despite many radical phrases, always supported the right Social Democrats against the Communists, thereby doing much to break up the revolutionary attacks of the workers upon capitalism. After the workers were defeated the "lefts" amalgamated with the Second International, of which, at all times, they were essentially a specialized part. Now, in this great crisis, they are attempting to come forth and repeat their treacherous role of 1918-23.

In the United States the principal representative of this insidious pseudo-revolutionary tendency is the Conference for Progressive Labor Action, or the so-called Muste group. This is made up of miscellaneous "progressive" petty trade union bureaucrats, remnants of the old Labor party movements, liberals and Brookwood intellectuals, dilettante churchmen, social workers, etc. Its chief political expression is the "left" Stanley group in the Socialist party and its principal activities are on the trade union field. Such Socialists as Thomas and Maurer flirt with the movement. On the fringes of the Muste group are the renegade Communist groups of Lore, Lovestone,

Cannon and Weisbord. They serve to give the whole tendency a more "red" tinge with their pretense at Communism; but their practice dovetails with the Muste group. The "left" Social Fascists are in reality specialized troops of the reactionary bureaucrats for struggle against the revolutionary sections of the working class.

The line of the Muste group is typical of such tendencies the world over. While criticising the betrayals of the A.F. of L. leaders and the Socialist party, they nevertheless give them practical support. They are bitter enemies of the Communist party and the Trade Union Unity League. They are special opponents of the policy of independent revolutionary unions, seeking to draw the unorganized workers under the control of the American Federation of Labor. They are the loyal "opposition" within the A.F. of L. They talk of starting a more radical Socialist party as a rival to the Communist party.

In its short life of about three years the Muste group has clearly shown the unity of its basic policy with that of the A.F. of L. How this "radical" group makes a division of labor with the A.F. of L. leaders is typically illustrated by the campaign of the A.F. of L. to "organize" the Southern textile workers recently. On the one hand, Mr. Green, accompanied by an efficiency engineer, Jeffrey Browne, proposed to "organize" the textile workers by offering to speed them still more

and to kill off radicalism among them.   Along this
line he spoke to many Southern Chambers of Commerce and employers' associations.   "The policies
he advocated," says the Memphis *Commercial Appeal,* "might have come with propriety from the
President of the American Banking Association."
On the other hand, the Muste group got into action
to help Green control the workers within his reactionary scheme.   Muste grew enthusiastic over the
campaign, called upon the workers to give the
A.F. of L. misleaders an organizing fund of $1,-
000,000, sent his speakers to talk radical to the
workers at the mill gates, and his organizers to
play a shameful role in the final strike sell-outs.
Thus this "progressive" wing of the A.F. of L.
cooperated perfectly with the top bureaucracy to
defeat the militant movement of the Southern
workers and to keep them away from the revolutionary National Textile Workers Union.

The recent Lawrence strike was another typical
example of the Musteites as auxiliaries of the
A.F. of L. leadership.   With the A.F. of L. accepting wage-cuts all over the country on principle,
manifestly it could not afford to have these 23,000
unorganized textile workers win their strike against
the wage-cut.   The A.F. of L. organizers went
into Lawrence to bring about the acceptance of the
cut, that is, to sell-out the strike.   The Musteites
helped them.   They viciously attacked the revolutionary union and aided the reactionary A.F. of L.

leadership to secure prestige among the masses by the Muste show of radicalism. In the 1931 Paterson strike of silk workers there was a complete united front of capitalist politicians, A.F. of L., Socialist Party, Muste group, Lovestoneites, etc., against the National Textile Workers Union.

Every "left" maneuver of the A.F. of L. bureaucrats to deceive the masses has the enthusiastic support of the Muste group and their renegade Communist allies. The putting over of the recent general wage-cut of the railroad workers provided a good example of Musteism in practice. From the outset of the negotiations between the companies and the union leaders it was evident that the latter intended to accept the cut after making a few maneuvers to create the impression among the rank and file that they were fighting the companies' proposition. Manifestly, the task of every militant was to expose this plot and to organize the workers against it. But no sooner did the latter begin their sham battle against the cut than Muste's paper, *The Labor Age,* Dec., 1931, declared: "The fact that the twenty-one railroad labor unions in this country have informed a committee of railroad presidents that they will not accept a 'voluntary' cut in wages of 10% is a hopeful sign. It may mean a turning point in American trade union history." This was plain aid and comfort to the enemy, deceiving the workers and making it easy for the leaders to betray them.

The Bankruptcy of Social Fascism

Now LET us see whether or not capitalism is developing in Social Fascism a means with which it can quench the class struggle and beat down the surging proletarian revolution. Even a cursory glance shows that with the narrowing of the economic base of Social Fascism, caused by the inability of capitalism to so widely corrupt the labor aristocracy, goes a narrowing of its mass base among the working class. Social Fascism is bankrupt in theory and practice and, despite (and because of) the support it gets from the employers and the State, it is entering into a period of disintegration.

By its daily role in the class struggle Social Fascism shows itself to be the road, not to Socialism but to the still deeper enslavement of the workers. The Social Democratic theory that the capitalist "democracy" would gradually evolve into a Socialist government leads in hard reality to Socialist support of growing Fascist dictatorships all over the capitalist world; its conception of a steadily rising standard of living for the workers under an organized capitalism leads, in the decaying capitalist system, to the acceptance of wholesale wage-cuts, starvation of the unemployed, preparations for war against the Soviet Union, etc.

Inevitably the meaning of all this is seeping into the minds of the masses of workers who have hitherto followed the lead of the Social Democrats. Although they still have many stubborn illusions, they are learning that the Social Democracy is their enemy, and they are starting to turn against it. Hence, there is beginning a world-wide decline in the mass influence and organizational strength of the Social Democracy and a growth of the Communist movement. In Germany, where the capitalist crisis is farthest advanced and the process of fasciszation of the Social Democracy most complete, the above trends are best illustrated. Thus, while the vote of the Social Democratic party steadily falls off, that of the Communist party, 4,982,000 in the recent election, as rapidly increases.

Nor is the United States an exception to this general tendency. Since the war the A.F. of L. has lost about 2,000,000 members. The United Mine Workers, once the backbone of the A.F. of L., has been reduced to one-fourth of its former membership and, because of its reactionary policies, it has become a stench in the nostrils of the miners. During the past two years the building trades unions have lost at least one-third of their members and other unions accordingly. Moreover, throughout the A.F. of L., there is brewing an explosive rank and file opposition to the reactionary policies of the leaders. Never was the prestige of the A.F. of L. so low among its members and the broad masses of workers. As against all this, there is the spreading mass influence of the Communist party and the Trade Union Unity League.

The capitalists, naturally, do not passively observe the disintegration of Social Fascism, but try to save it. Thus American employers are definitely cultivating the reactionary unions more and more. This amounts, in substance, to a modification of their historic open-shop policy. This tendency manifests itself in many ways, such as the "re-build the U.M.W. of A." movement; the "granting" of the check-off to the anthracite miners; the close collaboration of the bosses, the government and the union leaders in the fake needle trades strikes; the recognition accorded the shop unions by the railroad companies in the recent wage negotiations for many roads where they had no members, the close cooperation of the A.F. of L. and the Federal government, etc.

One of the most recent and striking manifestations of this tendency was the practically unanimous passage of the Norris-La Guardia Anti-Injunction bill. This bill, which presumably abolishes the "yellow dog" contract and limits the power of federal courts to issue injunctions, in reality does not do away with injunctions at all, but lays the basis for their application primarily against the revolutionary unions. It is a definite move to facilitate the organization of the A.F. of L. unions, and to give their reactionary leaders a "paper victory" to support the paralyzing non-partisan A.F. of L. political policy. It does not originate in a sudden burst of liberalism on the part of the government, but in a realization of the necessity to develop the A.F. of L. leadership still further as a strike-breaking organization.

The capitalist policy to strengthen Social Fascism as a barrier against the Communist party and the Trade Union Unity League is further expressed in the distinct cultivation of the Socialist party that is now to be seen all over the country. The S.P. has become a thoroughly respectable party of "opposition." The capitalists realize that the lack of a strong social reformist movement is a great disadvantage for them, hence, they are consciously building the Socialist party as a weapon against the Communist party. Its candidates and activities are given access to every avenue of publicity. The endorsement of Norman Thomas by most of the capitalist press in New York in the recent elections shows the way the wind is blowing. The capitalists know their own.

Such methods of galvanizing Social Fascism into life must fail. The masses of workers can never be dragooned into organizations that are so manifestly carrying out policies hostile to their interest. But this is not to minimize the danger. The Social Fascist method of obscuring the capitalist policy under the guise of Socialism is an insidious menace. It is now and will remain until the revolution the most dangerous capitalist influence among the working class, the most serious brake upon the class struggle. The progress of the revolutionary movement is to be measured by the breaking of the Social Democracy's grip upon the workers, ideologically and organizationally.

That there is such a breaking-down process now going on is self-evident, and this disintegration will increase with the sharpening of the general crisis of capitalism. The Social Democratic illusions of the masses are weakening, despite the frantic efforts of the "left" phrase-mongers to keep them alive. Less and less able are the employers to put into effect their traditional policy of corrupting the strategically situated labor aristocracy and thus to play them off against the rest of the working class. The differences between the skilled and unskilled are diminishing, the working class is becoming unified. More and more skillful become the newly-organized Communist parties in mobilizing the rebellious masses. Consequently, the employers are compelled to make ever greater use of open force against the workers, to resort to a policy of naked Fascism. '

The Futility of Fascism

ABOVE, we have pointed out the tendency towards the development of Fascism in all capitalist countries. Italy is the classical example of this tendency carried to its logical conclusion. Defenders of capitalism the world over have looked hopefully towards Italy for a solution of the capitalist crisis. Mussolini, as well as Ford, seemed to have the answer for capitalism's woes. But we shall see that this is not so.

Fascism is not an alternative to capitalism; it is capitalism, the most extreme expression of the capitalistic dictatorship. As Manuilsky says: "The Fascist regime is not a new type of State; it is one of the forms of the bourgeois dictatorship in the epoch of imperialism." [11] Fascism does not amend capitalist economics. The economic policy of Fascism is the familiar capitalist program of the exploitation of the workers and poor farmers. The difference between Fascism and a bourgeois democratic regime is that the former is more extreme and brutal in its exploitation of the toilers. As Manuilsky says further: "The main factor in Fascism is its open offensive against the working class with the employment of every form of violence and coercion." Thus, inevitably, Fascism deepens the contradictions of capitalist society. It must result in intensifying the economic crisis and in stimulating the revolutionization of the toilers.

The wide development of Fascism in various forms in the several capitalist countries is not a sign of capitalism growing stronger, but weaker. Fascism arises with the deepening of the capitalist

[11] *The Communist Parties and the Crisis of Capitalism*, p. 36.

crisis. It is the desperate means by which capitalism in its extremity of crisis vainly tries to save itself. It is significant that Fascism is most developed in exactly those countries that are the weakest links in the capitalist world chain. In some instances, to crush the workers, it incorporates the Social Fascist parties and unions into its machinery; in others, it destroys not only the Social Fascist organizations but also Liberal groupings.

Fascism is the instrument of finance capital. It speeds the development of State capitalism, linking the employers' organizations, "trade unions," etc. directly to the government. Here, indeed, is a heaven for capitalist "planners." Hence, all over the world, the advocates of an "organized capitalism" have looked hopefully towards Italy. We even find people who falsely dub themselves Communists asserting that Fascism can liquidate the economic crisis and do away with the class struggle. Thus V. F. Calverton says in *The Modern Quarterly*, (Jan.-Mar., 1931) : "In either case (Communism or Fascism, WZF) industry can be organized into a scientific unit, the present dissipation of energy be saved, and the friction of democratic struggle be destroyed."

But capitalism's hope in Fascist Italy has been no less futile than its enthusiasm for the "new capitalism" in the United States. Italy is just as deep in the mud of the capitalist crisis as other countries are in its mire. During the past year Italian industrial production has rapidly declined, examples of this decrease being steel 16%, cotton 30%, automobiles 50%, etc., the general average of decline being about 40%. Exports, notwithstanding government forced-draft methods of dumping, have dropped seriously. The crisis also manifests itself heavily in the realm of finance; the stocks of the largest and most important industrial undertakings having fallen off 50% to 75% since 1929; in November the Banca Commerciale Italiana, the largest bank in Italy, was saved from bankruptcy only by drastic government aid; in 1931 the government faced a deficit of 896,000,000 lire as against a surplus of 150,000,000 lire in 1930.

The living standards of the Italian workers and peasants have also catastrophically declined. An Associated Press dispatch of Mar. 15, 1932, says: "Italy's unemployed at the end of February totalled 1,147,000, a new high and an increase of 96,000 in a month." Only one-fourth receive the beggarly unemployment benefits. Wages have been slashed as much as 40% in the past four years. The prices paid to the peasants for their products have been similarly cut. So greatly have the masses been impoverished that Mussolini could cynically remark: "It is fortunate for Italy that the Italian workers and peasants are not in the habit of eating more than once a day."

The inevitable result of such conditions is a rising revolutionary movement in Italy also, despite the ferocious terror. The *Chicago Tribune,* (Feb. 20, 1932), says: "A wave of unrest is sweeping Italy from North to South and in many places disturbances have taken on the character of mass risings of the countryside against the authorities . . . the ordinary police forces are helpless and only the arrival of reserves prevented the rioters from lynching the authorities."

Fascism, the weapon of big capitalists, bankers and land-owners, finds its chief mass base among the petty bourgeoisie until these eventually become revolutionized by the intolerable conditions. The mass of the workers cannot be won over to Fascism. They see in Fascism a murderous enemy of the working class. The most that the Mussolinis and Hitlers can do is to temporarily win the support of sections of office employees and agricultural workers and others of the more backward and politically inexperienced toilers. As the workers free themselves from Social Democratic illusions they go to Communism, not to Fascism.

In his new book, *As I See It,* Norman Thomas develops the theory that the revolt of the workers cannot succeed in the face of the highly-destructive arms possessed by the capitalists, that the airplane can defeat the barricade. But this is only a call to the workers to surrender. The ruling class, also under Fascism, must have a mass base. It can not maintain power without one, notwithstanding all its airplanes and artillery. Fascism, as we have seen, has such a base in the petty bourgeoisie, and Fascism will disintegrate as this base collapses. In Italy, Poland and other Fascist countries this disintegration is clearly proceeding with the development of the capitalist crisis. The revolution attacks Fascism not only from without but from within.

The proletarian revolution cannot be crushed by force, even with the assistance of the most tricky Social Fascist and Fascist demagogy. Chang Kai Shek slaughtered 200,000 militant workers and peasants in the greatest reign of terror of modern history, but the wave of revolution in China mounts higher and higher. Poland, in spite of its extreme Fascist terrorism, goes rapidly to the revolutionary crisis. De Rivera in Spain learned something about trying to rule by violence, and the Russian Czar likewise. Hitler, if he comes to power in Germany, will eventually learn the same bitter lesson. And in Italy there is a revolutionary storm brewing that will blow Fascism to bits.

Mussolini was able to seize the power in Italy because of the Socialist betrayal of the great metal strike of 1920, which demoralized the workers who had hoped to make the revolution. Fascism is not an inevitable stage of the capitalist dictatorship; the revolution may forestall it. But it is possible that Fascism will secure the power in Germany, England, Japan, the United States and other countries through similar Socialist betrayals. In any event, however, Fascism will not be able to solve the capitalist crisis, and to save the present decaying social system. It cannot liquidate the class struggle; it cannot permanently hold down the workers and poor farmers by force. Faced by constantly worsening conditions and mass starvation, these masses will, under the leadership of the Communist party, eventually break through every system of Fascist terrorism and establish a Soviet regime.

CHAPTER IV

THE REVOLUTIONARY WAY OUT
OF THE CRISIS

IN THE preceding chapters we have seen that world capitalism, of which American capitalism is an integral part, sinks deeper and deeper into general crisis, with consequent widespread impoverishment of the masses, development of the menacing danger of imperialist war, and growth of a world-wide revolutionary upsurge by the exploited masses of toilers. We have seen, further, that every effort of the world bourgeoisie to halt or reverse these conditions only results, in the long run, in their intensification. Special measures to ease the present economic cyclical crisis — inflation, international moratoriums, State budget reductions, etc. — cannot permanently cure the basic general crisis of capitalism. This general crisis, with each recurring cyclical crisis, deepens and spreads.

In revolutionary contrast, we have seen the striking success of Socialism in the Soviet Union. There the workers and farmers have overthrown capitalism and established the dictatorship of the proletariat; they have found the solution to the

211

economic, political and social contradictions which are undermining the capitalist world. As the capitalist system internationally sinks deeper and deeper into crisis, the Socialist system in the U.S.S.R. achieves an even faster rate of progress to higher stages of well-being and culture for the masses.

The implications of all this are clear: to escape the encroaching capitalist starvation and to emancipate themselves, the workers of the world, including those in this country, must and will take the revolutionary way out of the crisis. That is, they will carry out a militant policy now in defense of their daily interests and, finally, following the example of the Russian workers, they will abolish capitalism and establish Socialism.

The Conquest of Political Power

BY THE term "abolition" of capitalism we mean its overthrow in open struggle by the toiling masses, led by the proletariat. Although the world capitalist system constantly plunges deeper into crisis we cannot therefore conclude that it will collapse of its own weight. On the contrary, as Lenin has stated, no matter how difficult the capitalist crisis becomes, "there is no complete absence of a way out" for the bourgeoisie until it faces the revolutionary proletariat in arms.

For the capitalists the way out of the crisis is

by forcing great masses of unemployed into semi-starvation, driving down the wage levels of the employed, waging desperate imperialist war, and instituting a regime of Fascist terrorism. This is the way the whole capitalist world development goes. For the workers, the capitalist way out means deeper enslavement and poverty than ever.

The capitalists will never voluntarily give up control of society and abdicate their system of exploiting the masses. Regardless of the devastating effects of their decaying capitalism; let there be famine, war, pestilence, terrorism, they will hang on to their wealth and power until it is snatched from their hands by the revolutionary proletariat.

The capitalists will not give up of their own accord; nor can they be talked, bought or voted out of power. To believe otherwise would be a deadly fatalism, disarming and paralyzing the workers in their struggle. No ruling class ever surrendered to a rising subject class without a last ditch open fight. To put an end to the capitalist system will require a consciously revolutionary act by the great toiling masses, led by the Communist party; that is, the conquest of the State power, the destruction of the State machine created by the ruling class, and the organization of the proletarian dictatorship. The lessons of history allow of no other conclusion.

It is the historical task of the proletariat to put a last end to war. Nevertheless, the working class

cannot itself come into power without civil war.
This is not due to the choice of the toilers; it is because the ruling class will never permit itself to be
ousted without such a fight. "Force," says Marx,
"is the midwife of every old society when it is preg-
nant with the new one; force is the instrument and
the means by which social movements hack their
way through and break up the fossilized political
forms." The *Program of the Communist International* thus puts the matter:

> "The conquest of power by the proletariat does not
> mean peacefully 'capturing' the ready-made bourgeois
> State machinery by means of a parliamentary majority.
> The bourgeoisie resort to every means of violence and
> terror to safeguard and strengthen its predatory prop-
> erty and its political domination. Like the feudal no-
> bility of the past, the bourgeoisie cannot abandon its
> historical position to the new class without a desperate
> and frantic struggle."

The Social Fascists make a great parade of
their theory of the "gradual" evolution of capitalism into Socialism through a process of peaceful
parliamentarism. Thus Mr. Hilquit, the million-
aire leader of the Socialist party says: "In the more
democratic countries, especially those in which the
Socialist and labor movements constitute important
political and social factors, the necessary transitional reforms, or at least a large part of them, may
be gradually conquered through the direct control
by the proletariat of important organs of the State,

such as municipalities or legislatures, or through the indirect influence of the growing labor movement." [1] Mr. Hillquit, like Social Fascists generally, goes on to say that the present imperialist government is actually the "Socialist transitional State, although it would be impossible for us to say just when we entered it."

We have seen in the previous chapter just what this "gradualness" theory of the Social Fascists means in practice — simply the creation of a united front with the capitalists to throw the burden of the crisis upon the workers, to try desperately to save the capitalist system and to crush back the revolution. Nor does the future hold any better perspective for this theory so far as the workers are concerned. Nowhere in the experience of the world class struggle can any justification be found for the conception that the capitalists have permitted or ever will permit themselves to be shifted from their ruling position without an open struggle. On the contrary, the evidence is entirely in the other direction. The capitalist class always brutally uses its armed forces against rebellious workers, meanwhile throwing its democracy and parliamentarism into the waste-basket.

What the capitalist class does when it is in a revolutionary situation is conclusively shown by the experience in Italy. In 1920 the Italian capitalists found themselves confronting a revolution-

---

[1] *Socialism in Theory and Practice*, p. 103.

ary crisis. Hence, they made no delay in scrapping their whole parliamentary system, adopting a program of Fascist violence and proceeding with fire and sword against the working class, previously betrayed and demoralized by the Socialist party. Workers and peasants were murdered and a reign of terror instituted on every front. Parliamentary representatives were expelled or assassinated, unions and cooperatives broken up, etc. Who but a political illiterate or a plain betrayer of the working class can assert that these Italian Fascist capitalist bandits can ever be voted out of power ?

The situation in Germany teaches the same lessons. The German bourgeoisie, fearing the revolution, are developing Fascism to drown it in blood. The Reichstag is only a democratic sham to hide the almost naked Fascist dictatorship. In England, although the crisis is not so far developed, Fascist trends are beginning to be seen. The English bourgeoisie, like the German, French, and others, will not surrender without the bitterest war against the proletariat. Or perhaps India and China present valid examples of how the toiling masses can achieve their emancipation without struggle? Chang Kai Shek would be especially responsive, mayhap, to parliamentary action by the workers and peasants ?

But the history of the American capitalist class offers ample evidence that the toilers can defeat the ruling class only in an open struggle. The American bourgeois revolution of 1776, even as the Russian Bolshevik revolution of 1917, was carried through on the basis of armed struggle. This fact the patriotic ladies of the D.A.R., fearful of the "bad" example set to the rising proletariat, would like to forget. "American history gives us another example of the same principle when, by the election of Lincoln, the overwhelming majority voted out of power in the United States government the southern slave holders, these slave holders took up arms to maintain their particular system of exploitation against the will of the majority." [2]

Nor has the American capitalist class ever hesitated to use violence against the toilers whenever its smallest interests were involved. Have we not seen that time and again when workers have struck against actual starvation conditions they have had to face troops, as well as armies of police, gunmen, etc. ? Ludlow, Paint and Cabin creeks in West Virginia, Gastonia, Kentucky, and innumerable other examples of the use of armed force tell their own story. If the capitalists of this country pass so quickly to the use of violence against the workers when the latter are fighting for the simplest economic demands, what will they do when they face a revolutionary situation in which their whole system is at stake ? To ask the question is to answer it.

[2] Statement of Communist Party to the Fish Committee.

In view of the universal lessons to the contrary, it is a crime to teach the workers that they can defeat such a ruthless capitalist class without open struggle. The Social Fascist theory that the economic and political contradictions of capitalism, will of themselves, by a gradual democratization of the State, bring about the automatic, peaceful, and painless transformation of capitalism into Socialism paralyzes the struggle of the workers and facilitates the rule of the bourgeoisie. The social Fascists, with the help of the Trotzkyist, Max Eastman,[3] vainly try to distort Marx in support of their theory.

This Social Fascist theory of "gradualness" is the most insidious that the workers have to deal with. But there are many others, if less important, that tend in a similar direction. Among these are the "folded-arm" general strike conception of the Syndicalists; the sectarian scholasticism of the Socialist Labor party and the Proletarian party; the petty bourgeois Anarchist theories of individual violence;[4] Gandhi's non-cooperation, non-violence program; the capitalistic utopias of Carver, Gillette and others for the workers directly to buy out the capitalist industries (expressed in their books respectively, *The Present Economic Revolution in the United States* and *The People's Corporation*); the fatalism of Veblen who, in *The Price System*

[3] *Marx and Lenin.*
[4] See *Living My Life*, by Emma Goldman, to learn how remote petty bourgeois Anarchism is from the proletarian revolution.

and the Engineers, maintains that capitalism will eventually, through the working of its inner contradictions, get into such a chronic and devastating crisis that in desperation society will spontaneously call upon the engineers to take over the operation of the industries and the government.

The question of the revolution is not merely one of a ripe objective situation. Such is, of course, a first requisite for the revolution. But the subjective factor is no less decisive. Capitalism will not grow into Socialism. The great masses of toilers must be in a revolutionary mood; they must have the necessary organization and revolutionary program; they must smash capitalism. This all means that they must be under the general leadership of the only revolutionary party, the Communist party. The real measure of a revolutionary situation in any given country is the strength of the Communist party.

Capitalism established itself as a world system by force. It defeated feudalism and laid the basis of its own power in a whole series of revolutionary civil wars in England, the United States, France, etc. Moreover, it has lived·by violence, its regime being marked by the most terrible exploitation and devastating wars in human history. And capitalism will die sword in hand, fighting in vain to beat back the oncoming revolutionary proletariat.

The Revolutionary Forces in the United States

Now LET us see if there are enough latent revolutionary forces in the United States to carry through the revolution, and what progress has been made in organizing them. In Chapter I we have seen how deep is the impoverishment of the toiling masses of workers and farmers and how tremendously this is being intensified by the economic crisis. We must, therefore, examine how extensive these impoverished classes are; see, in fact, who owns America, and who has a stake in the revolution.

The *Labor Fact Book,* basing its conclusions upon the report of the Federal Trade Commission, says, "The richest 1% of the population in the United States owns at least 59% of the wealth; the petty capitalists, (12%), own at least 31% of the wealth; and the great mass of industrial workers, working farmers, and small shop keepers, or 87% of the population, own barely 10%." These figures, constantly developing more favorably for the rich and spelling deepening exploitation, poverty and misery for the poor, show graphically enough who has a real stake in the country and who has not.

The choicest "flowers" of American capitalism are such multi-billionaires as the House of Morgan, which controls corporations worth $74,000,-

000,000, including innumerable railroads, banks, insurance companies, auto plants, steel mills, etc.; the Rockefellers with their billions in oil, chemicals, railroads, banks, etc.; the Mellon family, whose wealth control is estimated by W. P. Beazell, in the current *World's Work,* at eight billion dollars; the great Ford fortune, etc. "In 1929, 504 millionaires had incomes of $1,185,100,000, or more than the selling price of all American wheat and cotton in 1930." [5]

It is among the great masses of the 87% who own only 10% of the national wealth that the revolution will find a sufficiency of forces to overthrow capitalism. Capitalism in this country will learn to its undoing that the producing masses will not tolerate a condition where they are forced to work and starve while the great wealth they produce flows automatically, by the operation of the capitalist system, to still further swell the fortunes of a handful of wealthy social parasites. "Wars and panics on the stock exchange; machine gunfire and arson; starvation, lice, cholera and typhus; good growing weather for the House of Morgan," says John Dos Passos, in his book, *1919,* and the same can be said for capitalists generally. The statistics of the distribution of wealth in the United States and the general worsening of the toilers' standards are figures and conditions that speak in terms of eventual revolution.

[5] *America Faces the Future,* p. 356.

In analyzing the potentially revolutionary forces the first group to be considered are the workers. They are the very heart of the revolutionary movement and lead it in all its stages. Including the agricultural wage workers, the total number of wage and salaried workers in the United States is about 35,000,000, out of a total of approximately 43,000,000 "gainfully employed." With their families they constitute at least 70% of the total population of this country. Overwhelmingly they are low-paid unskilled and semi-skilled workers who are manifestly being radicalized rapidly under pressure of worsening conditions. The so-called skilled workers, although somewhat better off than the rest, are losing their privileged position. Unemployment, wage-cuts, etc., are also radicalizing these skilled workers, whose position in industry has steadily become less strategic through specialization, mechanization, etc. Their aristocratic isolation from the rest of the workers is being broken down; the crisis is unifying the working class. The most conservative sections of the working class are the office workers, who comprise about 10% of the whole. But here again, rapidly worsening conditions are having their inevitable results. Although in the first phases of the crisis these white collar elements offer a recruiting ground for Fascism, eventually, as events in Germany show, their trend is, in the main, in the direction that the working class travels.

Next to the workers in revolutionary importance are the poor farmers. Although not wage workers themselves, the poor farmers play a decisive revolutionary role in all countries as the allies of the proletariat. Especially important are they in the United States where agriculture occupies such a large position in the national economy. The estimated farm population on Jan. 1, 1931, was 27,430,000, a decline of 4,500,000 since 1910. The great masses are poor and getting poorer. The income of the whole group, including the richer farmers, amounts only to about 10% of the total national income of all classes in the United States, although the farmers comprise about 22% of the entire population. Capitalism has nothing to offer the poor farmer except more and more pauperization. An official of the Federal Reserve Bank, quoted in *Current History,* Mar., 1932, brutally states this as follows: "Our farmers should stop buying radios and Ford cars and live like peasants." Talk about collectivization of the farms under capitalism is utopian; this can take place only under a Soviet system. The way to the big farm under capitalism is by the starvation and expropriation of the small farmers, which goes ahead ever faster. Mr. Pitkin is wrong when he declares in *The Forum,* Aug., 1931, that "The American farmer must go the way of the coolie or the corporation." He will go neither way, but to Socialism. The American small farmer will play a vital role in the developing Communist movement in the United States.

The Negroes also constitute a great potentially revolutionary force. Comprising about 12,000,000, they are the poorest of the poor. They are made up of the most impoverished farmers, the lowest paid workers in the industries and in domestic service. They are the most bitterly exploited and persecuted element of the whole population. There is no section which has to confront such terrible economic, political, and social conditions. At his every turn the Negro faces a system of the rankest discrimination and exploitation. His outrageous position in society is a blazing indictment and exposure of the sham American capitalist democracy.

In industry the Negro is forced to take the hardest, dirtiest work for the lowest wages; he is denied access to the skilled trades; he is the last to be hired and the first to be fired during industrial crises; when unemployment relief is distributed he is shamelessly discriminated against. As an agricultural worker and share-crop farmer in the South, he is subjected to an almost chattel slavery exploitation and terrorism from landlords, bankers, etc. In his political life he is disfranchised; he is denied the right to hold office and to vote; he is refused the right of trial by jury; he is savagely lynched by mobs of whites, led by business men and landlords, and the State condones these shocking murders; in court his word counts for nothing against a white man's; when convicted, he receives sentences two or three times as severe as white men get for similar offenses. Socially the Negro is ostracized. Not only in the South but also in the North. He is systematically Jim-Crowed in hotels, restaurants, theatres, etc.; he is denied the right to an education; he is made to live in the most unsanitary sections of towns; his women-folk are the object of unpunished insult and assault from the whites.

The capitalists try to keep the Negroes isolated by cultivating race prejudice among the white workers; but this cannot permanently succeed. The white workers will learn that only in the most complete solidarity with the Negro masses can they make headway in defending their interests. The Negro masses will make the very best fighters for the revolution. The manner in which they are turning to the Communist party for organization and leadership constitutes one of the most important political facts in American life. The Negro petty bourgeois leaders are non-plussed by it. In a symposium of 17 non-Communist Negro editors in *The Crisis,* (April, 1932), a Social Fascist journal, on the issue of Communism among the Negroes, W. M. Kelly declares: "the wonder is not that the Negro is beginning, at least, to think along Communistic lines, but that he did not embrace that doctrine en masse long ago."

The revolution will not fail to recruit many sup-
porters also from the ranks of the lesser city petty
bourgeoisie. The advance of capitalism inevitably
crushes down into the proletariat great masses of
the small tradesmen, petty manufacturers, professionals, intellectuals, etc., that make up this big
class. The steady progress of trustified capital in
industry has long since broken the backbone of
the petty bourgeoisie in this field, and now the
chain store is ruthlessly invading its greatest
stronghold, retail trade. According to Ray B.
Westerfield in *Current History*, (Dec., 1931),
there were in 1930 in the United States 7837 chains
of stores with 198,145 units, and the movement is
growing like wildfire. This wholesale ruin of the
petty bourgeoisie, brought about by the normal
development of capitalism, is hastened by the industrial crisis, during which the process of the concentration of capital proceeds faster than ever.
Large masses of the petty bourgeoisie are being
impoverished. These elements are the natural recruiting ground for Fascism, but the Communist
party does not surrender them to the Fascists.
Experience, especially in Germany, where the expropriation, proletarianization and even pauperization of the petty bourgeoisie has developed to
unprecedented degree, shows that great numbers
of these people logically become convinced that
capitalism holds no hope for them and that only in
Communism is there a prospect for life and happi-

ness. The recent significant mass protest against the proposed Federal sales tax was principally a movement of the discontented petty bourgeoisie.

Especially is there a trend among the petty bourgeois intellectuals towards Communism. This is shown by the many prominent writers in Europe and the United States who in the past few years have declared for Communism. In the past period American imperialism provided a good living for the intellectuals and professionals generally. Those already carrying on their active work had easy pickings; those who were graduating from the innumerable colleges and universities found soft berths awaiting them. So the American intelligentsia, almost unanimously, united in a hymn of hundred percentism. But the capitalist crisis has changed all this. Many intellectuals and professionals now find their means of making a livelihood either wiped out or drastically curtailed, with consequent heavy drops in their standards of living. "A short time ago," says *The Nation,* (Mar. 3, 1932), "it was revealed that 45 members of the Detroit Bar Association were on-the-welfare — recipients of municipal charity." It is such conditions of keen competition, inferior remuneration and actual unemployment that the budding intellectuals still in the schools and colleges have to face. It is not surprising, therefore, that currents of radicalism begin to develop among intellectuals generally. Of this the recent student strike at Columbia University was an example. Even the intellectuals are being compelled to think. At first, in this discontent there may be strong Fascist or semi-Fascist currents, but eventually much of it will develop in the direction of the revolution and Communism.

In measuring the potential forces for and against the revolution, naturally the question of the role to be played by the army and navy is one of fundamental importance; for, in the final showdown, it is upon them that the bourgeoisie relies to maintain its control. If it loses the armed forces, then all is lost. Here, certainly, the revolution will recruit powerful forces, with fatal effects to capitalism. The armed forces are not impervious to Communism simply because they have patriotic propaganda dinned into their ears and are subjected to a rigid discipline. The great bulk of these forces originate in proletarian or farmer families and they eventually respond to the sufferings and miseries of their close relatives. Especially is all this true of conscript armies. Besides, they have their own deep grievances in the service. Experience teaches that such worker-peasant forces are very unreliable for the bourgeoisie. This was exemplified by the armies of the Czar and the Kaiser in the Russian and German revolutionary situations. It was only a few months ago that the capitalists of the world got a shiver of fright and a foretaste of the future by the revolts in the British and Chilean navies.

Within these great blocs of the population — the workers, farmers, Negroes, lesser city petty bourgeoisie — there are sufficient potential revolutionary forces to put an end to capitalism. They constitute the overwhelming majority of the people. And the deepening capitalist crisis will revolutionize them. The objective that the Communist party aims at in the mobilization of these forces is the winning of the majority of the working class. With a majority of the workers, which in a revolutionary situation would necessarily carry along with it large numbers of the other revolutionary elements, the Party would be within striking distance of the revolution.

But, of course, the American Communist party is only making a beginning in the accomplishment of this great task. Formed in 1919 by a split-off of the left wing of the Socialist party, it is now laying its foundations among the workers. Although the Party is still lagging very much behind the objective possibilities and has by no means mobilized the masses who are ripe for its leadership, it is, nevertheless, substantially increasing its membership and influence in all the key industries and localities. The actual strength of the Communist movement in the United States is not something that can be accurately stated in just so many figures. It has to be measured largely by the general mass influence of the Party and its program.

The membership of the Communist party is approximately 15,000. To this should be added 5,000 members in the Young Communist League. These figures represent the number of dues-payers, the body of Communists who are thoroughly conscious of the necessity of maintaining a permanent, disciplined Party. But the influence of the Party stretches far and wide beyond the limits of its actual membership. Thus the nine daily papers of the Party have a combined circulation of about 200,000. Besides this there are 20 weekly, semi-monthly, and monthly papers with about 100,000 circulation. This is the Party press proper. In addition, there are a large number of weekly and monthly papers in the revolutionary unions, defense, relief, fraternal and other organizations, with at least another 100,000 circulation.

In the 1928 elections, with the Party on the ballot in 34 states, it polled 48,770 votes. In the "off-year," 1930, in 18 states it polled 82,651. The Fish committee, in its report, with great alarm pointed out that there was an increase of 229% in 16 states. In the 1931 elections considerable increases were scored in many localities, two Communist councilmen being elected in Ohio and four in Minnesota. Doubtless, the 1932 national elections will register a large increase in the Party vote. But elections, for a number of reasons, are not an exact register of the Party strength. For one thing, large numbers of the poorer-paid workers, to whom naturally the Party makes the strongest appeal, are disfranchised because of shifts of residence, through unemployment, through tax delinquencies and foreign birth. Also, in a great many cases Communist votes are scornfully ignored by the usual ultra-reactionary election machines and are not counted. Moreover, in the ranks of revolutionary workers there are many who underestimate the great importance of voting in the elections.

The real power of the Party is seen in the mass movements which it initiates itself, or which, initiated by other revolutionary organizations, it gives its full support. The biggest of these are the movements of the unemployed. In the March 6th, 1930, national demonstration for unemployment insurance no less than 1,250,000 workers participated throughout the country. This huge outpouring was followed in the ensuing months by many large local demonstrations, state hunger marches, etc. A demand upon the federal government in 1930 for the adoption of the Workers' Unemployment Insurance Bill contained approximately 1,000,000 individual and collective endorsements. The big National Hunger March of December, 1931, put in motion during the many hundreds of local demonstrations held in connection therewith, at least 1,000,000 workers. The unemployed councils, organized under the National Committee of the Unemployed Councils and made up of workers of all political opinions, number at least 75,000 members.

The Communist party also exerts a wide and growing influence in the trade union field. Its main support is given to the building of the revolutionary unions of the Trade Union Unity League. It also lays great stress upon the formation of revolutionary minorities and movements inside the A.F. of L. unions. During the past several years the revolutionary unions and minorities have conducted a number of large mass struggles. Among these were the New York cloak (35,000) and fur (12,000) strikes in 1926-7, and the Passaic textile strike (15,000) during the same period. In the United Mine Workers of America, in 1926, the left wing candidate polled 101,000 votes, or an actual majority, but was robbed of the election by the corrupt Lewis machine. In the big U.M.W.A. strike of 1927-8 at least 100,000 miners followed the lead of the left wing. The important strike of the Gastonia textile workers in 1929 was conducted by the revolutionary National Textile Workers Union. In Lawrence, in Feb., 1931, the N.T.W.U. led a short strike of 10,000. It has since led a dozen smaller strikes in many New England textile towns and played a big role in the strikes later in the year in Paterson and Lawrence. During the Spring and Summer of 1931 the National Miners Union of the TUUL conducted a strike of 40,000 miners for three months in Western Pennsylvania, Eastern Ohio and Northern West Virginia. At present it is leading the heroic strike of the Kentucky miners. The foregoing are some of the larger struggles of the revolutionary union forces. The total membership of the unions of the TUUL is approximately 40,000, the minorities in the trade unions, less definitely organized, are double or triple that number. In the case of the TUUL unions and minorities, as with all the revolutionary organizations, their influence over the masses extends far beyond the borders of their actual membership.

Among the Negro masses the Communist party is developing a wide following. In the unemployment campaigns, especially in Chicago and Cleveland, many thousands of Negroes militantly participated. In the 1931, N.M.U. mine strike more than 6,000 of the strikers were Negroes. The Party leads the fight to defend the nine Scottsboro boys, whom the Southern capitalists are trying to legally lynch. It is estimated that no less than 1,000,000, a large percentage of whom were Negroes, took part in the innumerable mass meetings in which this case played a central role. The Negro membership of the Party and the Party's influence among the Negro masses are rapidly on the increase.

The Communist party also conducts movements and supports revolutionary organizations in many other mass activities and struggles. It is a strong and leading factor in the fight for the release of political prisoners, including Mooney and Billings, the Kentucky miners, the Centralia and Imperial Valley prisoners, etc. It has organized great demonstrations against imperialist war. Among the farmers, the Party carries on considerable work and is gradually laying the basis for a mass organization.

The foregoing facts and figures give at least a general idea of the strength of the Communist party at the present stage of the development of the class struggle in the United States. While they indicate that the Party has only made a start at the mobilization of the potentially revolutionary forces in the United States, they, at the same time, sum up into a picture of a Party gradually entrenching itself among the masses, especially the most exploited sections, and slowly building youthful bone and muscle in preparation for the gigantic revolutionary work that lies ahead.

The Communist Party; the Party of the Toilers

THE COMMUNIST PARTY is the only Party that represents the interests of these toiling masses of workers, farmers, Negroes, lower city petty bourgeoisie. It alone fights for their welfare now and provides the means for their ultimate prosperity and freedom. The other parties and groups — Republican, Democratic, Progressive and Socialist — are the enemies of these classes and the tools of the big capitalists.

The Republican party is the party of finance capital, of the great bankers and industrialists of Wall Street, of which the Morgan interests stand at the head. The Hoover government is the instrument of these owners and rulers of America. It uses all its power to oppress the producing masses for the benefit of the capitalist exploiters. The present situation, with its economic collapse and hunger and misery for the broad masses, is the logical result of this capitalist policy. From the Republican party no relief, but only a worsening of existing conditions may be expected.

The Democratic party is no less the party of the big capitalists. Raskob, the dictator of the Democratic party, is notoriously the representative of the Morgan - General Motors - Dupont interests. The corrupt and reactionary Tammany Hall of New York City is indistinguishable politically from the rotten Republican Vare machine in Philadelphia. The Democratic party is directly responsible for the unspeakable regime of lynching, Jim-Crowism and discrimination against the Negro masses in the South, although in this it has the full support of the Republican Federal Administration. Wherever the Democratic party is found in power its practical policies are identical with those of the Republicans and they sum up into a defense of the interests of the capitalists at the expense of the producing masses.

In recent years the Democratic party has ever more clearly exposed its big capitalist character. It long ago abandoned its demagogic attacks on the gold standard, imperialism and the trusts. And then, when the Morgan representative Raskob took over the party leadership a few years ago, this was immediately followed by the giving up completely of the old Democratic policy of low tariffs and the adoption of a high tariff policy on the Republican model. The thoroughgoing political unity of the two capitalist parties was further emphasized by growing tendencies to link them up organizationally without, however, abandoning the two-party principle which is so valuable to the capitalists. This developing organizational unity reached its highest point in the open alliance between the heads of both parties in the present Congress to put across the Hoover-Wall Street program of subsidizing the great banks, starving the unemployed, cutting the wages of the employed, shifting the tax burden upon the masses, preparing for imperialist war, etc. All went swimmingly for this two-party machine until it slipped a cog in trying to put across the sales tax.

In 1932 elections, the Democratic party is scheduled to play its historical role as the second party of capitalism. Although its basic policies are identical with the Republican party, it will make a great show of opposition. Large masses of the working class, farmers, Negroes and petty bourgeoisie are deeply discontented at their impossible conditions under the Hoover government. Therefore, it is the task of the Democratic party, with a flood of demagogy, to delude these masses, and to prevent their taking serious steps against the capitalists, by keeping them fettered with the two capitalist party system. This is the menace of the Roosevelts, Garners, Murrays, Bakers, etc. They are among the most effective instruments of the capitalists to enforce upon the producing masses a continuation of the present hunger regime.

The Progressive bloc also does not represent the interests of the producing masses. It represents the rich farmers and certain sections of small capitalists, and it supports the basic policies of Wall Street. During the present Congress the so-called Progressives supported the elementary proposals of the Hoover government to throw the burden of the crisis upon the producers. Their "fight" against the sales tax developed only when, in a broad movement of indignation, many millions of the small farmers, city petty bourgeoisie and workers demanded its rejection. Then, under the lash of Wall Street, they fled precipitately and proceeded, with later taxation, to undo the defeat of the sales tax. The only fight the Progressives ever make is for a few crumbs from the rich man's table.

The Progressive leaders, like their reactionary cronies at the head of the American Federation of Labor, fit themselves comfortably into the infamous two-party system. This constitutes a betrayal of the exploited masses into the hands of their capitalist enemies. The "non-partisan" policy is not simply an expression of political timidity, of hesitation to take the initiative in forming a new party; it is essentially based upon a political unity with the capitalists. We may be sure that if and when, under the pressure of the masses, a third party is formed, these elements will adopt the familiar devices of the Social Fascists to render it subservient to the capitalist class.

Practice shows that the Progressive policies are antagonistic to the interests of the exploited masses. They cultivate in the worst forms the democratic illusions so essential to capitalist control. For the unemployed the Progressives have produced the typical masterpieces of the massacre in Dearborn, for which Mayor Murphy, as well as Ford, is responsible; and the Wisconsin Groves Law, which, under the name of "unemployment insurance," provides even less relief for the unemployed than they now receive in many cities under the Hoover charity-hand-out system. For the employed the Progressives have provided wage-cuts, on the Hoover-Green model; example, the maneuvers of Pinchot in Pennsylvania with the U.M.W. of A. bureaucrats to break the strikes of the miners in the Pittsburgh and anthracite districts against wage-cuts. As for the farmers, the Progressives have kept them thoroughly disorganized by the non-partisan system: the Federal Farm Board, with its wheat and cotton speculation and enrichment of the rural bankers and rich farmers at the expense of the poor farmers, is the fine flower of Progressivism on the farms. Regarding the Negroes, the policies of the Progressives, although dressed up in radical phraseology, are in practice indistinguishable from those of the ultra-reactionaries: sufficient proof of this being the enthusiastic support given to the candidacy of Governor Roosevelt, Progressive Mogul, in the most Bourbon sections of the South.

Progressivism is a grave danger to the working class. This is because of the widespread existence of petty bourgeois illusions among the workers. The LaFollettes, Borahs, La Guardias, Norrises, Pinchots, Murphys, etc., are disorganizers and demoralizers of the workers and poor farmers. The Progressive bloc is just another lightning rod to shield the capitalist profit edifice.

The Socialist party is the third party of capitalism. This is amply demonstrated by its history in the United States and all other countries. The Socialist party has nothing constructive to offer the workers in their daily struggles now or for their ultimate emancipation. The fact that this party hides its capitalist face behind a pretense of radicalism makes it more, not less dangerous.

Already we have dealt in considerable detail with the policies and activities of the Socialist party. Its advocacy of capitalist trustification under slogans of nationalization, cultivation of illusions regarding "planned economy" under capitalism, support of the League of Nations, militarist imperialism cloaked with pacifism, alliance with the corrupt leadership of the A.F. of L., policy of putting through wage-cuts by fake strikes, rule of unions by gangsterism, systematic slander of the Soviet Union and minimizing of the war danger, etc., is all directly antagonistic to the working class.

That is why the capitalists and their press look with ever more favor upon the Socialist party. The Norman Thomases are being groomed to play in the United States some day the role of the Mac-Donalds in Great Britain, Boncours in France, Scheidemans in Germany, etc. The wage-cutting, dole-slashing activities of the British Labor party and the German Social Democracy in their attempt to bolster up the decaying capitalist system present clearly the perspective for which the Socialist party is being built in this country.

The Socialist party all over the world is a main pillar of the capitalist system. Its function is to demoralize the workers' defense in the face of the capitalist offensive, to break up the workers' counter-offensive against the capitalist system. The Socialist party is a specialized section of the capitalist machinery for exploiting the toiling masses. It is particularly dangerous in that it takes the workers, just breaking the ideological chains of capitalist slavery, and confuses them with a defense of capitalism under the pretense of fighting for Socialism. The Socialist party stabs the working class in the back. It, together with its fringe elements of Musteites, Lovestoneites, Trotzkyites, etc., has nothing in common with Socialism.

The Present-Day Tasks of the American Revolutionary Movement

THE TASKS of the Communist party in a given country at a specified time, in carrying out its program of class struggle, are, of course, determined by the objective situation and the state of the workers' mood and organization. Thus these tasks vary in the several countries, from the building of Socialism in the Soviet Union, open armed warfare in China, and preparations for an early revolutionary crisis in Germany, to the most elementary phases of mass education, organization and struggle in the United States, the stronghold of world capitalism.

In the United States — and this is basic in Communist strategy everywhere — the action program of the Communist party has its starting point in the every-day pressing economic demands of the workers. It is not enough that the Party should propagate its general slogans among the masses and then organize them for the eventual revolution. Such a course, as Lenin so forcefully pointed out in his famous pamphlet, *The Infantile Sickness of "Leftism" in Communism,* would condemn the Party to isolation and sectarianism. For the workers the class struggle is a never-ending matter of their daily lives; constantly they are confronted with the most urgent necessity to fight against the employers, in defense of their interests. The Communist party must lead in all these struggles. It is in such fights that the workers become class conscious and organized around the Communist party. Never would the masses recognize as their revolutionary Party one that ignored these daily fights and confined itself to a high and lofty agitation of revolutionary slogans.

It is a favorite slander, however, that the Communist party utilizes the daily struggles of the workers merely for agitational purposes. Norman Thomas repeats this, saying that Communist immediate demands are "designed to be impossible and so to 'show up' the capitalist system." [6] But the truth is just the opposite: the Communist party always places as immediate demands those mani-

6 *America's Way Out,* p. 152.

festly possible of achievement under capitalism and then it makes the most determined effort to win all it can of them in the struggle. This is because the Party has no interests apart from those of the working class; it also realizes that such victories, instead of destroying the militancy of the workers, stimulate it. Lenin called such reforms or concessions forced from the employers "by-products" of the revolutionary struggle. The Party understands clearly that the workers logically expect that a Party which proposes eventually to overthrow the whole capitalist system should know how to organize them to defend their interests here and now. As for "showing up" capitalism, this is done by agitation and propaganda and by the daily experiences of the workers in the class struggle, not by leading the workers to defeat in strikes and other movements.

The Social Fascists try to create the legend that the difference between them and the Communists is that while they fight for immediate demands, the Communists confine themselves simply to ultimate aims. This is not so. The difference is that while the Communists fight for the immediate demands as well as the final goal, the Social Fascists betray both.

In the present stage of development of the working class and of the revolutionary struggle in the United States the fight of the workers is essentially a defensive struggle against the capitalist offensive. On all fronts the employers, with the government in the lead, are worsening the living and working standards of the toilers through wage-cuts, throwing millions of workers into unemployment, seizing the lands of poor farmers, shifting the tax burden onto the producing masses, etc. It is the policy of the Communist party to organize the workers and farmers and to lead their resistance to the capitalist offensive, to prevent the capitalists from finding a way out of their crisis at the expense and further enslavement of the toiling masses. That is why the Communist party is to be found everywhere giving its fullest support to all struggles of the workers and poor farmers against the capitalist attack.

But the Communist party policy is not simply to organize the defense; it seeks also to transform the workers' defensive struggles into a counter-offensive. It strives to unite the scattered fights of the workers into broad class struggles and to give them more of a political character. This politicalization becomes the more urgent with the sharpening offensive of the employers and their increasing use of the State against the workers. The general effects of politicalizing the workers' struggle are to draw larger masses of workers into the fight, to direct this fight against the State as well as against the employers proper, and thus to strengthen the workers' struggle in every respect.

This politicalization is brought about by the raising of political demands which grow out of the very struggle itself, not merely by the active propagation of the ultimate revolutionary program of the Communist party. Thus during a strike demands are made for the right to meet, to picket, to strike, for the release of political prisoners, for the adoption, enforcement or repeal of labor legislation, against government arbitration, for the withdrawal of troops, etc., and the workers are mobilized in various ways for mass action in support of these demands. In this way, not only are the workers educated to the class character of the State, but the broadest class front and most militant action is secured in the struggle. In acute conditions of class struggle this line of strategy leads to the development of the mass political strike, during which the more fundamental political demands may be raised. In the question of political demands, as well as of economic demands, the central Communist strategy always turns around the winning of the immediate struggle in hand.

In the present period of intense capitalist offensive against the workers, the question of immediate, partial economic demands becomes of decisive importance. The workers have to fight desperately for the very right to live. Becoming ever more radicalized, they make this fight with constantly sharpening militancy. Even the smallest issues readily blaze into great conflagrations.

How quickly economic conflicts develop into major political struggles was evidenced again by the recent mutinies in the British and Chilean navies, both of which began over wage-cuts. It is interesting to recall, also, that the mutiny in the German fleet at the end of the World War, although prepared by the whole course of events, actually began in a flare-up of the men because their ration of soap had been cut off. All of which emphasizes the correctness of the stress that the Communist party places upon the question of practical partial demands and the necessity of developing the scattering economic fights of the workers onto a higher political level.

In thus politicalizing the struggle, the Communists come into sharpest conflict with the labor reactionaries of the Socialist party and the A.F. of L. type. As part of these misleaders' general policy of choking back the workers' struggles, they seek to keep these fights upon a purely economic basis. They resist all attempts of the workers to militantly fight the State, thus exposing them to the sharp political attacks of the employers. A typical example of this was the surrender of John L. Lewis to the government injunction in the national coal strike of 1920 under the slogan of "We can't fight the Government." Another outstanding example of this treacherous policy was during the British general strike of 1926. In this great fight, with the bosses using every power of the government to break the strike of the 5,000,000 workers, the Social Fascist leaders, eager to find a way to sell out the strike, put out the slogan that the struggle was purely an economic one and they bitterly fought every effort to give it a political character.   Thus the government was given a free hand and a terrific defeat was suffered by the workers.

The Communist Party Program of Immediate Demands

THIS is not the place for a detailed statement of the program of action of the Communist party. But at least an indication of its general character may be given.   As stated before, the Party bases its immediate struggle upon partial demands corresponding to the most urgent necessities of the toiling masses.   The most important of these demands are concentrated in the Party's 1932 election platform, as follows:

1. UNEMPLOYMENT AND SOCIAL INSURANCE AT THE EXPENSE OF THE STATE AND EMPLOYERS.
2. Against Hoover's wage-cutting policy.
3. Emergency relief, without restrictions by the government and banks, for the poor farmers, exemption of poor farmers from taxes, and from forced collection of debts.
4. Equal rights for the Negroes, and self-determination for the Black Belt.
5. Against capitalist terror; against all forms of suppression of the political rights of the workers.

6. Against imperialist war; for defense of the Chinese people and of the Soviet Union.

The Communist party puts the question of unemployment insurance in the very center of its immediate program. It demands that the federal government institute a system of insurance, on the basis of full wages,[7] for all unemployed and part-time workers, the necessary funds to be paid entirely by the employers and the State and to be raised by the allocation of all war funds, a capital levy, increased taxes upon the rich, etc. The Party, pending the enactment of adequate unemployment insurance legislation, demands special cash relief from the states and municipalities, lower rents, free food for school children of the unemployed, free street car fare, public works at union wages, abolition of forced labor on such jobs, etc. It demands that the insurance and relief systems be administered by the workers themselves. The Party also demands an adequate system of social legislation for old age, sickness, maternity, etc. These demands it supports by militant demonstrations, hunger marches, etc. It endorses the Workers' Unemployment Insurance Bill.

The Party concretizes its fight against the Hoover wage-cutting program into a militant strike policy. It also fights against the speed-up,

---

[7] In 1929 average American wages yearly did not exceed $1200, a figure ranging from $300 to $1000 less than bare cost-of-living budgets of the Labor Department and other capitalist institutions.

against mass lay-offs of workers, for the 7-hour day without reduction in weekly wages, (with a 6-hour day for the youth, for miners, railroaders, and workers in dangerous and unhealthful industries), for the adoption and enforcement of adequate legislation regarding safety and sanitation in industry.

The Party lays the utmost stress upon its demands for the Negroes. It demands full economic, political and social equality for them; it fights to eliminate the entire system of discrimination to which the Negroes are subjected in industry, in the distribution of unemployment relief, in segregated dwelling districts, in hotels and restaurants, in trade unions, in the courts, in political activities; that is, the whole Jim-Crow outrage; it demands death for lynchers, and it fights for the right of self-determination for the Negro nation in the Black Belt of the South.

For the farmers the Party demands immediate emergency cash relief from the government, for those crushed by the burden of low prices, high taxes, usurious debts, etc.; the exemption of poor farmers from the tax burden, abolition of foreclosures upon land for non-payment of mortgages, the full rights of organization and free speech, etc.

The Party fights against the monstrous tax burden being heaped from year to year upon the toiling masses and demands that this be shifted upon the rich. It opposes the sales tax and fights for higher inheritance taxes, surtaxes, etc. It demands drastic curtailment in the salaries of government officials and opposes all wage-cuts for government workers.

The Party fights militantly against the growing imperialist war danger. It mobilizes the workers to fight against the robber war in China and to defend the Soviet Union. It demands the withdrawal of American armed forces from China. It demands recognition of and trade relations with the U.S.S.R. It calls upon the workers not to transport war munitions for Japanese imperialism. It fights against all phases of American imperialism's program to militarize the American people. It gives active support to the masses in Latin-America in their fight against American imperialism. It educates the masses in the revolutionary Leninist strategy against war.

The Party fights against the developing terrorism and suppression of the workers' rights. It demands the rights of free speech, free assembly, and to strike and picket. It combats injunctions by a policy of mass violation. It organizes workers' defense corps in mass organizations to defend them from the violence of the employers and their agents. It fights against the finger-printing, deportation and other methods of discrimination used towards the foreign-born workers. It demands the release of all class war prisoners, the annulment of anti-Syndicalist laws, abolition of vagrancy laws, etc.

For the young workers the Young Communist League, supported by the Party, demands the abolition of child labor, the establishment of the 6-hour day, equal pay with adult workers, rest periods in industry, the right to vote, etc. In the various strikes the Y.C.L. always raises special youth demands. In schools and colleges it organizes the students and develops their struggle for better conditions. It also organizes the youth in their own Y.C.L. nuclei, and it works for the organization of special youth sections of local trade unions to deal with particular youth problems and to develop the necessary special activities involved in the organization of the youth.

The Party makes special demands for women workers, including equal pay with men, special protection in industry, maternity insurance, etc., and it incorporates them in its immediate program in given struggles. For the ex-service men it demands the full payment of the bonus; for those now in the army and navy service better wages, food, housing, etc. It demands the repeal of the 18th Amendment and the Volstead Act.

In short, in every phase of life where capitalist exploitation and persecution bear down upon the masses, the Communist party comes forward with partial demands corresponding to the most immediate needs of these masses. But in so doing, it does not fail to point out that the final solution of their intolerable situation can be achieved only by the overthrow of the capitalist system and the establishment of a Workers' and Farmers' government.

A Program of Class Struggle

THE COMMUNIST PARTY bases its activities upon the principles of the class struggle, both with regard to its every-day struggles and its ultimate revolutionary goal. It relentlessly fights against the policy of class collaboration practiced by the Socialist party and the A.F. of L. leaders. World-wide experience has fully demonstrated the fact that the workers cannot go along with the bosses as "friendly partners." The capitalists and the workers are class enemies, with mutually hostile interests. The exploiters and the exploited are natural political foes. The relations between them depend upon the question of power. The workers can get from the employers only what they have the power to take. The A.F. of L. theory (which corresponds to the Socialist party practice) of the "harmony of interest between capital and labor" is the theory of the surrender of the working class to the bourgeoisie.

Communist action is based upon the slogan of "Class Against Class"; that is, the working class against the capitalist class. This slogan expresses the elementary fighting policy of the revolutionary movement. In applying it, the Communist party actively promotes the mass organization of the workers, regardless of political opinion, into trade unions, unemployed councils, organizations to defend the rights of Negroes, ex-servicemen's leagues, labor defense and strike relief bodies, leagues of poor farmers, proletarian sports organizations, labor fraternal insurance societies, organizations to defend the foreign born, societies of working class culture, etc., etc. Where no mass organizations exist in these fields the Party takes the initiative in forming them; where such are already in existence and are headed by conservative officials, the Party follows the policy of building an opposition within them and fighting for the revolutionary program and leadership. This is the so-called boring-from-within policy.

The application of the "Class Against Class" policy requires the making of united front movements with workers who, while not prepared to accept the whole revolutionary program of the Communist party, nevertheless are willing to struggle for immediate, partial demands. It also means the carrying on of joint struggles with the poor farmers and impoverished sections of the city petty bourgeoisie. But in all such united front movements the aim always is for the workers to lead and for the attack to be directed against the capitalist class and its government. By the use of the united front the fighting ranks of the workers are extended far beyond the limits of the existing revolutionary organizations; the united front bridges the gap between the organized and unorganized workers and links them up for common struggle. United front organs may take a variety of forms, such as joint strike committees, shop committees, grievance committees, relief committees, defense committees, etc., being composed in each case of representatives of all the unions, A.F. of L. and revolutionary, as well as of the unorganized workers in the given situation. The united front is organized from the bottom; that is, not with the reactionary leaders of the various labor organizations, but with the rank and file workers.

The Communist party bases its work directly upon the mills, mines, and factories. Its principle is to make every shop a fortress for Communism. It follows closely the life of the workers in the industries, adapting its immediate program of struggle to their needs. It concentrates its work upon the heavy industries and those of a war character. The Party and the revolutionary unions are organized especially for this intense shop work. Instead of being based upon territorial branches, as is the Socialist party, the Communist party has as its basic unit the shop nucleus; the TUUL unions are based upon the shop branch, instead of the craft and general locals of the A.F. of L. type.

In carrying out its class struggle program the Communist party practices revolutionary parliamentarism. It places candidates during elections and makes every effort to elect them. It combines its parliamentary action inside legislative bodies with its mass action outside and fights to force all possible concessions from the government. It utilizes the election campaigns to educate the workers and to mobilize them for every phase of its program on the economic and political fields. It seizes upon these periods of general political discussion to confront the reactionary program of the capitalists and their Social Fascist agents with the revolutionary program of the workers. Where the Party elects its candidates to legislative bodies they make use of these public forums to expose the capitalist character of the government and to bring forward the Communist program in its various phases. In all its parliamentary activities the Communist party makes it clear to the workers that the capitalist democracy is a sham and that there must be no illusions about peacefully capturing the State for the working class.

The Communist party organizes its struggles upon the basis of mass action of the workers. It is opposed to individual acts of terror. Such terrorism weakens the workers' struggle by tending to substitute individual action for mass action and by exposing the movement to the destructive work of agents provocateurs. The workers' daily struggles are to be won and their emancipation finally achieved, not by the desperate acts of isolated heroes, but by the resolute action of the great masses of workers.

A cornerstone of the Communist class struggle policy is a ruthless fight against the Social Fascist leaders, especially those of the "left," phrase-mongering type. "Class Against Class" implies a war to the finish against such elements, who are part of the oppressive machinery of the capitalist class. They are enemies within the gates of the working class and must be treated as such. They head the labor movement only in order to behead it. They are a menace and an obstacle to all struggle by the workers. With their prestige as labor leaders, their demagogy is especially demoralizing; with their control of the workers' mass organizations, they are able to effectively sabotage the struggle. It is idle to try to "convince" the Social Fascist leaders or to "force them to fight by mass pressure," because they are class enemies of the workers. They must be politically obliterated. To accomplish this is a first condition for successful working class struggle and it is one never lost sight of by the Communist party.

The Communist party draws a clear line of distinction between the organized workers and their Social Fascist leaders. It calls upon the workers to take the control of their struggles into their own hands. The policy of independent leadership by the rank and file workers is fundamental in the general Communist action strategy. The Party promotes the formation of the revolutionary opposition in reformist trade unions; it organizes the workers to oust their reactionary leaders, to themselves take over the leadership of their strikes and other struggles, to break through the cliques of gangsters who control the local unions and suppress all trade union democracy, to disregard the maze of trade union legalism that has been built up by the bureaucracy to prevent the development of real struggles.

In the trade union field the necessity for independent rank and file leadership has led to the formation of several independent revolutionary industrial unions in the mining, textile, metal, marine, needle and other industries. These are united in a national center, the Trade Union Unity League, formed in 1929 through a reorganization of the Trade Union Educational League. The old TUEL was made up solely of revolutionary opposition groups in the reformist unions; the TUUL is composed of both revolutionary oppositions and industrial unions, with its center of gravity in the latter. The formation of the independent revolutionary unions was made imperative by the systematic sabotage of the struggle by the more and more Fascist A.F. of L. leaders through open strike-breaking, suppression of democracy in the unions, mass expulsions, be-

trayal of the unorganized, etc.   The TUUL is not
a dual organization in the sense of the I.W.W.
It does not make war upon the A.F. of L. unions
as such, but against their reactionary leaders.
With the A.F. of L. rank and file the TUUL
makes united fronts and conducts joint strike
struggles.   It organizes and supports the work of
the A.F. of L. opposition movements.   The TUUL
revolutionary unions concentrate their attention
upon the great masses of unorganized who make
up about five-sixths of the working class, building separate organizations where the fighting spirit
of the workers, lack of mass A.F. of L. unions,
etc., make this course the most practical one in
defense of their interests.   The TUUL is the
American section of the Red International of
Labor Unions.   It is made up of workers of all
political opinions.   Its relations towards the Communist party are those of mutual support and cooperation in the struggle, without organizational
affiliation.

The Communist party of the United States, in
line with its program of class struggle, unites with
the revolutionary workers of the world.   It is the
American section of the Communist International.
The Communist International carries out a united
revolutionary policy on a world scale, with the necessary adaptations for the special conditions in the
various countries.   The Communist International
is a disciplined world party; only such a party can

defeat world imperialism. Its leading party, by virtue of its great revolutionary experience, is the Russian Communist party. In its general work it applies the principles of democratic centralism, even as its affiliated parties do in their respective countries. That is, the policies of the International are worked out jointly with the several parties and then applied in the usual disciplined Communist way. Charges of the Matthew Woll brand that these parties "take orders from Moscow" are ridiculous. The united world revolutionary policy of the Communist International differs fundamentally from that of the Socialist Second International, whose autonomous sections follow the policies of their respective national bourgeoisie.

It is only with the foregoing Communist principles and program of class struggle that the workers can defeat the efforts of the capitalists to find a way out of the crisis through more unemployment, wage-cuts, and mass starvation, more Fascist terrorism and the unleashing of devastating war. Under the leadership of the Communist party and following out its class struggle policy, the workers can defend their interests here and now and they will ultimately traverse fully the revolutionary way out of the crisis by overthrowing capitalism and establishing a Soviet system.

The American Workers and the Revolution

THE CAPITALISTS and their henchmen in this country are very certain of the innate conservatism of the American working class. They confidently assure themselves that, no matter what may happen in other countries, the toiling masses here will have nothing to do with Socialism. And, on the surface of things, the workers of the United States are the most conservative of any great industrial country. This is primarily because, living in the land of the most powerful and rapidly rising imperialism, their standards of living have been somewhat higher than those in other countries. Besides, their class consciousness has been greatly hindered by the so-called democratic traditions in the United States, harking back to the days of free land. There has also been a retarding influence in the lack of homogeneity among the workers—many races, many nationalities, many traditions. All of which factors capitalism has thoroughly understood how to exploit in the unparalleled flood of propaganda that it has poured into the workers through the countless newspapers, schools, churches, labor leaders, politicians, radios, motion pictures, etc.

But this conservatism is more apparent than real; it is merely a surface and temporary indication. It is only a few years since the capitalists of Great Britain and Germany also boasted about the conservatism of their workers. They could do this because both of these countries were on a rising curve of imperialist development. It was possible at least for the masses of their workers to live. Illusions about the possibilities of capitalist development flourished among them. But now how changed is the situation. In Germany the workers are rapidly becoming revolutionized and in Great Britain they are traveling the same road, if at a somewhat slower tempo. This revolutionization of the workers develops because Germany and Great Britain have been caught deeply in the maelstrom of the general capitalist crisis: Germany, crushed by its imperialist rivals, approaches a revolutionary upheaval; Great Britain, ousted from its position as world industrial leader, slips deeper and deeper into chronic crisis. The erstwhile "conservative" workers of these countries, now facing mass starvation, are beginning to see the logic of the situation and are gradually preparing themselves for the fight to overthrow capitalism and to establish Socialism.

The American workers inevitably must go in the same direction and for the same reasons, although, for the causes above-mentioned, their pace is as yet much slower. A sure radicalization is being brought about by 30 to 40 cents a day wages for Kentucky miners,[8] $3.50 wages for a 70-hour week for Southern textile workers,[9] and similar condi-

[8] Theodore Dreiser, *Harlan Miners Speak.*
[9] *American Federationist,* Mar., 1932.

tions in the other industries.   Starvation wages are destroying the capitalistic illusions of American workers and 25 cent wheat is making the poor farmers their allies.   Especially are the hunger policies of the Hoover government in the unemployment question a potent factor in the growing radicalization.   The time will come when the capitalists of this country will realize that one of the greatest mistakes ever made by a ruling class was that of forcing the millions of unemployed to go without the necessaries of life while the warehouses were bursting with riches.

Under the pressure of the deepening crisis the workers are throwing off their conservatism with a speed and decisiveness that will soon startle the ruling class.   The British bourgeoisie were astounded at the recent sudden and significant mass upheavals in St. Johns and Auckland.   In Chapter I we have pointed out some of the signs of the new radicalization.   But doubtless the process has gone faster and farther than the open signs indicate and than even the closest observers realize. The radicalization is largely hidden because the American working class, almost completely unorganized industrially and politically, shamefully betrayed by the trade union leaders and terrorized in the industries, has great obstacles in the way of expressing its discontent.   It has to be of an explosive character before it appears upon the surface.   The pressure now rises dangerously.

The capitalists are congratulating themselves upon the lack of great mass struggles of the workers against the wholesale reductions in their living standards during the present crisis. *The Wall Street Journal,* (Jan. 5, 1932), states: "It is doubtful whether so rapid and extensive a deflation of the wage earner's income has ever before taken place in the United States, with so nearly a total absence of open conflict between masters and men. . . It seems a far cry back to the Homestead riots of 1892, to the Pullman and railroad strikes of 2 years later, or even to the Colorado mine disorders of 1914." Bourgeois economists and writers ascribe the dearth of big strikes to a lack of militancy on the part of the workers, and characteristically, the Socialist, Norman Thomas, agrees with them by giving as the reason "the docility of labor." [10]

The fallacy of this argumentation is readily apparent. At the door of the American Federation of Labor lies the chief responsibility for the failure of the working class to develop greater mass resistance against the huge lowering of their living standards. Had this organization, with its 2,500,-000 members and its standing as the traditional labor movement, issued a call to strike against wage-cuts and to fight for unemployment insurance undoubtedly many big strikes and unemployment demonstrations would have occurred. But

[10] *As I See It,* p. 166.

the A.F. of L., on the contrary, has used all its power and prestige to prevent struggle. Repeating the arguments of the bosses, it has unresistingly accepted wage-cuts and the unemployment hunger program of the government. Besides, it has unhesitatingly used strike-breaking methods (among the worst of which were the fake strikes, or lockouts in the Socialist-controlled needle trades) to defeat the workers who tried to beat the wage-cuts by struggle. This deadening influence of the A.F. of L. extended far beyond the ranks of its organization into the unorganized industries. The A.F. of L. leadership has been the principal instrument of the bosses to force the workers to accept lower conditions of living. All of which goes to show the great value of this leadership to the employers and to explain their systematic support of it.

The intensification of the crisis will inevitably bring with it a sharpening and broadening of the class struggle, despite all efforts of the bosses, the government and the A.F. of L.-S.P. leadership to check it. Consider the meaning of the Ford Hunger March, in which four workers were killed and many wounded by the police; just a few years ago the workers in the Ford plant were rated the best off in the world. Now they find themselves starving and ruthlessly shot down when they demand relief. Their answer is a violent mass resentment and a rapid building of the Communist party, the Unemployed Councils and the revolutionary Automobile Workers' Union.

Or take the case of the Kentucky miners: facing starvation wages, murderous terrorism by company gunmen and police thugs, wholesale arrest and railroading of militant workers, flagrant betrayal by the U.M.W. of A., they turned to the Communist party and the National Miners Union for leadership. These miners, almost without exception, are American-born. They and their forbears for generations back are of the old pioneer stock. They are intensely patriotic and religious; race prejudice against the Negro has been cultivated amongst them from their earliest childhood. The coal operators, realizing these facts and believing that they made the miners immune to revolutionary leadership regardless of their grievances, met the advance of the National Miners Union into the Kentucky-Tennessee coal regions with a frantic appeal to the prejudices of the miners. They made it appear that the developing strike was an attempt to overthrow the government, that it meant wiping out religion and the establishment of Negro domination. But the miners stood firm in the face of this unprecedented "red hysteria"; the strike went on despite all the demagogy and terrorism. Communism has established itself firmly among the American miners of the Kentucky and Tennessee coal fields.

Which way the farmers will go may be gathered

from the report of Professors Hutchinson and Holt on conditions in Michigan: "Then there are the farmers now talking the language of revolt. Their backs are against the wall and it will take only a few dramatic mortgage sales of lands held by families for two generations to start the fireworks. For them the passing of the American farmer to peasantry will not happen without a struggle in the spirit of 1776."

It is an illusion to think that the conservative American workers must first pass through the stage of social reformism before they will accept the Communist program. Doubtless, large numbers of them will fall victims to social reformism, hence, the great danger of the Socialist party and the A.F. of L. leadership. But experience already amply demonstrates that the Communist party, with its program of partial demands and united front policy, coupled with its ultimate revolutionary objectives, can and does successfully mobilize masses of these workers just breaking from the influence of the two old parties.

Dearborn, Kentucky, England (Ark.), Lawrence, Pittsburgh coal strike, etc., reflect the new spirit of the American class struggle. The capitalists, in the midst of the sharpening general crisis of capitalism, are determined to force the living standards of American toilers down to European levels, or lower. The workers will respond to this offensive by increasing class consciousness and mass struggle. More and more they will turn to the Communist party for leadership, and eventually they will be joined by decisive masses of the ever-more ruthlessly exploited poor farmers. The toiling masses of the United States will not submit to the capitalist way out of the crisis, which means still deeper poverty and misery, but will take the revolutionary way out to Socialism. The working class of this country will tread the path of the workers of the world, to the overthrow of capitalism and the establishment of a Soviet government. Lenin was profoundly correct when he said in his *Letter to American Workingmen,* of Aug. 20, 1918:

"The American working class will not follow the lead of its bourgeoisie. It will go with us against its bourgeoisie. The whole history of the American people gives me this confidence, this conviction."

CHAPTER V

THE UNITED SOVIET STATES OF AMERICA

THE MARXIAN principle holds true that the prevailing mode of production and exchange determines the character of the general organization in a given society. Thus the pioneer British capitalist society, based upon the private ownership of industry and the exploitation of the workers, forecast the type which, with only minor variations, came later to be developed by the whole capitalist world. Its parliamentary democracy, rampant patriotism, robot-like education of the masses, reformist trade unionism, etc., fitted naturally into the capitalist scheme of things everywhere.

By the same principle, the Soviet Union now forecasts the general outlines of the new social order that the world is approaching. The Soviet system was not an invention. Its basic institutions arose naturally from the economic and political necessities of workers and peasants freeing themselves from capitalist exploitation. Thus, for the United States as well as other countries, the Soviet Union is a plain indicator of the society that is to be, taking into account minor variations for special conditions in the several lands. It foreshadows the broad lines along which the future Soviet America will develop. Here our task is not to work out all the details of an American Soviet system, as that would exceed the scope of this book, but to trace out, upon the basis of actual experience to date, the general structure and workings of such a regime.

From capitalism to Communism, through the intermediary stage of Socialism; that is the way American society, like society in general, is headed. It represents the main line of march of the human race to the next higher social stage in its historical advance. It is the trend to which all the economic, political and social forces of today are contributing.

The American revolution, when the workers have finally seized power, will develop even more swiftly in all its phases than has the Russian revolution. This is because in the United States objective conditions are more ripe for revolution than they were in old Russia. In his work, *Imperialism,* Lenin states:

"Capitalism, in its imperialist phase, arrives at the threshold of the complete socialization of production. To some extent it causes the capitalists, whether they like it or no, to enter a new social order, which marks the transition from free competition to the socialization of production. Production becomes social, but appro-

priation remains private.   The social means of production remain the private property of a few."

This means that in such a highly-industrialized
country as the United States the industrial base for
Socialism is already at hand.   The great problem
before the workers is to get the political power.
The Russian workers, however, not only had to
conquer power but also to build a great industrial
system.   At the Eighth Congress of Soviets, in
1920, Lenin declared that, "Communism is the
Soviet power plus the electrification of the country."   In the United States, the problem of the
American working class in achieving Socialism
may be summed up, as Browder has put it, as
the present American industrial technique plus
Soviets.

Besides this more favorable industrial base,
American workers, once in control, will have other
advantages which will greatly speed the tempo of
revolutionary development.   These are, first, the
vast experience accumulated in the Russian revolution, and, second, the practical assistance of the
Soviet governments existing at the time of the
American revolution.   These are enormous advantages.   As for the Russian workers, they were
pioneers blazing the revolutionary trail.   They had
to work out for themselves a maze of unique
problems and to struggle against a whole hostile
capitalist world.   The sum of all which is that the
period of transition from capitalism to Socialism

in the United Soviet States will be much shorter and easier than in the U.S.S.R.

The American Soviet Government

WHEN the American working class actively enters the revolutionary path of abolishing capitalism it will orientate upon the building of Soviets, not upon the adaptation of the existing capitalist government. Capitalist governments have nothing in common with proletarian governments. They are especially constructed throughout to maintain the rulership of the bourgeoisie. In the revolutionary struggle they are smashed and Soviet governments established, built according to the requirements of the toiling masses.

The building of Soviets is begun not after the revolution but before. When the eventual revolutionary crisis becomes acute the workers begin the establishment of Soviets. The Soviets are not only the foundation of the future Workers' State, but also the main instruments to mobilize the masses for revolutionary struggle. The decisions of the Soviets are enforced by the armed Red Guard of the workers and peasants and by the direct seizure of the industry through factory committees. A revolutionary American working class will follow this general course, which is the way of proletarian revolution.

The American Soviet government will be organized along the broad lines of the Russian Soviets. Local Soviets, the base of the whole Soviet State, will be established in all cities, towns and villages. Local Soviets combine in themselves the legislative, executive and judicial functions. Representation, based on occupation instead of residence and property, comes directly from the shops, mines, farms, schools, workers' organizations, army, navy, etc. The principle of recall of representatives applies throughout. Citizenship is restricted to those who do useful work, capitalists, landlords, clericals and other non-producers being disfranchised.

The local Soviets will be combined by direct representation into county, state, and national Soviets. The national Soviet government, with its capital in Chicago or some other great industrial center, will consist of a Soviet Congress, made up of local delegates and meeting annually, or as often as need be, to work out the general policies of the government. Between its meetings the government will be carried on by a broad Central Executive Committee, meeting every few months. This C.E.C. will elect a small Presidium and a Council of Commissars, made up of the heads of the various government departments, who will carry on the day-to-day work.

The American Soviet government will join with the other Soviet governments in a world Soviet Union. There will also be, very probably, some form of continental union. The American revolution will doubtless carry with it all those countries of the three Americas that have not previously accomplished the revolution.

The Soviet court system will be simple, speedy and direct. The judges, chosen by the corresponding Soviets, will be responsible to them. The Supreme Court, instead of being dictatorial and virtually legislative, as in the United States, will be purely juridical and entirely under the control of the C.E.C. The civil and criminal codes will be simplified, the aim being to proceed directly and quickly to a correct decision. In the acute stages of the revolutionary struggle special courts to fight the counter-revolution will probably be necessary. The pest of lawyers will be abolished. The courts will be class-courts, definitely warring against the class enemies of the toilers. They will make no hypocrisy like capitalist courts, which, while pretending to deal out equal justice to all classes, in reality are instruments of the capitalist State for the repression and exploitation of the toiling masses.

The American Soviet government will be the dictatorship of the proletariat. In Chapter II we explained this dictatorship as the revolutionary government of the workers and toiling farmers. In the proletarian dictatorship the working class is the leader by virtue of its revolutionary program, superior organization and greater numbers. Towards the farmers, the attitude of the government will vary from an open alliance with the poor farmers and cooperation with the middle farmers, to open hostility against the big, exploiting landowners. Towards the city intelligentsia and petty bourgeoisie generally, its attitude will be one of friendliness and cooperation, insofar as these elements break with the old order and support the new. The new Workers' government, as part of its task of building Socialism, necessarily will have to hold firmly in check the counter-revolutionary elements who seek to overthrow or sabotage the new regime. To suppose that the powerful American capitalist class and its vast numbers of hangers-on will tamely submit to the loss of their power to the workers would be to ignore the whole history of that class. The mildness or severity of the repressive measures used by the workers to liquidate this class politically will depend directly upon the character of the latter's resistance. While the whole trend of the revolutionary workers is against violence, they always have an iron fist for counter-revolution.

In order to defeat the class enemies of the revolution, the counter-revolutionary intrigues within the United States and the attacks of foreign capitalist countries from without, the proletarian dictatorship must be supported by the organized armed might of the workers, soldiers, local militia, etc. In the early stages of the revolution, even before the seizure of power, the workers will organize the Red Guard. Later on this loosely constructed body becomes developed into a firmly-knit, well-disciplined Red Army.

The leader of the revolution in all its stages is the Communist party. With its main base among the industrial workers, the Party makes a bloc with the revolutionary farmers and impoverished city petty bourgeoisie, drawing under its general leadership such revolutionary groups and organizations as these classes may have. Under the dictatorship all the capitalist parties — Republican, Democratic, Progressive, Socialist, etc.— will be liquidated, the Communist party functioning alone as the Party of the toiling masses. Likewise, will be dissolved all other organizations that are political props of the bourgeois rule, including chambers of commerce, employers' associations, rotary clubs, American Legion, Y.M.C.A., and such fraternal orders as the Masons, Odd Fellows, Elks, Knights of Columbus, etc.

A Soviet government will provide the workers and poor farmers with the political instrument necessary to defend their interests. The whole purpose of such a government will be to advance the welfare of those who do useful work. This is not the case with the present government of the United States. It is dominated by the Morgans, Mellons and other big bankers and industrialists. Its function is to protect the interests of the capitalist class — in first line finance capital — at the expense of the working masses. Every piece of legislation, every strike, every demonstration of the unemployed illustrates this afresh. In no matter what field, wherever the interests of the workers are involved, they find the powers of the government arrayed against them. The American government is as much the property of the capitalists as their mills, mines, factories and land. Only a Soviet government can and will represent the will of the workers.

The establishment of an American Soviet government will mark the birth of real democracy in the United States. For the first time the toilers will be free, with industry and the government in their own hands. Now they are enslaved: the industries and the government are the property of the ruling class. The right to vote and all the current talk about democracy are only so many screens to hide the capitalist autocracy and to make it more palatable to the masses. Consider the economic and political gulf between the Southern textile workers slaving for $5 a week and the rich Southern capitalists; between the hungry unemployed workers in the Northern cities and the fat capitalist parasite masters lolling the Winters through at Palm Beach; between the semi-slave Negroes in the South and their exploiters; between the outrageous treatment visited upon Mooney and Billings, Sacco and Vanzetti and many other class war prisoners and the protection given to the Falls, Daughertys and the whole clique of capitalist robbers of the poor — then one gets the true measure of the American capitalist "democracy" and "freedom." Ambassador Gerard blurted out the truth that the American government is a capitalist dictatorship when he declared that 59 bankers and captains of industry are the real rulers of the United States.

The Expropriation of the Expropriators

"The victorious proletariat utilizes the conquest of power as a lever of economic revolution, i.e., the revolutionary transformation of the property relations of capitalism into relations of the Socialist mode of production. The starting point of this great economic revolution is the expropriation of the landlords and capitalists, i.e., the conversion of the *monopolistic property of the bourgeoisie into the property of the proletarian State*." [1]

After providing for the emergency defense and provisioning requirements, the first steps of an American Workers' and Farmers' government, which is the dictatorship of the proletariat, will be directed towards the revolutionary nationalization or socialization of the large privately-owned and State capitalist undertakings.

In industry, transport and communication this will mean the immediate taking over by the State of all large factories, mines and power plants,

[1] *Program of the Communist International.*

together with all municipal and State industries; the whole transport services of railroads, waterways, airways, electric car lines, bus lines, etc.; the entire communication organization, including telegraphs, telephones, post office, radio, etc.

In agriculture it will involve the early confiscation of the large landed estates in town and country, including church property, together with their buildings, factories, live stock, etc., and also the whole body of forests, mineral deposits, lakes, rivers, etc.

In finance it will mean the nationalization of the banking system and its concentration around a central State bank; the taking over of the department stores, chain stores, and other large wholesale and retail trading organizations; the setting up of a State monopoly of foreign trade; the cancellation of all government debts, reparations, war loans, etc., to the big foreign and home capitalists.

The socialization program will be carried through on the basis of confiscation without remuneration, except for special consideration to small investors. Such a program naturally evokes loud protest from capitalists and the defenders of private property, especially the Social Fascists. The latter's idea, again expressed by Norman Thomas in his book, *America's Way Out,* is for the workers to buy the industries and land from their capitalist owners. Thomas even proposes the absurd plan that, through holding companies, the workers can secure control with a minority of the stock.

Such Social Fascist proposals have nothing in common with Socialism. They represent a definite support of the capitalist class and the landlords in their claims for the right to exploit the workers; they seek to conserve the dominant position of these classes in a new form, State capitalism. The workers will never buy out the capitalists, nor could they if they would. There is no warrant in common-sense or historical precedent for the workers to buy the industries and natural resources from the present ruling class. In confiscating this property of the big landlords and capitalists, the workers and poor farmers will simply be taking back that which has been ruthlessly stolen from them. This lesson of expropriation without compensation by a revolutionary class has been amply taught in the British, French, Russian and many other revolutions. The revolutionary American colonists did not compensate the British landlords; the Northern capitalists did not pay the Southern planters when they transformed the Negro chattel slaves into wage slaves; and the working class will follow the same course of revolutionary confiscation.

The socialization of the key sections of industry, commerce, agriculture and finance will lay a solid economic foundation for the building of Socialism. Doubtless, private property will survive in small farms, in petty industry and in trade. But this will be only temporary. With the consolidation and growth of Socialism and the general spread of well-being all the land will eventually and without serious difficulty be nationalized, and all industry will be concentrated into the Socialist Soviet economy.

The Improvement of the Toilers' Conditions

THE CENTRAL purpose of the revolution is to conquer political power for the workers and to fundamentally improve the economic and social conditions of the producing masses. Immediately an American Soviet government is established, the shut-down factories will be opened. Production will be started to relieve the impoverished workers and farmers. The great stores of necessities, now piled up and unsaleable, will be released to the masses. The unemployed will be fed, housed and given work. Pending any delay in putting the industries into full operation, the unemployed will be paid social insurance on the basis of full wages. The general policy of the Soviet government will be to at once put into effect at least the immediate demands that the workers are now demanding of capitalism, and which we have discussed in the previous chapter. Wages will be sharply raised, especially for the lower-paid categories; then there will be established the 7-hour day or, very probably, less, with a correspondingly still shorter workday for young workers and those engaged in dangerous occupations; there will also be the development of the system of social insurance against unemployment, old age, sickness, accidents, etc., on a full wage basis; the abolition of the many discriminations against Negroes, women, and young workers in industry; the establishment of free medical services, vacations for workers, etc.

The Soviet government will initiate at once a vast housing program. All houses and other buildings will be socialized. The great hotels, apartments, city palaces, country homes, country clubs, etc., of the rich will be taken over and utilized by the workers for dwellings, rest homes, children's clubs, sanatoria, etc. The best of the skyscrapers, emptied of their thousand and one brands of parasites, will be used to house the new government institutions, the trade unions, cooperatives, Communist party, etc. The fleets of automobiles and steam yachts of the rich will be placed at the disposition of the workers' organizations. A great drive will be made to demolish the present collection of miserable shacks and tenements and build homes fit for the workers to live in.

The Soviet government will immediately free the poor farmers from the onerous burdens of mortgages and other debts which now hold them in slavery. Of the total income of all farmers in

1927, 17% went for loans and mortgages.[2]   Land rent will be abolished, both in the form of cash and share-crops.   The land will be to the users.   The present monopolistic prices for agricultural machinery, fertilizer, etc., will be drastically cut. Taxes will be slashed and shifted off the backs of the poor farmers.   For the millions of "one-horse" farmers now living at the verge of starvation in many states, more land will be allotted; they will also be furnished with the necessary seed, machinery, fertilizer and expert instruction.   Food and other necessities of life will be given to those in need.   Production of foodstuffs will not be curtailed, but greatly stimulated.

Such a program is not a matter of mere speculation.   This is the line that developed in the Soviet Union and it is the one that will develop here. Even in the face of their gigantic tasks, the necessity to build industry from the ground up in the teeth of world capitalist opposition, the Russians, as we have seen in Chapter II, have been able vastly to improve the conditions of the toilers of factory and farm.   In the United States, however, the revolution, because of the superior industrial equipment here, will be able to advance the American workers' standards of living much more quickly and drastically.   It will also make it possible to lend assistance to the more undeveloped countries.   It is true that the powerful and ruth-

[2] *Recent Economic Changes,* Vol. II, p. 784.

less American capitalist class will seek to prevent all this by destroying the industries during the revolution, which only emphasizes the need for breaking their resistance the sooner.

The above measures of improvement for the workers and farmers will represent only a bare beginning. Already the material conditions are at hand in the United States for an enormous increase in the well-being of the masses. The barriers to this advancement are the incredible robberies, wastes and the general idiocies of the capitalist system. The revolution will clear away this mass of exploitation, inefficiency and reaction, and will open the road for such an industrial development and general rise in material and cultural standards of the masses as now seems only the stuff of dreams.

The Liquidation of Capitalist Robbery and Waste

THE REVOLUTION will put a stop to the whole series of capitalist leaks, wastes and thieveries which now prevent the rise in standards of the masses. It is the marvel of the capitalist world how the Soviet government, with virtually no foreign credits, manages to raise the many billions necessary to finance the Five-Year Plan. The explanation is to be found in the gigantic economies inherent in the Socialist system as against the inefficiencies and grafts of capitalism. These economies will be much greater in the United Soviet States of America.

First of all, the American Soviet government, by taking over the ownership of industry and the land, will put a sudden stop to the manifold forms of robbing the workers and farmers of monster masses of value on the basis of private ownership of the social means of livelihood. All forms of capitalist interest, rent and profit will be abolished. Capitalists, mortgage holders, landowners and coupon clippers perform no useful function in society. Their rake-off from industry and the land is sheer robbery. This is one of the great lessons of the Russian revolution. They are a deadly detriment. The first requirement for further social progress is to abolish this class of parasites. Veblen states the case very mildly when he says that "the capitalist financier has come to be no better than an idle wheel in the economic mechanism, serving only to take up some of the lubricant." [3] In reality, the capitalists, with their program of mass poverty, exploitation and war, are a menace to the human race.

Ending the gigantic robbery which is the very base of the capitalist system will at once release vast values for useful social ends. How vast may be realized from the fact that in 1928 the total national income in the United States was approxi-

[3] *The Price System and the Engineers*, P. 66.

mately 90 billion dollars, of which, it is estimated by Varga that no less than 46% was taken by capitalist exploiters in the shape of corporation profits, ground rents, interest on mortgages, official salaries and bonuses, etc. An American Soviet government, stopping this monstrous expropriation of the toilers, will turn these great sums to the improvement of the living and cultural standards of the producing masses.

Secondly, the setting up of a Socialist system will greatly increase the productive forces and production itself. By liquidating the contradiction between the modes of production and exchange, it does away with economic crises, with all their waste and loss. Where there is no capitalist class to demand its profit before production and distribution take place, and where the producers as a whole receive the full product of their labor, there can be no economic over-production and crisis. Consequently, unemployment, with its terrible misery and suffering, will become a thing of the past. The many millions who now walk the streets unemployed will have fruitful work to do, to the benefit of all society. With the deadly limitations of the capitalist market removed, the road will be opened to virtually unlimited expansion of industry and mass consumption.

Thirdly, Socialism will result in an enormous increase in industrial and agricultural efficiency. It is the proud boast of the capitalists, particularly the Americans, that their system represents the acme of economy and efficiency. But this is so untrue as to be grotesque. The Socialist system of planned production, based upon social ownership of industry and the land, is incomparably more efficient than the anarchic capitalist system founded upon private property, competition and the exploitation of the workers. In his book, *The Tragedy of Waste,* Stuart Chase estimates that of the 40,000,000 "gainfully employed" in the United States about 20,500,000, or 50%, waste their labor totally. Recently *Iron Age* stated that by putting all the industrial plants in the United States on the basis of modern technique it would be possible to shorten the working day to one-third of the present, while at the same time doubling the output. Socialism will wipe out these great wastes, inherent in the planless, competitive capitalist system. It will liquidate the hundreds of useless and parasitic occupations, such as wholesalers, jobbers, and the entire crew of "middlemen," real estate sharks, stock brokers, prohibition agents, bootleggers, advertising specialists, traveling salesmen, lawyers, whole rafts of government bureaucrats, police, clericals, and sundry capitalist quacks, fakers, and grafters. It will turn to useful social purposes the immense values consumed by these socially useless elements.

Socialism will also conserve the natural resources of the country which are now being ruthlessly wasted in the mad capitalist race for profits. Chase points out, among many examples of such criminal waste, that by wrong production methods 16 billion barrels of petroleum have been lost; every year 5 billion feet of lumber are likewise wasted; and although as yet only 2% of the total coal in this country has been mined, 33% of the best beds has been gutted. Natural gas and the various minerals are being similarly wasted. A Soviet government will, of course, put a stop to this criminal recklessness and have as one of its principal aims the careful conservation of all the natural resources.

Finally, the eventual victory of the workers on a world scale will liquidate the monster, War, with all its agonies and social losses. The ghastly bill of the World War comprised, in terms of human life, 12,990,000 dead and a total casualty list of 33,288,000, not counting the thirty millions more who died in various countries from famine and pestilence as a result of the war. The direct property loss and general financial cost of the war is estimated at 340 billion dollars.

It is along these broad channels that the American Soviet government will find the means for the early and far-reaching improvement of the toilers' standards. The abolition of the monumental robbery of the workers by the capitalists in all its myriad forms; the liquidation of the capitalist economic crisis, with its mass unemployment and general crippling of the productive forces; the development of an industrial efficiency and a volume of production now hardly dreamed of; the careful conservation of natural resources; the abolition of war; — these revolutionary measures will provide the material bases for a well-being of the toiling masses of field and factory now quite unknown in the world.

The Reorganization of Industry

AMONG the first tasks of the American Soviet government will be the reorganization of the chaotic capitalist industries upon Socialist lines. To do this the banks will all be centralized in one great system. The railroads will be completely consolidated; duplicate lines will be eliminated; bus, truck, airplane, interurban electric and steamship lines will be scientifically coordinated with the railroads, thereby making a saving of at least 50% in transportation efficiency. The scattered units of the other industries will be similarly organized, with an eventual program of rebuilding industry into larger units, regrouping of plants at more strategic points, elimination of small and uneconomic plants, etc.

The industrial system as a whole will be headed by a body analogous to the Supreme Economic Council of the U.S.S.R. The S.E.C. is made up of a series of "united industries," "trusts," and "combines." There is the necessary sub-division for the special character of the industry, local conditions, etc. Each industrial unit, with an established budget and allocated capital and credit, operates upon the principles of cost accountancy and individual and collective responsibility. The whole industrial apparatus — production, distribution, financing — while each part retains the necessary organization, specialization and initiative required for the fulfillment for its particular functions, constitutes a great industrial machine, each cog of which fits into and works harmoniously with the rest.

The superiority of such an organized Socialist industry over the present piece-meal and anarchic American industrial system is evident at a glance. Compare this scientific industrial organization, as a coordinated and cooperating whole, with the present maze of 206,556 separate American manufacturing concerns, including coal mining 6,000; textiles (cotton, wool, silk, rayon) 5,833; metal (main branches) 23,000, etc.,[4] not to speak of the hundreds of thousands of separate retailing, jobbing and financing concerns. And all these multitudinous units are engaged in a dog-eat-dog competition with each other, blindly producing and throwing their products aimlessly into the markets. Socialist industry means system, cooperation, effi-

---

[4] Figures based on U. S. Department of Commerce Census Bulletin, Dec. 31, 1930.

ciency; capitalist industry means chaos, conflict, waste.

Naturally, American Socialist industry will be operated upon the basis of a planned economy. The aim of the whole industrial machine will be to achieve the highest possible standards for the producing masses, not the welfare of a few capitalists. Production will be scientifically calculated in advance. The needs of the people and the possibilities of the industries will be carefully studied and met. With a thoroughly organized industrial system the carrying out of the production plans will be easy and natural. A Socialist society without a planned economy is unthinkable, even as it is unthinkable that a capitalist society should work on the basis of scientific planning.

Under the American Soviet government with such an organized industrial system, economic crises, clogging of the markets through over-production, cannot take place. The toilers as a whole receiving the values they produce and there being no parasitic capitalists whose special class interests have to be preserved, gains in production will express themselves automatically and immediately in higher wages, shorter working hours and generally improved conditions. In a Soviet America there could not possibly exist the present hideous anomaly of millions of workers and their families unemployed and starving while the markets are glutted with commodities and the great industries stand idle.

The operation of Socialist nationalized industry is, of course, not to be compared with government-operated industry under capitalism. This is because the capitalists, fearing to endanger their beloved system of private ownership, always see to it that industries operated by their governments are thoroughly sabotaged, mismanaged and generally discredited. But under Socialism the whole interest of the government is to manage the industries efficiently and to eliminate bureaucratism, and this is done to a degree quite unknown in the capitalist world.

In Socialist society the trade unions play a fundamental role. They are a gigantic factor in the Soviet Union. They draw the masses directly into the work of Socialist construction, in the building of the new society. They attend to the protection of the immediate needs of the workers. They constitute the mass basis for the Soviets. They are the great schools for Communism. No important activities are embarked upon without their consent and cooperation. No labor law can go into effect without their endorsement. Their representatives occupy key positions in every stage of the economic, political and social organization. Compared to these great mass bodies, the American Federation of Labor, which presumes to sneer at the Russian unions, plays an insignificant role in the life of the working class.

The Russian trade unions base their organization directly upon the industries through shop committees. Their general structure follows the lines of the economic organization of their industries. There are 45 national industrial unions in the U.S.S.R. They are not State organs, being based entirely upon the principles of voluntary membership.

The trade unions look after the formulation and enforcement of the whole elaborate body of social insurance (unemployment, sickness, old age, maternity, accident, etc.). They enforce the government sanitary and safety regulations. And especially they work out the wage scales jointly with the government economic organs. This is not a matter for strikes and struggles, there being no ruling, owning class to contend with; it is a question of amicable arrangement upon the scientific basis of the general returns from industry and agriculture, taking into account the needs for the further expansion of industry, the upkeep of the government, etc.

In industry the trade unions perform a very important part. But they do not of themselves actually lead the production, this being the task of the government economic organs, with close local and national supervision from the Party and the unions. The Syndicalist theory that the trade unions could directly carry on production is one of the many theories that were proven false by the actual practice in the Russian revolution. The unions, locally and nationally, hold periodic production conferences with the technical heads of the industries, hearing reports from them and checking up on their work. They have representatives in all the higher economic organs, as well as in the Soviets proper. The trade unions are the very basis of the vast mobilization of the working class in the industries for the carrying through of the Five-Year Plan.

The trade unions are also a vital means in the education of the masses. They have a great network of factory schools, newspapers, libraries and theatres. They have thousands of rest homes, clubs, sanatoria, hospitals, gymnasiums, etc. They swell in many directions the great wave of enlightenment, organization and prosperity among the toilers.

In building Socialism in this country the trade unions will play essentially the same role as in the U.S.S.R. The revolutionary unions of the Trade Union Unity League are the nucleus of the eventual great labor organizations of Soviet America. Whatever remnants of the present A.F. of L. may exist at the time of the revolution will be merged into the series of industrial unions based on all-inclusive factory committees. The revolutionary workers, both before and during the revolutionary crisis, will ruthlessly drive from office the reactionary A.F. of L. leaders as the most servile and dangerous of all tools of the bourgeoisie.

The cooperatives are also a foundation stone in the Socialist economic system. The cooperatives form the great retail distributing mechanism; they are directly connected with the factories, thus cutting out all useless and parasitic middlemen. Entering into every city and village, they constitute a gigantic distributing agency, beside which even the biggest American chain stores and mail order houses are only small potatoes. The cooperatives also play a very important role in production, especially in agriculture. The tremendous collective farm movement in the U.S.S.R. represents the cooperative grown to revolutionary maturity.

As in the case of the American trade unions, the existing cooperatives in this country will have to be profoundly reorganized and rebuilt to perform their new tasks. They will be developed from the skeleton organizations they are today into a gigantic mass movement. This will be one of the first and most urgent tasks of a revolutionary American government.

In building Socialist industry the greatest problem the workers will have to solve, as the Russian experience shows, is to secure mastery over industrial technique. Although the great industrial base will be on hand, despite capitalist efforts to destroy it in the revolutionary struggle, there will remain the task of giving the industries Socialist form and leadership. It will be impossible to take over, as is, the capitalist economic organs and personnel and start them off running as Socialist institutions.

But in the United States this problem of developing the new Socialist forms and cadres will not be so acute as in the Soviet Union. This is because of the general reasons previously cited: the greater ripeness of the objective situation and the existence of Soviet countries and a great body of revolutionary experience. Inasmuch as American industry is much more developed, the workers have more skill and experience than the Russians had; the trusts and the advanced industrial technique will lend themselves more readily to Socialist reorganization, and besides there will not be the need for such swift industrial expansion as in the U.S.S.R. Also the American capitalist engineers do not form such an air-tight clique as the Russians did and they will not be so strategically situated to sabotage the industries; in the existing surplus of technicians doubtless large numbers of them, suffering from unemployment and generally bad conditions, will go along with the revolution and they will be given every opportunity to use their skill in the industries. Besides, and this is of decisive importance, the American Soviet government will have at its disposal the vast experience of the Russian workers in the building of Socialist industry and also, if necessary, actual help from their engineers.

The American Soviet government will immediately proceed with the difficult task of creating an adequate supply of reliable technicians and managers for the industries. The scattered technical institutes, trade schools, correspondence schools, etc., will be organized, expanded and linked up directly with the industries. Technical schools will be established at all factories. Workers and their children will be given the preference in the study of industrial technique.

The Collectivization of Agriculture

THE SOVIET system provides a scientific method of organizing agriculture as well as industry. Stalin says: "To create an economic basis of Socialism — that means to unite agriculture with Socialist industry into a single economy, and to place agriculture under the leadership of Socialized industry." Private property, production for profit, competition and all the rest of the capitalist chaos and robbery, have no more place on Soviet farms than in the factories. An immediate and fundamental problem to confront the American Soviet government, therefore, will be to carry through the Socialist collectivization of the land.

This, for the poor and middle farmers, will be done upon a voluntary basis.

In the agrarian question the experience in the Soviet Union is of the most fundamental importance. In their vast movement of collectivization, described in Chapter II, the Russians have developed several forms of farm organization. Chief among these are the "kolkoz," or artel, with land, draft animals and implements pooled and the joint returns distributed upon the basis of the work done, and the State farm, ("sovkhoz"), with the land farmed directly by the State, (State Farm Trust), and the workers paid upon a wage basis. There are also the societies for the joint cultivation of the land (TSOS), with private property in draft animals, crops, etc., and finally, there are the communes, with common property in tools, horses, products and dwellings. In all cases the land is owned by the government. The State agriculture organization is grouped under the Commissariat of Agriculture, and is formed into trusts for various crops and geographical divisions of the industry; such as Grain Trust, Cotton Trust, Flax Trust, Livestock Trust, Hemp Trust, Tea Trust, etc. Crops are sold either directly to the government, to the cooperatives, or, in a very rapidly lessening extent, upon the open local markets.

All these forms have been widely applied. But the most adaptable and basic are the artels and the State farms. The State farms are an unquestioned success, but it is especially along the lines of the artel that the many millions of Russian peasants are now regrouping themselves. The collectives and State farms, despite the still existing shortage of machinery, etc., have already proved, by greatly increased output, their vast advance over the old forms of farming.

The superiority of such an organized agriculture over the present unorganized American system is evident at a glance. It is like comparing a modern automobile with an ox cart. The Russian farmers, with their vast farms, are producing crops under increasingly scientific conditions and then disposing of them to a government which they, together with the industrial workers, completely control. American farmers, on the other hand, in 6,300,000 separate units destitute of organization except for a few cooperatives and other associations largely controlled by the bankers, capitalist politicians and rich farmers, are all producing, helter-skelter, and then, harassed by capitalist loan sharks, industrial trusts, and a hostile government, are selling their crops in open competition with each other and the whole world. It is no surprise, therefore, that while the Russian farmers are blazing ahead to progress and prosperity, the American farmers slump deeper into poverty, stagnation and crisis.

The central policy of the American Soviet government in agriculture will be to reorganize the farming system primarily upon the basis of State farms. The position of American agricultural technique and the experience in the U.S.S.R. will justify such a policy. The great ranches of the Far West, the big corporation farms of the Middle West, the huge private estates of the millionaires in the East — all confiscated by the new government — will provide immediate bases for many such great State farms. These will be vast model farms, equipped with the most modern machinery and technique. They will raise the level of agriculture production generally to a new and higher stage. But, doubtless, the artel type of collective farm will also be widely organized. It will be the policy of the government to stimulate the collectivization movement, furnishing the poor farmers with the necessary implements, etc. The artel form of farm will provide a convenient bridge, leading away from individualist, competitive farming and towards the State farm.

Once the political power is in the hands of the workers and peasants the collectivization of American agriculture, the winning of the poorer categories of farmers for the building of Socialism, will proceed very rapidly. It is true that the American farmer on the average has a bigger farm than the Russian peasant had and that the private property idea is perhaps more deeply ingrained in him, but he is, as we have already seen, caught between the millstones of capitalist exploitation and is being crushed. The vast majority of the farmers will have everything to gain from the outset by a Socialized agriculture. Today, despite popular notions to the contrary, the average farmer seriously lacks machinery. The one million American tractors, not to speak of other costly machines, are now concentrated very largely in the hands of the well-to-do and rich farmers. The poor farmer also lacks fertilizers and has little or no chance to apply modern methods.

Collectivization under a Soviet system will radically change all this. Not only will it furnish the farmer with a boundless market for his products, but it will also provide him with machinery, fertilizers, selected seed and general scientific methods on a scale entirely unknown even on the largest present-day American farms. The marginal mountain and rocky farms in the South, New England, etc., will be abandoned and the farming industry concentrated and intensified in the most adaptable sections. The revolutionary collectivization of the land will effect a profound advance in American agriculture and cause a veritable leap forward in the living standards of the farmer.

The Liberation of the Negro

THE CAPITALIST class not only robs the workers as a whole, but it visits special exploitation upon those sections of the working class — Negroes, foreign-born, women, youth, the aged, etc.— who, for one reason or another, are the least able to defend themselves in the class struggle. The American Soviet government will drastically eliminate such special discrimination, along with capitalist exploitation generally.

Above all, as we have remarked, it is the Negro who is singled out for the bitterest exploitation and persecution by the capitalists. His condition is comparable only to that of the "untouchables" of India and is the most crying outrage of American capitalism. He is set apart as a pariah, an object of contempt and scorn, a victim of the most systematic suppression and enslavement to be found anywhere in the modern industrial world.

The purpose of all this tyranny and repression is, of course, the most intense robbery of the Negro toilers; for the vast majority of Negroes are either poor farmers or workers. The Jim-Crow system, with all its cultivated snobbery of race, is a device of the ruling classes to whip extra profits out of the hides of the oppressed Negroes by splitting them off from the rest of the toilers.

The Republican party, boasted friend of the Negro, is equally responsible with the Democratic party for the maintenance of this criminal outrage. Such Negro organizations as the Urban League and the National Association for the Advancement of Colored People, dominated by the white and Negro capitalists and petty bourgeoisie, also have this responsibility; they live by cultivating segregationalism; they sabotage every real fight for the liberation of the Negro.   In the case of the framed-up nine Scottsboro Negro boys, the attorney of the N.A.A.C.P. made a purely formal defense, practically coinciding with the prosecution.

As for the American Federation of Labor, its record on the Negro question is one of shame and treachery; it falls into step with the whole capitalist policy by barring Negroes from its unions, by blocking their entry into the better-paid jobs, by refusing to fight for their burning demands, by cultivating the insidious white chauvinism. The measure of the policy of the A.F. of L. on the Negro question is to be seen, for example, in Atlanta, where Negroes are not even allowed to enter the local labor temple.

The Socialist party, despite all its parade of radicalism and alleged friendship of the Negro, follows the same basic Jim-Crow line as the A.F. of L. This was clearly shown by Heywood Broun, Socialist leader, when he said:

"If I were a candidate for high executive office, or judiciary office, I would say, even without being cornered, that I would not now sanction the efforts to enforce the 14th and 15th Amendments to the Constitution of the United States." [5]

The Communist party, alone of all the political parties, fights for the liberation of the Negro, both

5 *New York Telegram,* Apr. 28, 1930.

in the present-day struggle and as an ultimate goal. The American Soviet government, immediately it takes power, will deal a shattering blow to the whole monstrous Jim-Crowism. To destroy it ruthlessly will be one of the real joys of the victorious proletarian revolution. Every remnant of slavery will be abolished. In a Soviet system, the Negro will have the most complete equality — economically, politically, socially. The doors to every occupation, to every social activity, will be wide open for him. He will have ample land, confiscated from the great white landlords. He will be free to do and go as any other citizen, without let or hindrance. Attempts to maintain the capitalist white chauvinism and ostracism of the Negroes will be punished as a serious crime against society. Socialism will mean the first real freedom for the Negro. He is beginning to realize this, hence his mass turning to the Communist party for leadership, and the consequent deep alarm of the capitalists and big landowners at this growing unity of white and black toilers.

The status of the American Negro is that of an oppressed national minority, and only a Soviet system can solve the question of such minorities. This it does, in addition to setting up real equality in the general political and social life, by establishing the right of self-determination for national minorities in those parts of the country where they constitute the bulk of the population. The constitution of the Soviet Union provides that, "Each united republic retains the right of free withdrawal from the Union." The *Program of the Communist International* declares for:

"The recognition of the right of all nations, irrespective of race, to complete self-determination, that is, self-determination inclusive of the right to State separation."

Accordingly, the right of self-determination will apply to Negroes in the American Soviet system. In the so-called Black Belt of the South, where the Negroes are in the majority, they will have the fullest right to govern themselves and also such white minorities as may live in this section. The same principle will apply to all the colonial and semi-colonial peoples now dominated by American imperialism in Cuba, the Philippines, Central and South America, etc.

And logically, foreign-born workers, now denied the right to vote and ruthlessly deported, will enjoy the fullest rights of citizenship. One of the most monstrous features of the present attack upon the working class is the deportation of tens of thousands of foreign-born workers by Doak's Department of Labor. These masses of workers, torn away from home and families, are sent back to countries with which they have lost all touch. Doak's deportation campaign, part of the capitalist offensive, is an attempt to terrorize the foreign-born workers, to crush every semblance of resistance among them, to split them off from the American-born workers. The wholesale deportation of radical workers and leaders is an attempt to illegalize the Communist party and the TUUL.

The experience with self-determination of national minorities in the Soviet Union shows that the Russians have solved this problem with the revolution. The many national minorities have the right of self-determination; they have their own languages, their own culture. Yet they all live together in the strongest unity under the general constitution of the U.S.S.R. Where there is no capitalist or feudal exploitation there can be no suppression of weaker nationalities. The radical liquidation of the "insoluble" Jewish problem in the U.S.S.R. testifies to the completeness of the Bolshevik cure. Murderous pogroms, a curse of old Russia, are now totally eradicated. The Jews enjoy absolute equality with all other nationalities. The solution of the question of suppressed nationalities, a question which causes untold misery in the capitalist world, is one of the greatest achievements of the Russian revolution.

The American Soviet will, of course, abolish all restrictions upon racial intermarriage. The arguments of Ku Klux Klanners and the like that Negroes are an inferior race and that "mongrel" peoples are less capable, have no justification in science and social experience. Those "scientists" who endorse such "white supremacy" theories are only so many bought-and-paid-for upholders of the prevailing mode of exploitation. The facts are that all the big peoples of today are already hopelessly "mongrel" and that wherever Negroes have half a chance they demonstrate their intellectual equality with the whites. Geographic isolation of the early human stock into widely separated groups brought about its differentiation into individual races; contact between these various races, bred of modern industrialization, is just as irresistibly breaking down these racial differences and bringing about racial amalgamation. The revolution will only hasten this process of integration, already proceeding throughout the world with increasing tempo.

The Emancipation of Woman

WHEN woman emerged historically from feudalism she was burdened with a whole series of customs, prejudices and restrictions enslaving her in her work, her personal life and her political status. Characteristically capitalism, which respects nothing in its greed for profits, quickly seized upon all these handicaps of woman and used them to doubly exploit her. This is true of the United States as well as other capitalist countries. The so-called freedom of the American woman is a myth. Either she is a gilded butterfly bourgeois parasite or she is an oppressed slave.

The life of the working class woman and poor farmer's wife is one of drudgery and exploitation. Capitalism sees in her mainly a breeder of wage slaves and soldiers. The boasted American home, enslaving the woman through her economic inferiority and her children, makes her dependent upon her husband. On all sides she confronts medieval sex taboos, assiduously cultivated by the church, State and bourgeois moralists. When she goes into industry she has to toil for from a third to a half less than the male worker; she works at a killing pace under unhealthful conditions and she is barred from many occupations under the hypocritical and reactionary slogan, "The woman's place is in the home"; the A.F. of L. betrays her every attempt to organize and to defend her interests. Politically, she is practically a zero, having little or no opportunity to educate herself or to function in an organized manner. Finally, to cap the climax of woman's enslavement, capitalism maintains in full blast the "oldest profession," prostitution.

The proletarian revolution will profoundly change all this. The American Soviet government will immediately set about liquidating the elaborate network of slavery in which woman is enmeshed. She will be freed economically, politically and socially. The U.S.S.R. shows the general lines along which the emancipation of woman will also proceed in a Soviet America.

The Russian woman is free economically, and this is the foundation of all her freedom. Every field of activity is open to her. She is to be found even in such occupations as locomotive engineer, electrical crane operator, machinist, factory director, etc. There are women generals in the Red Army, women ambassadors, etc. Two-thirds of the medical students are women. In industry the women are thoroughly organized in the trade unions. They get the same pay as men, and are protected by an elaborate system of maternity and other social insurance. In politics the women of the Soviet Union are a major and militant factor.

The Russian woman is also free in her sex life. When married life becomes unwelcome for a couple they are not barbarously compelled to live together. Divorce is to be had for the asking by one or both parties. The woman's children are recognized as legitimate by the State and society, whether born in official wedlock or not. The free American woman, like her Russian sister, will eventually scorn the whole fabric of bourgeois sex hypocrisy and prudery.

In freeing the woman, Socialism liquidates the drudgery of housework. So important do Communists consider this question that the Communist International deals with it in its world program. In the Soviet Union the attack upon housework slavery is delivered from every possible angle. Great factory kitchens are being set up to prepare hot, well-balanced meals for home consumption by the millions; communal kitchens in apartment houses are organized widespread. Every device to simplify and reduce housework is spread among the masses with all possible dispatch.

To free the woman from the enslavement of the perpetual care of her children is also a major object of Socialism. To this end in the Soviet Union there is being developed the most elaborate system of kindergartens and playgrounds in the world — in the cities and villages, in the neighborhoods and around the factories. Of this development, Anna Razamova says:

"All these institutions for child welfare mean a great deal in the life of the working woman. They free her from the necessity of spending all her time at home, cleaning, cooking and mending. While she is at work she can be sure that her child is being well taken care of, and that it is supervized by trained nurses and teachers, and gets wholesome food at regular hours." [6]

The free Russian woman is the trail blazer for the toiling women of the world. She is beating out a path which, ere long, her American sister will begin to follow.

Unshackling the Youth

A RULING class which did not hesitate to send more than twelve million young men to their death in

[6] *Russian Women in the Building of Socialism*, p. 13.

the World War to further its greed for wealth and power, naturally does not stick at the most ruthless exploitation of the youth at all other times. Capitalism, whose great god is profit, poisons society at its source; it destroys the seed corn of the human race, the young.

The condition of the children of the American working class is a damning indictment of capitalism. Recently even President Hoover admitted that in the United States, the richest country in the world, 6,000,000 children are chronically undernourished. The starved masses of workers, harassed by low wages and unemployment, are unable to feed their children properly, and the State callously shrugs its shoulders at the problem. Great masses of them slave in the industries, while their parents go around jobless. The position of the workers' children has naturally grown immeasurably worse during the present industrial crisis. *The Nation,* (Mar. 23, 1932), exposes a typical condition when it declares: "5,000 to 10,000 children in Detroit are daily in child bread lines." Regarding a recent investigation of conditions among continuation school boys in New York, Grace Hutchens states:

"Of 2,700 working boys, less than one in seven was found free from physical defects. One-fifth of them were under-weight from under-nourishment. Three-fifths needed dental care. Defective eyesight, adenoids, undeveloped chest, poor muscle tone, diseased tonsils, anemia, heart conditions, and tuberculosis scars were common. Most of these difficulties could have been prevented." [7]

The Labour Research Association says in its Bulletin of Nov. 9, 1931:

"In Detroit, in a single school in the working class district, 500 children refused to report for classes. Investigation showed that more than half of them lacked even clothes and shoes. In Chicago, children are fainting from lack of food and 15,000 are starving. In Cleveland, the number of under-nourished children in the elementary schools will reach 15,000 before the end of the present term. A recent study of 290 typical children in West Virginia coal towns by Dr. Ruth Fox of the Fifth Avenue Hospital in New York City, showed that in Ward, W. Va., their average weight was 12% below the standard."

The generally disastrous effects of such conditions may be better imagined than described. Capitalism, besides thus feeding, vampire-like upon children, no less ruthlessly exploits the youth, who are becoming an ever-greater factor in industry. It drives their immature bodies at a pace in production which even adult workers cannot endure; it forces them to work at lower wages than grown-ups; child labor laws are "more honored in the breach than in the observance." Special victims in this raw exploitation are the Negro youth.

Such barbarous conditions for the youth are, of course, utterly alien to Socialism. Just as inevitably as a profit-seeking, anarchic, socially-

[7] *Youth in Industry,* p. 14.

irresponsible capitalism ruins the young of the
people, so inevitably, does an ordered and responsible Socialism take the greatest care of its youth.
In the very center of the whole Communist
program stands the systematic protection and development of the children and young workers.
Even the sharpest enemies of the Soviet Union
have to admit the truth of this. Not even in the
darkest days of the civil war, when hunger and
pestilence were rampant, was the welfare of the
youth ever lost sight of in the U.S.S.R. They
always had plenty, although often their parents
were semi-starved. A bourgeois correspondent,
Julia Blanshard, says:

"Youth is one of the first concerns of Soviet Russia.
You, as an elder, might live on cabbage soup, but your
children would have meat stews and even sweets. Russia
looks to the future, not the past. . . The children look
clean, well-nourished, neatly dressed and alert." [8]

Under Socialism the care of the children rests
directly with the parents — stories of the nationalization of children in the Soviet Union are ridiculous. But the State does not let matters rest
entirely with the parents. It throws such additional
safeguards around the children in the schools, kindergartens, etc., of city and village that none can
possibly go hungry, be denied medical care or lack
education.

[8] *New York Telegram*, Nov. 8, 1931.

The Soviet government, the trade unions and the Communist Youth League, as well as the Party and other organizations, vigilantly protect the youth employed in Russian industry. The general conditions they have set up indicate the lines of development in the United States. There is no industrial child labor. And such driving as exists among the millions of young workers in American industries is unheard of. The Russian young workers work only six hours daily; they are shielded from night work and especially dangerous or heavy toil. The Soviet Union is the only country in the world where the youth are paid equal wage rates with adults for similar work. The health and education of the young workers is promoted by vast sport and cultural organizations. In politics the youth are a real factor, the franchise being based upon the principle, "Old enough to work, old enough to vote." In every walk in life the antiquated prejudices that the "elders" alone must lead have been broken down and the path is clear for the development of full leadership on the basis of ability and regardless of age. In the United States, as in the U.S.S.R., the Soviet system will open up a new world for the youth.

The Cultural Revolution in the United States

PRESENT-DAY culture in this country is an instrument by which the capitalist class consolidates its dominant position. The prevailing systems of education, morality, ethics, science, art, patriotism, religion, etc., are as definitely parts of capitalist exploitation as the stock exchange. The schools, churches, newspapers, motion pictures, radio, theatres and various other avenues of publicity and mass instruction are the organized propaganda machinery of the ruling class.

The chief aims of bourgeois culture, so far as it is directed towards the working class, are to develop the workers into, (1) slave-like robots who will accept uncomplainingly whatever standards of life and work the owners of industry see fit to grant them; (2) unthinking soldiers who will enthusiastically get themselves killed off in defense of their masters' rulership; (3) superstitious dolts who will satisfy themselves with a promise of paradise after death as a substitute for a decent life here on earth. To these ends the workers are regimented in the schools, poisoned by the militaristic Boy Scouts and C.M.T.C., enmeshed in fascist-like sport organizations, herded into the strike-breaking Y.M.C.A., stuffed with endless rot in the newspapers and movies, jammed into religious training before they are able to think for themselves, etc. As for real education, about all the workers get of it in school is the minimum of the three R's required to enable them to perform the tasks allotted them in industry.

So far as this culture is directed to the bourgeoisie

and petty bourgeoisie, it results in a mass production of capitalist intellectual robots. The schools and colleges, firmly in the grip of finance capital, as Upton Sinclair so completely showed in his book, *The Goose Step,* are great manufactories of Babbitts. In no country is culture so debased by capitalism as in the United States. Essentially a gigantic effort to perpetuate the robbery of the workers, it is sterile, hypocritical, colorless, lifeless. America's capitalistic writers are engaged in trying to convince the working class what a glorious thing it is to be a wage slave; her artists and poets are busy glorifying Heinz's pickles and the advertising pages of *The Saturday Evening Post;* her dramatists and musicians are cooking up patriotic slush and idiotic sex stories to divert the masses from their troubles and the hopeless boredom of capitalist life; her scientists are trying to prove the unity of science and religion, etc., etc.

The proletarian revolution in the United States will at once make a devastating slash into this maze of hypocrisy and intellectual rubbish. Not less than in the Soviet Union, it will usher in a profound cultural revolution. For the first time in history the toiling masses will have the opportunity to know and enjoy the good things of life. With prosperity assured for all, with no slave class to stultify intellectually and with no system of exploitation to defend, Communist culture will have a mass base and will flourish luxuriantly and free. It will call forth the artistic and intellectual powers of the masses, always hitherto repressed by chattel slavery, feudalism and capitalism. Superstition, and ignorance will vanish in a realm of science; "Culture will become the acquirement of all and the class ideologies of the past will give place to scientific materialist philosophy." [9]

Among the elementary measures the American Soviet government will adopt to further the cultural revolution are the following; the schools, colleges and universities will be coordinated and grouped under the National Department of Education and its state and local branches. The studies will be revolutionized, being cleansed of religious, patriotic and other features of the bourgeois ideology. The students will be taught on the basis of Marxian dialectical materialism, internationalism and the general ethics of the new Socialist society. Present obsolete methods of teaching will be superseded by a scientific pedagogy.

The churches will remain free to continue their services, but their special tax and other privileges will be liquidated. Their buildings will revert to the State. Religious schools will be abolished and organized religious training for minors prohibited. Freedom will be established for anti-religious propaganda.

[9] *Program of the Communist International.*

The whole basis and organization of capitalist science will be revolutionized. Science will become materialistic, hence truly scientific; God will be banished from the laboratories as well as from the schools. Science will be thoroughly organized and will work according to plan; instead of the present individualistic hit-or-miss scientific dabbling, there will be a great organization of science, backed by the full power of the government. This organization will make concerted attacks upon the central problems, concrete and abstract, that confront science.

The press, the motion picture, the radio, the theatre, will be taken over by the government. They will be cleansed of their present trash of sex, crime, sensationalism and general babbitry, and developed into institutions of real education and art; into purveyors of the interesting, dramatic, and amusing in life. The press will, through workers' correspondents on the Russian lines, become the actual voice of the people, not simply the forum of professional writers.

The American Soviet government will, of course, give the greatest possible stimulus to art in every form, seeking to cultivate the latent powers of the masses. Painting, sculpture, literature, music — every form of artistic expression — will flourish as never before. The great art treasures of the rich will be confiscated and assembled in museums for the enjoyment and instruction of the toiling masses.

Cultural societies of all kinds will be developed energetically.

One of the basic concerns of the workers' government will be, naturally, the conservation of the health of the masses. To this end a national Department of Health will be set up, with the necessary local and State sub-divisions. A free medical service, based upon the most scientific principles, will be established. The people will be taught how to live correctly. They will be given mass instruction in diet, physical culture, etc. A last end will be put to capitalist medical quackery and the adulteration of food.

A main task of the American Soviet government will be to make the cities liveable. This will involve not only the wholesale destruction of the shacks that millions of workers now call homes, but the building over of the congested capitalist cities into roomy Socialist towns. These will develop towards the decentralization of industry and population, the breaking down of the differences between city and country. There will be no great landed, financial, and transportation interests to maintain the monstrous congestion typical of capitalist cities. The present "city beautiful" plans of capitalism will seem puny and trivial to the future city builders of Socialism.

Only a few years ago many of the foregoing proposals would have seemed fantastic, merely utopian dreams. But now we can see them growing into actuality in the Soviet Union. In making the cultural revolution in the United States, the workers and farmers, facing the same general problems as the Russians, will solve them along similar lines.

Curing Crime and Criminals

CAPITALISM, by its very nature, is a prolific breeder of crime. It is a system of legalized robbery of the working class. The whole process of capitalist business is a swindle and an armed hold-up. In capitalist society what constitutes crime and what does not is a purely arbitrary distinction. The capitalists do not recognize any line of demarcation for themselves. They do whatever they can "get away with." The record of every large fortune and big corporation in this country is smeared not only with brutal robbery of the workers but also statutory crime of every description, from the bribery of legislatures to plain murder. Wall Street is full of uncaught Kreugers.

In a society where each grabs what he can at the expense of the rest, naturally the government offers a wide field of corruption. It is a well-known fact, emphasized afresh by the Seabury investigation in New York, that every city and State in this country is controlled by grafting politicians, allied with the criminal underworld. The Teapot Dome scandal, not to mention numerous others, shows that the national government is also permeated with this gross corruption. Such corruption is not a special condition, but of the very tissue of capitalism.

It is not surprising that in a system of society where the aim is to get rich by any means, crime of every kind should flourish. Faced by low wages and other impossible economic conditions on the one hand and by the corrupt example of capitalism generally on the other, many naturally take to lives of open crime and try to seize at the point of a gun what the capitalist "big shots" steal through exploiting the workers, by a corner on the stock exchange, or by corrupting the government. The main difference between their operations is primarily one of dimension. Al Capone is an altogether legitimate child of American capitalism, and it is no accident that he is an object of such widespread admiration.

The American Soviet government will liquidate the mounting crime wave which, according to the Wickersham committee, costs the government a billion dollars yearly. Socialism, by putting an end to capitalist exploitation, deals a mortal blow at crime of every description. The economic base of crime is destroyed. The worker is enabled to live and work under the best possible conditions. There is no place for human sharks to prey upon their fellow men. Not only does the abolition of capitalism destroy the basis of the so-called crimes against property, but the revolutionized economic and social conditions, involving an intelligent moral code and effective educational system, also greatly diminish the "crimes of passion."

These facts are already demonstrated in the Soviet Union, which is fast becoming a crimeless country. While the exigencies of the revolutionary struggle against the counter-revolution made it necessary, from time to time, to confine a considerable number of political prisoners, this need is now fast passing with the consolidation of the Socialist regime and the liquidation of the last remnants of the exploiting classes in the Soviet Union. Life and property are safer now in the U.S.S.R. than in any other country in the world. Crime is rapidly sinking into abeyance and this will be more and more the case as the new society becomes strengthened.

Capitalism blames crime upon the individual, instead of upon the bad social conditions which produce it. Hence its treatment of crime is essentially one of punishment. But the failure of its prisons, with their terrible sex-starvation, graft, over-crowding, idleness, stupid discipline, ferociously long sentences and general brutality, is overwhelmingly demonstrated by the rapidly mounting numbers of prisoners and the long list of terrible prison riots. Capitalist prisons are actually schools of crime. Even the standpat Wickersham committee had to condemn the atrocious American prison system as brutal, medieval and fruitless.

Socialist criminology, on the other hand, attacks the bad social conditions. While the American Soviet government will ruthlessly break up the underworld gangs that brazenly infest all American cities and will also give short shrift to grafting politicians, its prison system will be essentially educational in character. In the new Russian prisons, for example, the prisoners have the right to marry and to live with their families; they are taught useful trades and are paid full union wages for their work; there are no guards or walls or bars; the discipline is organized entirely by the prisoners themselves. The prisoners are also allowed freely to visit their friends in other towns. The lengths of the terms to be served are determined by the prisoners' committees, on the basis of the fitness of the given prisoners to resume their places in society. The whole terminology of crime, criminal, prison, etc., has been abandoned in such institutions. Upon release, a prisoner is not only able to make his way in society but is welcomed. He is eligible to belong to the Communist party. It requires very little imagination to see the great advantages of this Socialist system over the barbarous prisons of capitalist countries. Congressman W. I. Sirovich, (Dem., N. Y.), said, after a recent visit to the Soviet Union, "The Russian prison system sets an example that is worthy of emulation by any nation in the world." [10]

Prohibition, based upon a criminal alliance between capitalists, crooked politicians and gangsters, has bred a growth of criminals such as the world has never seen before. And the "best minds" of the country stand powerless before the problem. The American Soviet government will deal with this question by eliminating prohibition, by establishing government control of the manufacture and sale of alcoholic liquors; these measures to be supported by an energetic campaign among the masses against excessive drinking.

This way of handling the prohibition question is working successfully in the Soviet Union. Shortly after the October revolution the Soviet government prohibited the sale or manufacture of alcoholic drinks. But soon bootlegging began, with familiar demoralizing consequences: poisonous liquor was made, much badly-needed grain was wasted, open violation of the law existed on all sides. Then, with characteristic vigor and clarity of purpose, the government legalized the making and selling of intoxicating beverages. At the same time, a big campaign was initiated by the government, the Party, the trade unions, etc., to educate the workers against alcoholism. This program is succeeding; the evils of alcoholism are definitely on the decline. Doubtless, the Russians have found the

10 *New York Journal*, Dec. 1, 1931.

real solution of the liquor question. Just as Socialism is abolishing so many other evils, it is also rapidly wiping out alcoholism and the mass of misery and degradation that accompanies it.

The Abolition of War

ONE OF the revolutionary achievements of victorious world Communism will be the ending of war. In Chapter I we have seen the great and growing danger of a new world war and also the utter futility of all the capitalist peace pacts and disarmament schemes as war preventives. We have also seen the economic forces of imperialism behind the war danger. So long as capitalism lasts war must continue to curse the human race. It is the historical task of the proletariat to put an end to this hoary monster. This it will do by destroying the capitalist system and with it the economic causes that bring about war.

It is characteristic of capitalism to justify all the robbery and misery and terrors of its system by seeking to create the impression that they are caused by basic traits in human nature, or even by "acts of god." Thus we find current many metaphysical and mysterious explanations of the present crisis and unemployment. These preventable disasters are made to appear almost as natural phenomena over which mankind has no control, like tornadoes and earthquakes. The same general attitude is taken with regard to war. War is put forth as arising out of the very nature of humanity. Man is pictured as a war-like animal, and therefore capitalism escapes responsibility. War becomes more or less inevitable.

This is all nonsense, of course. Man is by nature a gregarious and friendly animal. He does not make war because he dislikes others of his own species, differing from him in language, religion, geographical location, etc. His wars have always arisen out of struggles over the very material things of wealth and power. This is true, whether he has been living in a tribal, slave, feudal or capitalist economy, and whether he has obscured the true cause of his wars with an intense religious garb or with slogans about making the world safe for democracy. The cause of modern war is, as we have already seen, the imperialistic policies of the capitalist nations to rob the colonial peoples, to smash back the growing revolutionary movement, to crush each other in the world struggle for markets, raw materials and territory. In a society in which there is no private property in industry and land, in which no exploitation of the workers takes place and where plenty is produced for all, there can be no grounds for war. The interests of a Socialist society are fundamentally opposed to the murderous and unnatural struggle of international war.

Under capitalism the workers, by militant and

well-organized struggle, can check the development of war. By the threat of revolution they can,
for a time, force the capitalists to hold in leash
their dogs of war. This fear has contributed basically to holding the capitalist governments so long
from making another open armed attack upon the
Soviet Union. But pressure from the workers can
only delay the war, not stop it permanently. The
irresistible and incurable antagonisms of the capitalist countries inevitably force them into war,
revolution or no revolution. Only the proletarian
revolution itself can solve these war-breeding contradictions and put a final end to war. Not chris-
tianity but Communism will bring peace on earth.

A Communist world will be a unified, organized
world. The economic system will be one great
organization, based upon the principle of planning
now dawning in the U.S.S.R. The American
Soviet government will be an important section in
this world organization. In such a society there
will be no tariffs or the many other barriers erected
by capitalism against a free world interchange of
goods. The raw material supplies of the world will
be at the disposition of the peoples of the world.

Politically, the world will be organized. There
will be no colonies, no "spheres of influence," no
hypocritical "open doors." The toilers will then
have fully realized Marx's famous slogan, "Workingmen of the World, Unite!" The interests of
the toiling masses in the various countries will not

be in conflict, but in harmony with each other. Those who speak of "red imperialism" repeat the calumnies of capitalism. Once the power of the bourgeoisie is broken internationally and its States destroyed, the world Soviet Union will develop towards a scientific administration of things, as Engels describes. There will be no place for the present narrow patriotism, the bigoted nationalist chauvinism that serves so well the capitalist war-makers. Armies and navies, rendered obsolete, will be disbanded. Grim war will meet its Waterloo.

At the meeting of the League of Nations' Preparatory Commission for Disarmament at Geneva in November, 1927, the representatives of the Soviet Union presented a proposal for complete world disarmament. It was later re-enforced by the Soviet Union's proposal for a general economic non-aggression pact, by its non-aggression treaties with individual governments, and by its generally firm peace policy in the face of imperialist provocation.

But, of course, the imperialist capitalist nations did not accept the Soviet Union's plan for doing away with war. The U.S.S.R. is the only country that genuinely struggles for peace; the capitalist powers need war in their business. War is not to be ended in capitalist peace conferences, but by revolutionary struggle of the toiling masses against capitalism itself. Hence, inevitably, the capitalists at Geneva ridiculed the Soviet 1927 proposals and shortly afterwards adopted as a substitute the supremely hypocritical Kellogg Peace Pact, meanwhile intensifying their own war preparations. They have again rejected the Soviet Union's disarmament proposal at the present Geneva conference. Thereby they expose afresh to the workers of the world the fact that they do not want peace, but war. It will be only when the workers and peasants have finally defeated international capitalism and are assembled to re-organize the world on a Socialist basis that a proposal for general disarmament will be adopted and carried into effect. This event, being irresistibly prepared by the deepening capitalist crisis and the growing mobilization of the world's toilers under the leadership of the Communist International, will take place sooner than the world bourgeoisie dare think and it will be one of the very greatest steps forward ever taken by the human race.

Socialist Incentive

ONE OF the classical capitalist arguments against Socialism is that it would destroy incentive; that is, if private property in industry and the right to exploit the workers were abolished the urge for social progress, and even for day-to-day production, would be killed.

But the Russian revolution has shattered this

contention irreparably. The Russian workers and peasants are building Socialism with a mass energy and enthusiasm quite unparalleled in history. Manifestly, they are propelled by a great incentive. This is a marvel to the bourgeois newspaper correspondents. But it is just as Marx, three gen erations ago, said it would be under Socialism.

The incentive of the Russian toilers is easily explained. They own the country and everything in it. There is no exploiting class to rob them of the fruits of their toil. They welcome better production methods because they get the full benefit of them. They have broken the chain of capitalist slavery and are building a new world of liberty, prosperity and happiness for themselves and families. It is equally understandable why the producing masses in capitalist countries betray no such enthusiasm in their work. The latter are robbed of what they produce; for them improvements in production mean wage-cuts and unemployment. Incentive under capitalism is confined practically to the exploiting classes and their hangers-on. It is only with the advent of Socialism that the great masses develop real incentive.

Socialist incentive in the Soviet Union explains why the workers so militantly defended the revolution against the many capitalist armies in 1918-20, and why they have endured famine and pestilence for the revolution. In the industries it is an intelligent mass incentive that provides the basis

for the keen Socialist competition, for shock-bri-
gades to speed production, for the self-imposed
labor discipline, for the heroic present-day self-
denial in putting the Five-Year Plan into effect so
that a solid base of heavy industry may be quickly
laid for the Socialist prosperity.

In view of all this mass interest and initiative
of the workers in Soviet industry current capitalist
charges about "forced labor" in the U.S.S.R. stand
exposed as ridiculous. Forced labor is native to
capitalism, not Socialism. The whole Socialist
system is utterly antagonistic to any enslavement
of the workers. Even bourgeois writers and politicians are beginning to admit this. H. R. Mussey
says: "If anybody wants a bargain in forced labor, or any other kind of labor, I should advise
him not to look for it in Russia just now, as far as
I have seen it; for it is a seller's market in labor
if ever there was one." [11] Rep. H. T. Rainey,
Democratic House leader, declares: "Labor is
freer in Russia than in any other country in the
world." [12]

The differentiated wage scales, including piece-
work, in the Soviet Union constitute no contradiction to the prevalent strong mass incentive.
Temporarily, they must serve to stimulate the less
conscious elements to acquire skill and to produce.
The wage system as a whole is a hang-over from

[11] *The Nation*, Nov. 4, 1931.
[12] *New York World-Telegram*, Apr. 8, 1932.

capitalism, part of the baggage that has to be discarded during the transition from capitalism to Communism. Improved production methods and general education will solve that problem. Recently Stalin said, in polemizing against tendencies to at once equalize wages:

"Marx and Lenin said that the differences between skilled and unskilled work would continue to exist even under Socialism and even after the classes had been annihilated, that only under Communism would this difference disappear, that therefore, even under Socialism 'wages' must be paid according to the labor performed and not according to need." [13]

Besides the revolutionary enthusiasm and initiative of the masses and many other indications already present of the eventual wageless system there is the "Party maximum." That is, the members of the Communist party have a set wage limit above which they cannot go. Thus Stalin gets the same wages, as many hundreds of thousands of other workers and much less than large numbers of non-Party mechanics and engineers. "Russia," says Stuart Chase, "has achieved more progress and developed more initiative on $150 a month, the official Party salary, than any other nation has ever dreamed of in an equal period." [14]

It is exactly in the incentive of the workers and poor farmers that the proletarian revolution has

[13] Speech delivered on June 23, 1931.
[14] *The Philadelphia Record*, Nov. 22, 1931.

its great motive force.   This is what gains it the support of the masses, what carries it through a thousand trials and tribulations, what is driving through the Five-Year Plan successfully and what will eventually build a world system of Communism.   Mussey, in the above-quoted article from *The Nation,* issues the following warning to the capitalist class:

"If the rulers of the western world would retain their leadership, even in part, then I am persuaded that they and their apologists would do well without further delay to recognize the profound significance of that combination of motives on the basis of which the Russians have accomplished the impossibilities of the past 14 years and to cease their parrot-like iteration of the impossibility of successful appeal in industry to anything except individual cupidity.   The Russian construction marvels of 1931 — and they are marvels — are not built on individual cupidity."

Collectivism and Individualism

DEFENDERS of capitalism declare that Socialism destroys individualism.   But when they speak of individualism they have in mind the right of freely exploiting the workers.   They mean that the anti-social individualism of capitalism will go.   Under Socialism no one will have the right to exploit another; no longer will a profit-hungry employer be able to shut his factory gates and sentence thousands to starvation; no more will it be possible for a little clique of capitalists and their political henchmen to plunge the world into a blood-bath of war.

Yes, such deadly individualism is doomed. But the revolution will create in its stead a new and better development of the individual. The collectivist society of Socialism, by freeing the masses from economic and political slavery will, for the first time in history, give the masses an opportunity to fully develop and express their personalities. Theirs will be an individuality growing out of and harmonizing with the interests of all. It will not have the objective of one's getting rich by robbing the toilers, but will develop itself in the direction of achievement in science, industrial technique, art, sports, etc. A typical example of this new motive was the case of Lensky, a worker in the "Pneumatics" factory of Leningrad who recently invented a very valuable electric-pneumatic meter: given 120,000 rubles as a reward, he immediately presented the money to various cultural organizations.

The boast of capitalist apologists about the equal opportunity which their society affords, that it is a case of the survival of the fittest, is a tissue of lies. What equality is there between a Vanderbilt and a poor miner? And as for the fittest surviving, under capitalism, this means those strongest financially. Harry K. Thaw is a glowing example of capitalist survival of the fittest. Only Socialism can provide equality of opportunity, which means a genuine occasion for the masses to enjoy life and to develop their latent personalities.

Socialism, it is also argued, kills the spirit of competition in society. That is more nonsense. Under Socialism men and women strive for superiority in achievement just as naturally as boys do in a foot race. But not on the basis of privately-owned, competitive industry. Indeed, Socialism will introduce the first real competition since the days of primitive Communism. Lenin, in an article written in 1918, says:

"Socialism does not only not extinguish competition but on the contrary for the first time creates possibilities to apply competition widely, on a real mass scale, to draw the majority of the workers into the field of this work, where they can really show themselves, where they can develop their abilities, disclose their talents which are an untouched source among the masses and which capitalism trampled upon, crushed and strangled by thousands and millions."

Stalin thus describes the basically different capitalist and Socialist competition:

"The principle of capitalist competition is defeat and death for some and victory for others. The principle of Socialist competition is, comradely assistance to those lagging behind the more advanced, with the purpose to reach general advancement."

The history of the Russian revolution to date entirely bears out these statements of Lenin and Stalin. Socialist competition is one of the main driving forces of the revolutionary development. In view of the basic tasks now confronting the Soviet Union, it is inevitable that the most striking manifestation of the new Socialist competition should relate to the buildng and operation of the industries. This, which we have described in Chapter II, is a gigantic factor in carrying through the Five-Year Plan. But Socialist competition runs into every other field of endeavor as well, and it will play an increasing role as the new Socialist system gets a more solid foundation.

The existence of a strong mass incentive and a lively spirit of competition under Socialism effectually disposes of the time-worn "dead level of Socialism" theory. Not Socialism, but capitalism, with its exploitation, terrorism, war, superstition, and cultivated illiteracy, creates a dead level in its poverty and ignorance for the uncounted millions of toilers of field and factory. It is precisely Socialism that will destroy this dead level.

But the capitalists, as is their wont, seek to justify their destructive type of competition by asserting that it is rooted firmly in human nature. Such appeals to "human nature," however, must be taken cautiously. By that method of reasoning it would be quite easy to conclude that the rich capitalist who heartlessly casts workers out of his shops penniless and gives no thought as to their future has quite a different "human nature" than the African Negro hunter who, with his high sense of clan soli-

darity, before eating his kill, calls loudly in the
four directions in case perchance there may be
another hungry hunter nearby. Changed social
conditions develop different "human natures."
Thus competition, a ruinous, anti-social thing under capitalism, becomes, under Socialism, highly
beneficent.

In recent years the argument against the approaching "dead level" of Socialism has taken on
a new development. Now machinery itself is being roundly denounced as a "dead leveller." Wide
fear is expressed that we are going into a regime
of such standardization and mechanization that life
is becoming merely a machine-like process and the
people so many robots.

This fear is essentially a class fear. The petty
bourgeoisie, including their writers and poets,
dread the machine because it wipes out their class
base, small industry; because it brings the further
subjugation of their class to the bankers and big
industrialists. Many capitalist economists, like
Foster and Catchings, Tugwell, Chase,[15] etc., also
fear the machine and modern methods of mass production, because they sense their revolutionary consequences. They see the growing volume of
production, the shrinking markets, the increasing

---

[15] Chase, although stating that, on the whole, the effect of the
machine has been progressive, is manifestly alarmed. In *Men and
Machines*, p. 318, his fear and confusion are expressed by his
empty program of meeting the problem of the machine without a
plan, "with nothing to guide us but our naked intelligence and a
will to conquer."

unemployment, the radicalization of the producing masses, the growing revolutionary struggle, and they tremble at the prospect. In Montreal, according to a United Press dispatch of Feb. 23, 1932, the Canadian government buried a toy steam-shovel ceremoniously, declaring that its "future policy will be to engage manual laborers and to scrap machinery wherever advisable."

Anti-machine propaganda like that of Gandhi, Spengler, etc., is the absurdity of capitalism in despair and decline. None such will be found in the Soviet Union. The Soviet workers do not fear the machine. They see in it an emancipator from the drudgery and poverty of the past. They have no dread of ensuing industrial crises and unemployment. They will control the machine; not let it enslave them as it has done under capitalism. Nor do they fear that it will create a "dead level," standardized, uninteresting world. Such conditions can only develop under capitalism where everything is made for profit's sake. Capitalism naturally develops a hopeless babbittry in every direction; but Socialism produces inevitably the intelligent and the beautiful.

Under Socialism the machine will be used on the broadest scale possible to produce the necessities of life in the great industries, transport systems and communication services. It would be the sheerest nonsense and quite impossible not to take advantage of every labor and time-saving device.

But Socialist society will also know how to develop the variegated and artistic. Where the creative impulses of the masses are not checked by poverty and slavery, where the arts and sciences are not hamstrung by the profit-making motive, where the masses are not poisoned by anti-social codes of morals and ethics, and where every assistance of the free community is given to the maximum cultivation of the intellectual and artistic powers of the masses — there we need have no fear that society will be robotized by the machine.

Life under a Communist society will be varied and interesting. Individual will vie with individual, as never before, to create the useful and the beautiful. Locality will compete with locality in the beauty of their architecture. The impress of individuality and originality will be upon everything. The world will become a place well worth living in, and what is the most important, its joys will not be the niggardly monopoly of a privileged ruling class but the heritage of the great producing masses.

Building a New World

THE PROLETARIAN revolution is the most profound of all revolutions in history. It initiates changes more rapid and far-reaching than any in the whole experience of mankind. The hundreds of millions of workers and peasants, striking off their age-old chains of slavery, will construct a society of liberty and prosperity and intelligence. Communism will inaugurate a new era for the human race, the building of a new world.

The overthrow of capitalism and the development of Communism will bring about the immediate or eventual solution of many great social problems. Some of these originate in capitalism, and others have plagued the human race for scores of centuries. Among them are war, religious superstition, prostitution, famine, pestilence, crime, poverty, alcoholism, unemployment, illiteracy, race and national chauvinism, the suppression of woman, and every form of slavery and exploitation of one class by another. Already in the Soviet Union, with the revolution still in its initial stages, the forces are distinctly to be seen at work that will eventually liquidate these handicaps to the happiness and progress of the human race. But, of course, only a system of developed world Communism can fully uproot and destroy all these evils.

The objective conditions, in the shape of scientific knowledge and the means of creating material wealth, are already at hand in sufficient measure to do away with these menaces to humanity. But the trouble lies with the subjective factor, the capitalist order of society. Capitalism, based upon human exploitation, stands as the great barrier to social progress. Communism, by abolishing the capitalist system, liquidates this subjective difficulty.   It releases thereby productive forces strong enough to provide plenty for all and it destroys the whole accompanying capitalist baggage of cultivated ignorance, strife and misery.   Communism frees humanity from the stultifying effects of the present essentially animal struggle for existence and opens up before it new horizons of joys and tasks.   The day is not so far distant when our children, immersed in this new life, will look back with horror upon capitalism and marvel how we tolerated it so long.

Communist society, in its battle onward and upward, will attack and carry through many profound measures besides those mentioned.   Among these will be the organization of the economics of the world upon a rational and planned basis, the systematic conservation and increase of the world's natural resources, the development of a vast concentration upon all the great problems now confronting science, the beautification of the world by a new and richer artistry, the liquidation of congested cities and the combination of the joys and conveniences of country and urban life, and the solution of many other great problems and tasks now hardly even imagined.

Communist society, however, will not confine itself simply to thus developing the objective conditions for a better life.   Especially will it turn its attention to the subjective factor, to the fundamental improvement of man himself.   Capitalism,

UNITED SOVIET STATES OF AMERICA 341

with its wars, wage slavery, slums, crooked doctors, etc., undermines the health of the race and destroys its physique. Communism, with its healthful dwellings and working conditions, its pure food, physical culture, etc., will make good health, like thorough education, the property of all. Already this is becoming so in the Soviet Union. But this will be only a beginning. Communist society will go farther. It will scientifically regulate the growth of population. It will especially speed up the very evolution of man himself, his brain and body. Capitalism has checked the evolution of the human species, if it has not actually brought about a process of race degeneration. But Communism will systematically breed up mankind. Already the scientific knowledge is at hand to do this, but it is at present inapplicable because of the idiocy of the capitalist system, its planlessness, its antiquated moral codes, its warp and woof of exploitation.

For many generations the long list of utopians, the Platos, Mores, Fouriers, Owens, and Bellamys, have dreamed and planned ideal states of society. Their strong point was that they sensed mankind's capacity for a higher social life than the existing wild scramble. But their weak point, and this was decisive, was that they did not know what was the matter with society nor how to cure it. They had not the slightest conception of either the objective or subjective conditions necessary for social revo-

lution. Their utopias, mere speculations discon-
nected from actual life, fell upon deaf ears.

It has remained for the modern proletariat, under the brilliant leadership of Marx and Lenin, to
find the revolutionary way to the higher social
order, on the basis of the industrial and social conditions set up by capitalism. Marxians have been
able to analyze capitalism scientifically, to work
out a correct program and strategy of struggle, to
establish effective organization among the workers
and peasants, to master generally the laws of social development. Consequently, with the objective situation becoming ever more ripe, the
revolution no longer appears as an abstraction, a
mere theory. Today, Socialism is a great living
world reality. As Polakov says, "The Russian
'experiment' is an experiment no more." In the
Soviet Union the first great breach has been made
in the walls of capitalism. The rest will follow
apace. And we may be sure that the revolution,
in its upward course, will carry humanity to heights
of happiness and achievement far beyond the
dreams of even the most hopeful utopians.

American imperialism is now strong. Its champions ridicule the idea of a revolution. But their
assurance is not now quite so sure as it was a couple
of years ago, before the great industrial collapse.
They are beginning to feel a deadly fear. The
Russian revolution is to them such a terrible reality.
But they console themselves with the thought that

"it can never happen in this country," and they scorn the at-present weak Communist party. But they overlook the detail that the same attitude was taken towards the pre-revolution Bolsheviki. Especially did the Socialist Moguls of the Second International look upon them as narrow sectarians and upon Lenin as a fanatical dreamer. But one thing is certain, American capitalism is part and parcel of the world capitalist system and is subject to all its basic weaknesses and contradictions; it travels the same way to its destruction as capitalism in general.

The world capitalist system is in decay. All the king's horses and all the king's men cannot·save it. Its general crisis deepens; the masses develop revolutionary consciousness; the international revolutionary storm forces gather. Capitalism, it is true, makes a strong and stubborn resistance. The advance of the revolution is difficult, its pace is slow, and it varies from country to country, but its direction is sure and its movement irresistible. Under the leadership of the Communist International the toilers of the world are organizing to put a final end to the long, long ages of ignorance and slavery, of which capitalist imperialism is the last stage, and to begin building a prosperous and intelligent society commensurate with the levels to which social knowledge and production possibilities have reached.

THE END

21059947R00188

Made in the USA
Lexington, KY
01 March 2013